WRITING AND POLITICS IN FRANCO'S SPAIN

WRITING AND POLITICS IN FRANCO'S SPAIN

BARRY JORDAN

ROUTLEDGE
LONDON AND NEW YORK

First published 1990
by Routledge
11 New Fetter Lane, London EC4P 4EE

Simultaneously published in the USA and Canada
by Routledge
a division of Routledge, Chapman and Hall, Inc.
29 West 35th Street, New York, NY 10001

©1990 Barry Jordan

Data converted by Columns of Reading
Printed in Great Britain by TJ Press (Padstow) Ltd. Padstow, Cornwall

British Library Cataloguing in Publication Data
Jordan, Barry
Writing and politics in Franco's Spain.
1. Spanish literature, 1900–1960. Influence of politics, 1936–1960
I. Title
860.9′0062

Library of Congress Cataloging in Publication Data
Jordan, Barry, 1950–
Writing and politics in Franco's Spain / Barry Jordan.
p. cm. — (Writing and politics)
Bibliography: p.
Includes index.
ISBN 0–415–02503–6
1. Spanish fiction—20th century—History and criticism.
2. Politics and literature—Spain. 3. Literature and society—
Spain. I. Title. II. Series.
PQ6144.J67 1990
863′.6409358—dc20
89–10417
CIP

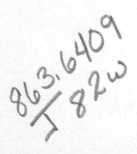

CONTENTS

v

INTRODUCTION

In postwar Europe, with the defeat of fascism, the emergence of power blocs and the Cold War, the rapid rise and fall of popular front governing coalitions, the replacement of anti-fascism by anti-communism as the dominant ideology of the West, and the general shift towards conservative governments under American hegemony, the left-wing intellectual once again began to pose the question of the writer's responsibility. In France, in the late 1940s and against a background of an intensification of the Cold War and the emergence of political movements demanding European neutrality, Sartre developed the notion of *engagement*. In *Qu'est-ce que la littérature?* (1948), which constituted his polemical treatise on the writer's role in the advancement of socialist revolution, Sartre saw literary commitment as crucially dependent on the ability of language to communicate, of writing to speak. Echoing Lukács's position, Sartre, regarded writing (by which he meant prose) as providing a transparent medium, fully adequate to represent the world as it is, through which the writer revealed a situation to others in order to change it. Literature's radical potential thus lay in its ability to contain the heterogeneity of language and to guarantee the reader's untroubled access to meaning. By contrast, in his *Combat* essays of the late 1940s (collected in *Le Degré zéro de l'écriture* (1953) and usually regarded as a critical riposte to Sartre's manifesto),[1] Barthes maintained that the world *as it is* did not exist independently of its construction in language; that is, that the real was not naturally *there*, but culturally produced. Moreover, recalling Brecht, Barthes also maintained that writing was no simple copy of things, no neutral vehicle for the transmission of determinate, pre-existing meanings, but annoyingly slippery, unstable, indeterminate: in short, an anti-communication. Thus, the idea of writing as a shared communication between author and reader was an illusion, based on the fallacy that writing speaks. In consequence, a literature committed to social revolution, in the Sartrian sense, was seen as self-deluding, as a form of linguistic naïveté, unrealizable because technically impossible. For Barthes, what was at stake for the radical writer was not so much a commitment to revolution in the world, but to revolution in the word. What mattered was not to reveal the world *out there*, i.e. to produce a literature of the referent, but to lay bare the rules, codes, and systems by which the real is constructed. Writing was thus to be regarded as a radical experience of language.

In postwar France, despite his considerable influence in left intellectual politics and anti-American protest movements, Sartre's manifesto on literary commitment failed to inspire a significant literary school or trend. In fact, the novel trend that did emerge in France in the 1950s, the *nouveau roman*, seemed to confirm not Sartre's ideas but those of Barthes, who would proceed to defend and champion the new literary modernism. In the French novel, this was the age of suspicion, *l'ère du soupçon*, as Nathalie Sarraute had put it, which fundamentally queried the ability of the novel to render the real.[2] According to this view, writing was essentially about itself, concerned with its own nature as language and not as reference. For well over a decade the French novel would be effectively disengaged from worldly concerns; and while artistically and technically progressive in terms of its new dehumanizing objectivism the *nouveau roman* was, none the less, introspective, ahistorical, self-regarding, and inescapably elitist.

Where the Sartrian project did make an impact was in Spain, providing opposition writers with a set of guidelines for the creation of their own indigenous, anti-modernist, committed literature. Under the Franco dictatorship, literature took over many of the roles and responsibilities which, in a democratic society, would normally have been discharged by the press. It tried to act both as a source of information on daily realities and social issues which were absent from the official media and also as an instrument of socio-political critique. Writers and artists opposed to the regime thus believed that the literary work could function as a tool of demystification and as a means of raising public consciousness. A younger generation of writers, emerging in the early 1950s and drawn largely from the families of the winning side, began to devote their literature to exploring the problems of rural poverty and migration, working-class oppression and urban deprivation, social marginalization, and so on. Denied access to the 1930s debates on aesthetics and politics and to basic Marxist literary criticism, young Spanish writers found a rationale for their own dissent and for the writer's social and ethical function in Sartre, whose ideas gradually filtered across the Pyrenees in the early and mid-1950s. And it was Sartre's claim that writing communicates, that it was capable of revealing the real, grasping the truth, and allowing the voiceless to speak which crystallized and gave a focus to the young writers' aesthetic and ethical concerns. However, in repressive conditions and under the vigilant gaze of censorship, writers could only deal with Spain's hidden realities indirectly, adopting writing strategies which, as far as possible, avoided editorial comment in favour of direct, objective reporting. It was then left up to the reader to read between the lines and to raise questions concerning the responsibilities for the situations and conditions portrayed. In this way, it was assumed that writing would operate directly on the consciousness of the reader who, with a new awareness, would then act in the real world in order to transform such conditions and eliminate social injustice. This, in rather crude summary form, was the general idea behind Spain's realist novel of the 1950s, commonly referred to as the *novela social*. The present study sets out to examine the early development of this literary movement. In particular, it aims to reconstruct those historically specific contexts, influences, platforms, and writing practices that provide the conditions of possibility for the new realism of the 1950s. Also in broader terms, it is concerned with the relations between texts, contexts, and wider cultural and social processes, including the relations between the *novela social* and previous novel trends, the generational determinations on the movement, its location within the rise of an intellectual opposition, and so on. In short, by looking at the beginnings of the *novela social*, I hope to show how it operates as complex, dynamic, gradually unfolding process; I also hope to

INTRODUCTION

draw some more general conclusions regarding the relations between writing and politics in Franco's Spain.

Though it is one of the few books in English on the subject, the present study is not the first attempt by any means to account for the nature and development of the *novela social*. Since the 1960s, countless critical works have appeared with the same or related objectives. However, the vast majority of them, which are mainly in Spanish, tend to be of the general, panoramic type, consisting of broad surveys of authors, texts, and trends, usually classified according to generational criteria. One of the effects and limitations of this approach is that many of the available studies are little more than catalogues or inventories. Another difficulty is that, because of their emphasis on pigeon-holing writers and works, most studies have neglected to explore important and available source material. As a result, there has emerged a dominant, consensus view that proposes that the *novela social* of the 1950s and 1960s represents the culmination of a trend which began in the 1940s, if not before, and that illustrates a *progressive recovery of realism* in the postwar Spanish novel. By contrast, my own hunch is that the development of artistic forms, their rise and fall, rarely operates in such an apparently straightforward, cumulative, linear fashion. So that, rather than a simple continuation, I want to argue that the *novela social* represents a *break* with previous writing styles in certain crucial respects: in its narrative perspective and presentation of material, its implicit attitude towards the function of writing and the writer, and its understanding of the nature of social reality. My proposition is that Spain's *novela social* constitutes a form of *littérature engagée*, not previously known, which takes its aesthetic and political direction from a series of factors, influences, and inputs which begin to surface and coalesce in the early 1950s.

As regards the organization of this study, chapter 1 provides an overview and critique of the dominant critical perspectives on the postwar novel and the *novela social*. Chapter 2 relates the beginnings of the *novela social* to the formation of an intellectual opposition and considers the various routes along which young writers and intellectuals reach opposition attitudes. Chapter 3 consists of a detailed study of two reviews which are always mentioned in relation to the rise of the *novela social* but are rarely analysed. I refer to *Laye* (1950–3) and *Revista Española* (1953–4), based in Barcelona and Madrid respectively and which act as focal points for the early writers and intellectuals of the movement. Chapter 4 is concerned with the main influences on the formation of the movement which again are always mentioned, but never seriously scrutinized. First, there is Sartrian *engagement* and its reception in Spain, principally through the critical writings of José María Castellet. Second, Italian neo-realism, particularly in film and its role in providing the early social novelists with the technical resources for their much-disputed objectivism. Third, the North American realist novel of the inter-war period (e.g. Hemingway, Dos Passos, Faulkner, Hammett), which offered practical examples of realist writing for Spain's young writers. The fifth and final chapter offers a detailed textual analysis of a series of novels which seem to represent the varied writing options that characterize the rise of the *novela social*. In particular, I single out *Los bravos* (1954) and *El Jarama* (1956) as texts which become important reference points and which set the pattern for the subsequent evolution of the movement.

The *novela social* quickly became an important, even dominant, trend in the late 1950s, being accompanied by developments in other cultural forms and supported by a private publishing industry, anxious to cash in on a type of writing that was relatively profitable and fashionable among a small, middle-class, reading public. We cannot talk in any strict terms of a series of distinct phases or stages in the development of the *novela social*; it is perhaps better understood as a literary movement, a plural, contradictory, shifting phenomenon, that exists as a varied series of attempts to develop a formula for a politically committed literature. At bottom, the aim of the new novelistic realism was to encourage in the reader a 'toma de conciencia' of Spain's unrecorded realities, on the assumption that such an awareness could be translated into a political awareness and thus, eventually, into political action in the real world, as Sartre had argued. As it turned out, the attempt to exploit the novel as a means of raising consciousness suffered from its own mystifications and by the early 1960s broke up under the weight of its own contradictions and a recognition of its lack of impact on social and political change in Spain. This was hardly surprising in a country like Spain, with a minuscule literary reading public and where the novel, even if it could inform and help to transform, was simply too remote from too many people. So, though historically justified, the *novela social* was arguably the victim of its own linguistic innocence, populist sentimentalism, revolutionary romanticism, and the confusion, already evident in Sartre, between the literary and revolutionary deed. However, we cannot dismiss the fact that, during its lifetime, many writers and intellectuals were quite convinced of the power of writing to transform consciousness and to act, indirectly, on reality. If this proved in the end to be a chimera, we still have to acknowledge the honesty and integrity of those who believed it possible.

To sum up, my main interest in the *novela social* has to do with where this realist writing came from. How did it get started and why did it emerge at one moment and not another? How did it relate to other indigenous literary forms? What was new and different about it? How did it carve itself a space in the 1950s literary economy? In short, what were its beginnings? I use the term 'beginnings' rather than 'origins' in the light of Edward Said's useful methodological distinction between the two.[3] He poses the distinction in terms of logocentric versus anti-logocentric concepts or, put another way, the difference between an essentialism and an anti-metaphysical concept. Said is sceptical of inaugural, primal concepts such as origins in that they suggest a single centre, an irreducible core from which all else flows; they hint at a foundational moment, a kind of literary–historical Big Bang. By contrast, the concept of beginnings allows him to avoid the essentialist, metaphysical implications of origins and to shift attention away from texts and writing to the enabling conditions which make these practices possible. So, for Said, beginnings operate as a multilayered set of forces and conditions; they are dispersed but, at the same time, they are loosely held together by means of complex networks of linkages and affiliations. Said thus attempts to avoid a dominant tendency in literary–critical writings, that of relying on models of completion and coherence, by invoking an alternative model sensitive to the impact of historical and contextual determinations. So, for example, the radicalism or otherwise of a piece of writing would not simply inhere in the words on the page but be contextually articulated; in other words, it would be the context that would lend that writing its subversive potential as well as predetermine the sort of writing strategies appropriate to the creation of an oppositional literature. This has obvious relevance to the case of the *novela social*, a mode of writing whose radicalism and rationale are contextually defined and which, in a different context, would be unlikely to generate the same sort of meanings and purposes. So, following Said, I would wish to argue that the beginnings of the *novela social* can best be understood, not according to a pattern of order, but in terms of their dispersion and diversity. Moreover, I believe a model of order inclines towards ideological misrepresentation and that if the goal is to achieve a non-reductive view of a literary–historical process, then a model of dispersion is a far more appropriate and sensitive means of doing so.

Chapter One

PROGRESS OR PROCESS?

As already mentioned in the Introduction, the majority of critical studies broadly coincide in their view of the development of the postwar novel.[1] This, as Nora first pointed out, consists of a 'movimiento de recuperación del realismo, que en conjunto caracteriza la novela de postguerra'.[2] In one way or another, critics seem to accept the idea of a gradually evolving realism in the novel from the 1940s onwards. Some, like Gil Casado, relate this development to 'el retorno al realismo que se había iniciado en la preguerra'; others, like Corrales Egea and Sobejano talk of a 'renovación dentro de una línea realista' or 'la adopción de este nuevo realismo' in the 1940s.[3] Sanz Villanueva perhaps offers the clearest formulation of this idea: 'Parto pues, de la hipótesis de la existencia de un proceso evolutivo en torno a la cuestión del realismo en la novela de postguerra', a process which emerges from a 'literatura testimonial escasamente crítica hasta el surgimiento de unas formas realistas críticas – e incluso socialistas. . . . En esa sucesión, la estética del realismo social ocupa el núcleo central.' Referring to the latter, he adds: 'hay que tener en cuenta que este innegable resurgimiento a partir de mil novecientos cincuenta y tantos, hay que considerarlo como la cima de un proceso que había empezado en años anteriores y que ahora culmina.'[4]

The dominant critical consensus thus rests on the idea of a progressive recovery of realism in the postwar novel, which is seen as a fairly stable, linear, evolutionary development. It is also

1

widely accepted that the realism of the 1950s and early 1960s, the so-called *novela social*, is but a continuation and culmination of a realist trend already in evidence in the 1940s. The process is usually explained in the following way.

After what is generally regarded as a crisis in novel writing during the Dictatorship period of the 1920s (engendered by a dominant, anti-mimetic, 'dehumanized' literary aesthetic, associated with Ortega and other modernist disciples), there emerged a new critical realist trend in the 1930s. This was exemplified in the works of Sender, Arconada, Benavides, Carranque de Ríos, Díaz Fernández, etc., which Nora refers to as the 'novela social de preguerra'.[5] Unfortunately, the development of this new social realism was cut short by the civil war. The postwar novel is thus seen as a gradual and continuous attempt, starting from scratch, to recover the realism of this pre-war 'promoción truncada', as Nora puts it, which is finally achieved in the 1950s.[6] The process of recovery is slow but cumulative, beginning in a rather timid fashion in two pioneering novels: *La familia de Pascual Duarte* (1942) and *Nada* (1945); it passes through a transitional phase of tentative or moderate realism in such novels as *El camino* (1950), *La noria* (1952), and *La colmena* (1951); and finally culminates in the mature, fully-fledged realism of Fernández Sántos, Sánchez Ferlosio, Aldecoa, Goytisolo, and others, the so-called 'novela social'. The critics usually divide up the process into stages, corresponding to decades. Talking of a generalized trend of 'nuevo realismo' in the postwar novel, Sobejano distinguishes two sub-types: a 'novela existencial' in the 1940s and a 'novela social' in the 1950s; Corrales Egea talks of 'los primeros esfuerzos por restaurar el realismo' in the 1940s and 'el giro decisivo' of the 1950s; Buckley divides up the period between 'la etapa existencialista y tremendista' in the 1940s and 'el neorrealismo o realismo social' of the 1950s; Curutchet mentions 'el realismo crítico de la primera generación' and 'el realismo histórico de la generación testimonial'; Sanz Villanueva identifies a 'primera conciencia realista' in the 1940s, giving rise to a 'literatura escasamente crítica', which is followed, in the 1950s, by 'el surgimiento de unas formas realistas críticas'.[7]

Though perhaps rather crudely summarized, the above interpretation raises a number of questions concerning the postwar novel which, while generally implicit and often addressed in existing critical writings, deserve to be briefly re-examined:

1 As a general explanation of the development of the postwar novel, the idea of a gradually evolving realism in the novel seems altogether too simple and straightforward, too neat and unproblematic, especially under dictatorship conditions. Is it sufficient, we may ask, to see the realism of the 1940s as merely a less mature, less evolved version of 1950s realism?

2 If the pre-war social realists begin a process, albeit truncated, which is reactivated after the civil war and culminates in the *novela social* of the 1950s, then what connections, relationships, influences, etc., exist between 1950s realism and its assumed pre-war origins?

3 Critics tend to identify early signs of a recovery of realism in novels that concentrate on the more sordid aspects of life and allegedly express a gloomy, pessimistic outlook. In other words, the recovery process supposedly begins with what is usually referred to as *Tremendismo*, a trend which some critics also relate to existentialism. Is it here, then, that we find the pioneering realist works that establish the parameters and styles for later developments in the novel? Critics also maintain that certain novels occupy a transitional phase in the forward movement of the recovery of realism. In both cases, in what ways and to what extent is the realism of the 1950s indebted to these antecedents? Is it the case, as Sanz Villanueva argues, that without the example of authors 'cuya vinculación con el realismo social es escasa', such as Cela, Laforet, Zunzunegui, Azcoaga, Landínez, Suárez Carreño, etc., 'el grupo joven que en los comienzos de los cincuenta lo protagoniza no hubiera sido posible'?[8]

4 Regarding the social realism or *novela social* of the 1950s, critics still tend to subscribe to the basically formal definition first proposed by Gil Casado and later elaborated by Sobejano.[9] How adequate are such definitions? How useful are they in accounting for the *novela social* as a multifaceted, dynamic, and historically changing literary and cultural phenomenon? In more recent work, notably in Sanz Villanueva, considerable efforts have been made to do just this and to locate the *novela social* more fully in the surrounding conditions of its emergence and development, thus overcoming some of the limitations inherent in earlier formal definitions. Yet, there is still a tendency to regard the *novela social* as a relatively homogeneous trend, whose only major internal change

(as argued by Sanz Villanueva) involves a distinction between an early neo-realist phase, merely ethical in orientation, followed by a more robustly social or politicized phase.[10] Again, how useful are such separations, how far do they explicate or render opaque the nature of the *novela social*, especially its beginnings and emergence, which form the main focus of interest in this analysis?

REALISM AND ITS RECOVERY

As an explanatory model, the idea of an evolving realism suggests that from certain rather 'primitive', early realist forms, the postwar novel evolves in a series of incremental steps or stages to a mature, fully-developed organism in the 1950s. The question arises as to how these less developed forms are recognized as such and marked out as links in the evolutionary chain. This can only be done, it seems to me, from the vantage-point of an already completed process, a frame of reference in relation to which certain novels are regarded as gradual steps towards it. The recovery of realism would seem to be posited, then, according to the end-point of an already completed formal model. In practice, what seems to happen is that critics adopt the *novela social* as the apex of the recovery process, the end-point of its development. From here, and working backwards, they select those novels which exemplify their *a priori* schema, i.e. an already posited evolving realism in the novel. Literary data are made to fit the schema and this is then labelled a recovery. Such an interpretation, I believe, proposes an unusually coherent, continuous, almost seamless line of literary development. The recovery of realism is, it seems, a remarkably smooth-running, uncomplicated process. However, if realism in the novel *evolves*, we are given no satisfactory account of how this happens. If internal criteria alone are insufficient to explain the evolution of literary forms, then what is it that keeps the evolution going, what is it that makes it move? Is it changing historical conditions, changes in the relations between writers and the state, publishers, critics, etc., questions of censorship, new influences and models, shifts in attitudes towards the role of the writer, etc.? Critics on the whole are quite happy to recognize such determinations, but because of their broad commitment to the idea of an evolving realism, they are often unable to deal adequately with the specificities of literary and extra-literary relationships. Besides, the

4

evolutionary model raises other questions to do with the connections between evolved and unevolved forms and the differences between them. Leaving aside the question of what actually makes certain novels become more mature, realist works, what is it that prevents other novels from evolving? What linkages exist, for example, between the *novela social* and those unevolved forms? The dominant consensus view of the postwar novel appears rather ill-equipped to deal with such questions. Indeed, in the end, the explanation of the novel of the 1940s according to the schema of the realist novel of the 1950s is a teleology. The past is selectively reorganized in terms of an assumed present; the possible discontinuities, contradictions, and breaks of literary history – indeed, a whole alternative conception of historical change – is politely disregarded in favour of a *progress* in the novel, a critical narrative of continuity. However, as Edward Thompson reminds us, history cannot be reduced to a single, continuous, unilinear development; equally, the notion of process – which has become fashionable among critics – is misunderstood if seen simply as an ascending path towards some pre-established point; rather, it suggests for Thompson an unstable flow, replete with liaisons and contradictions, dominant and subordinate elements, declining and ascending energies, in short not a coherent development.[11]

To sum up, the dominant view of a progressively evolving realism in the postwar novel may not be totally mistaken or lacking in validity. It all depends, of course, on how widely or otherwise *the novel* is conceived. But, as an explanation of literary developments and changes over two or three decades, the view is arguably just too general and crude. It operates on too selective a textual basis, by excluding large amounts of material and thus radically simplifies a far more irregular, uneven, and contradictory situation. Above all, given its reliance on a model of continuity and coherence, it is unable to provide a more detailed, nuanced account of difference and discontinuity both at the textual and extra-textual levels.

NOVELA SOCIAL DE PREGUERRA

It was Nora who first put forward the concept of 'novela social de preguerra', applying it to works by such writers as Arconada, Arderíus, Benavides, Carranque de Ríos, Díaz Fernández, and

Sender, which emerged in the early years of the Republic. This trend (which Nora also calls a 'literatura revolucionaria', in contrast to a 'literatura conservadora', exemplified by Ledesma Miranda, Zunzunegui, Sánchez Mazas, etc.) signalled 'una rápida recuperación del realismo' in the 1930s and represented 'una ruptura más o menos efectiva y consciente con el mundo burgués, ruptura de tipo humanista y anarquizante generalmente, más bien que racional o apoyado en un pensamiento dialéctico.'[12] In other words, a non-communist or non-Marxist-inspired trend. Nora claims that the 'nuevo realismo' of this 'promoción truncada' stands as 'un eslabón insoslayable entre el realismo clásico y el actual, como avanzada prestigiosa de la actitud estética, de las preferencias temáticas y del temple moral, si no del enfoque ideológico' of 1950s realism, 'el neorrealismo de hoy'.[13] At the same time, Nora regards Sender, 'en muchos aspectos, como el precursor y el maestro efectivo de los más jóvenes'.[14]

For Nora, then, the pre-war social realism represents an important precedent for the realism of the 1950s; also, he seems to propose some degree of continuity between both trends. Unfortunately, Nora nowhere attempts to go beyond his assertions and show more detailed connections between both trends; nor does he explore the relation between realism and his 'literatura conservadora' or follow up the role of Sender as an influential figure in postwar social realism. A number of other critics have taken up such questions and one would have expected them to have explored more fully, with further evidence, Nora's contentions. This has not happened. Indeed, critics have been happy to follow Nora's views, without adopting his more cautious standpoint. For example, Ferreras, like Nora, regards Sender and company as 'la continuación natural de la gran tradición realista de la novela' and the pre-war social realism as 'precursor' of the 1950s realism. Domingo also refers to 1930s social realism as the 'preanuncio' of the 1950s variety. Gil Casado, who has perhaps made the most emphatic claims for influence, stresses the revolutionary character of the pre-war realism. But he fails to clarify whether such works are revolutionary because of their realism, their left-wing politics, or both. Yet, he still connects the trend via Sender ('el escritor intermedio entre la tendencia social de preguerra y el realismo social de la actualidad') to the social realism of the 1950s. Gil Casado is also concerned to 'establecer el proceso de continuidad, la evolución de la tendencia (social) para ver cuál es el punto de partida de la actual novela social'.[15]

On the whole, critics who claim a relationship between pre- and postwar realisms tend to do so on a very general level, using terms such as precedent and precursor, but rarely spelling out in detail what these terms imply. Only Gil Casado has gone as far as to say that 'La novela social actual muestra una directa influencia de la novela social de la década de 1930', arguing, for example, that López Pacheco's *Central eléctrica* (1958) 'se inspira directamente en *La Turbina* de César M. Arconada', or that Ferres' *Con la manos vacías* (1964) is a re-working of the plot of Sender's *El lugar de un hombre*.[16] However, beyond a rather sketchy comparison of subject matter and themes, Gil Casado offers little or no supporting evidence. One cautionary factor in this question of influence is that writers such as López Pacheco and Ferres, as well as Sánchez Ferlosio and Fernández Santos, give no indication in the 1950s of knowing or of having read Sender and company. Direct influence – via a knowledge of these pre-war writers – thus seems rather unlikely. This is arguably compounded by post-civil war conditions in which such writers simply ceased to exist. After 1939, works by writers and poets such as Sender, Aub, Chacel, Blasco Ibáñez, Alberti, Hernández, and Cernuda, as well as the pre-war social realists were officially outlawed. They were not to be found in libraries, given that the works of *non-sancti* writers were purged from the shelves and their names removed from the catalogues. Some copies would have survived in private collections, though it is likely that their circulation would be rather limited due, among other things, to the fear of sanctions for handling banned books. The slow process of rehabilitation and recovery of 'enemy' writers (Machado being perhaps the classic case) and the traffic in proscribed books would not substantially fill the vacuum.

In general, it would seem that the works of the pre-war social realists were unlikely to be available to the social novelists of the 1950s and consequently were not read by them. An indication of this state of ignorance appears in the debate between Guillermo de Torre and Juan Goytisolo, concerning the issue of a 'literatura nacional popular' and appearing in articles published in *Insula* in 1959.[17] Arguing that modern Spanish writers had reneged on their responsibilities towards the reading public and its needs, Goytisolo laid much of the blame on the pernicious influence of Ortega's ideas, which had inspired an elitist, aestheticist, and escapist literature. Pre-war modernism, so Goytisolo alleged, had established a stranglehold on the novel and had reinforced the already considerable divide between writer and public, as well as between writer and social reality. Rising to Ortega's defence, Guillermo de Torre reminded Goytisolo that the so-called 'dehumanized' conception of art had been contested in its time by writers such as Sender, Díaz Fernández, Arderíus, Benavides, Arconada, etc., adding 'En ellos . . . tiene Goytisolo sus inmediatos antecesores realistas; ahí encontrará el eslabón que juzga perdido en la línea de esa literatura "humana", "nacional" que reclama'.[18] Here, either Goytisolo knew of these pre-war writers and neglected to mention them for tactical reasons or, far more likely, he was simply ignorant of them. On this same question, Sanz Villanueva states:

> Estos novelistas sociales de preguerra quedaron dentro de la península del todo olvidados, con el fin de la contienda. Su labor se continuó, en algún caso, en el exilio y la obra anterior a 1939 no circuló en absoluto entre nosotros, por lo que difícilmente han podido influir en los escritores de los cincuenta . . . su influencia en los novelistas del realismo crítico es nula.[19]

Corrales Egea also points out 'las nuevas generaciones de postguerra ignoraron esos intentos de los años 1930 al 1936 en pro de una novela testimonial, enraizada e incluso comprometida.'[20] To these doubts about influence can be added the fact that, when dealing with pre-civil war writers, Castellet and Goytisolo refer only to Baroja as being of any significance. On Sender and company, they are silent. All of which leads to the conclusion that the claim for influence is at least unlikely, if not mistaken. Indeed, efforts to establish connections, it seems to me, have more to do with critical practice than historical fact, in particular with the critical investment in models of literary development based on notions of coherence and continuity. However, as regards the question of influence, it seems likely that a minimal, indirect, second-hand awakening inside Spain to the pre-war social realists came about only with the publication of Nora's pioneering study and with Marra López's *Narrativa española fuera de España* in 1963.[21] Before that, it seems, ignorance prevailed.

TREMENDISMO

As previously mentioned, the development of the postwar novel is usually divided up into stages, the first of which corresponds to the 1940s. Here, a re-emerging realism is said to focus on the individual and while subjective and only very tenuously critical, it expresses a profound *desengaño* or *desencanto*. This gloomy, pessimistic outlook supposedly reflects a genuine collective attitude or consciousness prevalent in postwar Spain and is associated with a developing realism in that it seems to run counter to official triumphalism. In more concrete terms, this outlook is expressed in the novel through an emphasis on the most unpleasant, repulsive, sordid, and violent aspects of human behaviour. The recovery of realism supposedly begins, then, under the banner of *Tremendismo*. As Sanz Villanueva puts it:

> Frente – y a la vez paralela – a una literatura evasiva, la notación tremendista ponía de relieve la existencia de una realidad mísera, amarga, que no ocultaba lacras . . . descubre aspectos poco halagüeños de la realidad – sin intencionalidad crítica ni mucho menos social – que pueden ser un lejano precedente para el testimonio que realiza la generación del medio siglo.[22]

Though only tentatively proposed, Sanz Villanueva seems to argue that *Tremendismo* constitutes a 'lejano precedente' for the realism of the 1950s because of a general similarity of content: the depiction of mainly unsavoury aspects of a marginalized, hidden, otherwise unreported reality. This may well be the case, but what the quest for similarities leaves out of account is the manifest differences between trends, especially questions of style, treatment, and purpose, as well as the varying contextual determinations. Also, even if *Tremendismo* is accepted as a precedent for 1950s realism, the critic would still have to recognize the variations and changes in its subsequent development and the possibility that 1950s realism might well be formally and ideologically unrecognizable in relation to its novelistic ancestor. Moreover, in trying to connect *Tremendismo* with the *novela social* in terms of an evolving realism, there is the temptation to designate the tendency as realist simply by contrasting it with the manifestly escapist nature of much of official culture in the 1940s. That is, *Tremendismo* is realist because it seems not to conform to official literary models. Apart from being an oversimplistic correlation, this view tends to ignore the fact that, like other official cultural products, *Tremendismo* was produced by writers of the winning side in the civil war and under the same political auspices as the more triumphalist, optimistic works to which it is contrasted. In other words, *Tremendismo* was just as much an official literature as other trends and genres.

To accept the linkage between *Tremendismo* and the *novela social* would imply seeing, say, *La familia de Pascual Duarte* as a less evolved form of 1950s realism, such as *Los bravos*. This, it seems to me, is both formally and historically doubtful, even allowing for the intervening process of variation and change mentioned above. Indeed, to do so is to privilege superficial similarities over considerable differences, not the least of which is the fact that Cela and Fernández Santos belong to different generations and formative movements, with different purposes and priorities guiding their writing. Besides, when we compare their respective treatments of their subject matter, their construction of the 'real', the differences seem to outweigh the similarities. In contrast to the more detached mode of narration characteristic of *Los bravos* and its attempt objectively to render the 'real', the realism of *La familia de Pascual Duarte* is filtered quite visibly and self-consciously through the playful re-working of conventions taken from the epistolary novel and confessional literature. Several different narrative viewpoints (the 'nota del transcriptor', the letter from Pascual to the friend of the conde de Torremejía, the letters from the chaplain and the Civil Guard, etc.) complement the unusually articulate written record of the narrator–protagonist, a figure who seems to embody the terror and the tenderness of a timeless hispanic machismo. This is articulated through an almost sensationalist emphasis on sex, violence, murder, sadism, irrationalism, and death – all of which, paradoxically or not, is given a highly lyrical, sensual, and peculiarly voyeuristic treatment. In short, a mixture of 'estilo brutal' and a view of life reduced to its barest, most elemental, biological determinants.

Cela's novel may well be the spark that ignites the recovery of realism, but to say as much without more detailed comparison and without taking into account the multiple transformations in technique and outlook occurring between *Pascual Duarte* and *Los bravos* is to ignore the workings of history and historical change. It is also to evade the possible conclusion that a 1950s realism has evolved in quite unexpected directions and ways in comparison to its supposed progenitors. Indeed, the supposed continuity between trends, based on the common feature of 'the discovery of a hidden reality', arguably corresponds to quite different conceptions of reality and radically different treatments. In other words, an assumed identity of content in no way implies an identity of form and ideological or political perspective. In the end, to say that *La familia de Pascual Duarte* is a distant precedent of the *novela social* is not saying very much; in fact, unless the intervening determinations and connections can be made in a detailed fashion, it seems rather gratuitous. One rough, rather inconclusive indicator of the lack of connection between trends is that social novelists, like Fernández Santos, totally disregard *Tremendismo* as a precedent. Of course, they do not ignore Cela; but that is a different matter as we shall see shortly. In short, a reasonably convincing case, supported by evidence, is yet to be made for the role of *Tremendismo* as precursor of 1950s realism.

THE TRANSITION TO SOCIAL REALISM

As we have seen, the notion of a progressive recovery of realism in the postwar novel assumes a basic continuity between a supposedly timid, moderate, existential realism in the 1940s and a more robust, thorough-going social realism in the 1950s. In other words, beneath the surface variation in forms, there exists a kind of essential realist identity in all the novels which represent the recovery process. The difference between the realisms of the 1940s and 1950s then, would necessarily be one of degree rather than kind. While many critics simply take this relationship for granted and enquire no further, others have attempted to flesh out the possible linkages between stages in the recovery process. They do so by positing a type of transitional phase between one realism and another, singling out certain novels as setting the pattern for the social realism of the 1950s. Three novels in particular are invariably mentioned: *Las últimas horas* (1950) by José Suárez Carreño, *La noria* (1952) by Luis Romero and heading the list *La colmena* (1951) by Camilo José Cela.[23]

At the outset, it has to be admitted that in a model of literary development based on notions of continuity and progress, the idea of a transitional phase or the positing of immediate precedents might respond more to a desire for theoretical consistency than to historical reality. Also, the assumed role of these precedents, as definers of the frame in which the social realism of the 1950s emerges, might tend towards simplifying a rather more complex, nuanced situation; indeed, rather than a smooth passage from one stage to another, a transition might well contain elements of discontinuity and rupture which, because of the model adopted, are disregarded. In the present case, one slightly disconcerting factor is that those young realist writers who were developing their craft in the early 1950s and thus were likely to be influenced by novelistic precedents, e.g. Fernández Santos, Aldecoa, Goytisolo, Sánchez Ferlosio, never actually acknowledged the first two of the three novels cited, nor regarded them as important antecedents. At the same time, in the early critical writings of such a crucial figure as Castellet, e.g. *Notas sobre literatura española contemporánea* (1955), Suárez Carreño is merely mentioned by name, while Romero is reviewed only to be rejected out of hand.[24] Among the early figures usually connected with the social novel trend then, there appears to be a degree of ignorance, or indifference, if not a conscious dismissal of the first two novels taken as antecedents.

As for the novels themselves, it is difficult to see *Las últimas horas* as exploiting the sort of features commonly attributed by critics to the *novela social*, i.e. collective protagonist, city as main focus, objective technique, social critique.[25] Rather, the novel concentrates on three, well-defined, individual characters (Carmen, Aguado, and Manolo *el golfo*), subjects them to detailed psychological scrutiny and takes up the themes of sexual frustration, moral propriety, and guilt. The city of Madrid acts largely as a backcloth and the scenarios it provides for the action (the elegant, nocturnal haunts of the rich and the dingy passageways and street corners inhabited by *el hampa*) are arguably exceptional rather than representative. Of course, the novel deals in contrasts, not only of setting, but of character and social grouping. However, rather than grasp the opportunity to explore social divisions and class differences in any depth, the author chooses to travel in the opposite direction. That is, the novel focuses largely on emotional and psychological identifications between characters of different social levels, and on situations in which social inequalities are overcome by moments of common suffering and 'simpatía humana'. At the same time, Suárez Carreno perhaps reinforces certain stereotyped images of rich and poor by indulging in *costumbrista* treatments of characters and presenting them, especially the poor, in rather picturesque, exotic ways.

As for *La noria*, we do indeed find a collective protagonist (37 characters in all), all of whom are inhabitants of Barcelona; they also seem to be drawn from a fairly wide cross-section of city-dwellers, but without exception they are affected by exactly the same type and degree of alienation produced by city living. The author's own writerly artifice is highly visible, not only in the use of the technical device by which one character is rather mechanically linked to the next in line, but also in the intrusive narratorial voice and its often moralistic asides. Also, rather than being representative and more nuanced, character portrayal tends towards superficiality and uniformity, as differences and variations are flattened out by a rigid application of the same technique. But if *La noria* scores well on its collective protagonist, city focus, and its scope, the visibility of its formal conventions does not suggest a significant step towards objective narration. As for its outlook, rather than provide a critical view of the pressures of city living, it seems to indulge in a certain resigned acceptance of things as they are, in a clichéd, moralistic tone. Reviewing the novel shortly after publication, Castellet adopted a very hard, uncompromising view, virtually accusing Romero of plagiarizing the technical novelties of Cela's *La colmena*. He also regarded the linking device between characters as too crude and obvious and character portrayal as too close to stereotype, objecting strongly to their moral and psychological uniformity, 'son pues títeres, nunca hombres'. For the future guru of the *novela social*, *La noria* was nothing less than 'un lamentable *bluff*, un engaño más para el lector español de novelas, tan sufrido, tan desamparado el pobre, cuya especie lógicamente va desapareciendo'.[26]

As regards *La colmena*, its position and status as a transitional novel is rather more complex. This is especially so when the author himself has defined the novel's narrative attitude and purpose in terms tantalizingly reminiscent of the prescriptions of neo-realism: 'Esta novela mía no aspira a ser más – ni menos ciertamente – que un trozo de vida narrado paso a paso, sin reticencias, sin extrañas tragedias, sin caridad, como la vida discurre, exactamente como la vida discurre.'[27] Add to this Cela's other remarks that *La colmena* is 'la novela de la ciudad . . . Madrid, en una época cierta y no imprecisa, 1942', 'una novela sin héroe', 'una novela reloj',[28] (which relies on a complex system of linkages and cross references, temporal and spatial compression, as well as a collective protagonist of 296 characters, whose multiple perspectives regarding the struggles for survival in the 1940s are rendered in fragmentary, impressionistic, and humorous fashion, etc.) and we would appear to have the very prototype of the *novela social*.[29] However, this view requires a certain amount of qualification. To begin with, part of the case for seeing *La colmena* as a pioneer social novel relies on the fact that it was published at the beginning of the 1950s, the latter being the decade of the social novel. But the equally relevant fact that Cela produced a first version of the novel in 1945 (as well as four subsequent versions), puts the actual production of the novel in a very different writing context chronologically.[30] Indeed, it relocates the novel squarely alongside such works as *Pabellón de reposo* (1944), *Nuevas andanzas y desventuras de Lazarillo de Tormes* (1945), the short stories of *Esas nubes que pasan* (1945) and *El bonito crimen del carabinero y otras invenciones* (1947). In other words, when placed in a different intertextual setting, the classification and meanings usually practised on the novel begin to alter. Rather than heralding the dawn of a new social realism, *La colmena* becomes re-readable in terms of the *Tremendismo*, vitalist irrationalism, black humour, lyricism, and aestheticism which featured prominently in Cela's work in the 1940s.

There is also the fact that having been rejected by Censura on several occasions, *La colmena* was finally published, not in Spain, but in Buenos Aires in 1951. This caused Cela himself to be temporarily expelled from Madrid's Press Association, deprived of his journalist's card, and his name prohibited in Spanish newspapers.[31] Such apparently harsh treatment no doubt fuelled interest in the novel and was probably influential in portraying it as a work of serious social criticism. However, what is curious about the publication of *La colmena* is that, having had to appear abroad, copies for review were made available almost immediately afterwards inside Spain to official reviews and magazines such as *Correo Literario* and *Cuadernos Hispanoamericanos*.[32] So despite his disgrace, Cela could still rely on the support of a wide network of friends and connections (in particular Juan Aparicio, his literary godfather) in reviews, publishing houses and the state bureaucracies. Castellet, however, seemed to view Cela as innocent victim of a corrupt and irresponsible system. And angered by the novel's publication abroad, he greeted it with uncharacteristic admiration and enthusiasm:

> Con *La colmena*, Camilo José Cela ha escrito la primera, la única novela española, que en los últimos 15 años lleva consigo la problemática del hombre español actual, la única novela que se expresa en un lenguaje literario cuya técnica y estilo están al día dentro de su tiempo ... y C.J.C. ha conseguido – y en ello estriba su originalidad – todas estas características, que no lograron otros novelistas de hoy, escribiendo precisamente un libro que está dentro de la mejor, quizá la única línea posible de nuestra novela: la que arranca de la picaresca para acabar, inmediatamente antes de *La colmena*, en Baroja.[33]

For Castellet, Cela's novel signalled a major breakthrough. It seemed to contain the prerequisites for a new type of novel, hitherto unknown in Spain, which he had been advocating for the young writers of his own generation: a critical intention, a focus on postwar Spain, a modern, up-to-date technique and a connection with a certain literary tradition, exemplified by Baroja and the picaresque regarded as examples of a committed literature. Like Castellet, the young Goytisolo also considered *La colmena* as something of a pioneering work, placing it alongside *Los bravos* and *El Jarama* as another example of a new novel, whose chief merit lay in 'el descubrimiento de los sectores menos favorecidos'.[34] Of course, both Castellet and Goytisolo take a rather selective and highly idiosyncratic view of Baroja and the picaresque. In fact, the sort of reading they engage in – one which emphasizes realism, focus on the lower classes, combativity, commitment – seems to constitute a projection of the type of novel they were demanding for their own time and from their own generation. The reading they make of *La colmena* is just as distinctive and *sui generis*, placing the novel within the same *desired* tradition and the same set of concerns. Moreover, as Castellet again points out,

> tanto *Viaje a la Alcarria* como *La colmena* son dos libros que han sido repetidamente leídos por los jovenes narradores y de ellos han sacado no pocas lecciones que, después, han utilizado a su

manera y que incluso, como determinada concepción de la literatura, han intentado superar por otros caminos.[35]

It would seem then that *La colmena* did indeed represent a significant stimulus initially to the emergence of the new realism of the 1950s. But Cela's influence was arguably limited to the prestige he enjoyed as Spain's only serious writer and due to the fact that *La colmena* dealt with postwar Madrid with a degree of technical sophistication. And as Castellet admits, the younger writers would later come to reconsider and even reject Cela as an influence, owing largely to differences in ideology and treatment of subject matter.[36] Curiously, if we are to talk of influence at all, it seems not to emerge in the novels of Fernández Santos, Sánchez Ferlosio, or the early Goytisolo, i.e. writers who we would expect to take into account the example of *La colmena*. In Aldecoa, there may be vague connections and resemblances in style and subject matter, not in the early novels, but in some of his short stories.[37] Indeed, if there is a debt to Cela incurred by the realism of the 1950s, it springs not so much from *La colmena* as from the travelogue (the *libro de viajes*) genre begun in *Viaje a la Alcarria*. Here, we might well find a precedent for such works as Goytisolo's *Campos de Níjar* (1960), *Caminando por las Hurdes* (1960) by López Salinas and Ferres, or *Por el río abajo* (1964) by Ferres. Whether Cela's work provides the younger writers with a 'model' for the travelogue is hard to say; in fact, any similarity seems to stop at the adoption of the travelogue approach, since the younger writers arguably set out from very different ideological standpoints and exploit the approach rather than adopt Cela's model. On the whole, the case for seeing *La colmena* as a crucial precedent in the emergence of the *novela social* seems rather less compelling than many critics would have us believe. Cela was no doubt regarded by 1950s social novelists as a good writer, but not as a good novelist;[38] more importantly perhaps, he seemed not to share their commitment to developing an oppositional realism nor their ideas on the writer's social responsibility. So while writers like Suárez Carreño and Romero seem to have been ignored by the young social novelists, Cela appears to have been initially influential (especially in the critical writings of Castellet), but is later rejected.

NOVELA SOCIAL

The term *novela social* has long been recognized as inadequate and unsatisfactory to designate the realist novel of the 1950s and 1960s.[39] Its deficiencies and imprecision are partly attributable to the historical context of its emergence, i.e. dictatorship conditions, and to that distinctive language of indirection adopted by writers and critics working within a censorship regime. *Novela social* is thus a euphemism, a trope used to refer to a type of writing and, just as importantly, to its standpoints and purposes which, while recognizable to writers, allies, and also opponents, could not be openly declared. As Soldevila-Durante suggests,

> De hecho, bajo el título de novela social se ha tendido a encubrir lo que en términos más precisos convendría llamar novela socialista, cuya intención, no por implícito menos real, es despertar o iluminar la conciencia frente a las injusticias de la clase dominante burguesa en el estado dictatorial.[40]

In broad terms, Soldevila-Durante is clearly right to point to the consciousness-raising objectives of the *novela social* and to equate 'social' with 'socialista'. But to do so *tout court* is, on the one hand, perhaps to beg the question of 'socialista' and its meanings (does it refer to 'realismo socialista' or perhaps to the PSOE of the 1950s?) and on the other, to head for a single, unitary definition of the term, forgetting that it has been a highly contested category and variously defined over time. In other words, during its life as a culturally active, received, circulating term, a number of conflicting and contradictory meanings have been imposed, resisted, and negotiated on and around it, both conceptually and in practice. For this reason, it is difficult to affirm that *novela social* means this or that or to posit an originary, pure, stable meaning, to which we can all refer as a starting point, but which has since been distorted or devalued. But what is clear is that the varied appropriations and re-inflections of the term have left us with quite a complex and confused picture.

For example, by the late 1950s, at a time when the *novela social* was clearly beginning to achieve a degree of autonomy and recognition as an identifiable trend, writers such as Zunzunegui and Darío Fernández Flórez were proclaiming themselves as 'novelistas sociales'.[41] In fact, like many other writers, they were responding to the unusual success and growth of the trend and

17

arguably jumping on the bandwaggon. For writers such as Ferres, López Salinas, and López Pacheco, however, Zunzunegui and company were distinctly unlikely, if not incongruous fellow travellers, especially in terms of their careers and their known ideological affiliations. So, not surprisingly, faced with the prospect of being grouped alongside these erstwhile stalwarts of official cultural values, many social novelists understandably baulked at the term and ended up rejecting it. As Marfany has argued, by challenging the adjective 'social' or by affirming that all literature is by definition social, the young writers of the 1950s were trying to respond to certain confusions: first, that *novela social* was being used in too narrow a fashion, thus excluding from the grouping writers whose work, though formally different, was exploring territory and issues similar to those taken up by the 'sociales', with similar purposes. Second, the term was often applied in too inclusive a fashion, embracing writers whose work, while formally similar, was none the less ideologically at variance with that of the 'sociales'. Third, *novela social* was frequently used in a pejorative sense to marginalize or disqualify as artistically invalid novels whose 'social' content was too explicit or direct.[42] This invariably gave rise to tactical defences of the aesthetic dimension of novel writing, but not as an end in itself; rather, art was subordinate to what it expressed. As García Hortelano stated in 1959, 'No admito la novela artística como entidad independiente; creo en la belleza únicamente en funcion de la expresividad.' And the latter, as López Salinas put it, was to attempt to 'revelar las relaciones sociales, mostrar el mundo tal como es'.[43]

Challenged, denounced, and frequently rejected in its time, the term *novela social* has none the less survived, having become historically sedimented and incorporated into the critical writings on the subject. But it has survived and been understood not so much as a sign variously occupied by different meanings, i.e. as the summation of its historical activations and reorganizations. Rather, critics such as Gil Casado and Sobejano have tended to opt for the single, unitary, comprehensive definition, distinguished by phases perhaps, but generally accepted as valid and applicable to the whole of the treñ.[44] That is, the *novela social* has mostly been defined from the *inside*, as a group or class of texts, based on a number of finite features more or less common to all members of that class. The problem here is that in terms of dealing with the political and ideological aims and underpinnings of the *novela social*, the sort of definitions used by Gil Casado and Sobejano are arguably too wide and vague. In fact, Gil Casado's definition is unable to approach the question in a more precise, focused way. Sobejano, on the other hand, attempts to provide an interpretation, but his advocacy of a democratic humanism is perhaps rather misleading and distorts the specifically political and revolutionary character of the *novela social*, in the late 1950s and early 1960s.[45] In this connection, critics tend to divide up the development of the *novela social* between an early, social, moral, or humanist phase and a later radical, critical, politicized phase, the division being implicit not only in the chronology adopted but also in the critical terms used. Gil Casado, for example, while claiming that the *novela social* forms part of wider 'realismo crítico o social', talks of a 'novela social de crítica' as a first stage, followed by a 'novela social de denuncia'. Amorós, who is perhaps more explicit in his terminology, proposes an early 'realismo social no politizado' (which includes Aldecoa, Matute, Fernández Santos, and Sánchez Ferlosio), followed by a 'realismo crítico'. Esteban Soler distinguishes between an early 'neorrealismo', and then a 'realismo social', followed by a 'realismo crítico'.[46] In similar fashion, Sanz Villanueva also proposes an early 'grupo neorrealista', which leads into a more clearly delineated 'social' grouping. It is worth quoting his formulation at length since it seems to encapsulate this widespread critical view:

Pero la diferenciación entre un grupo neorrealista y otro de más netos propósitos sociales creo que es una de las distinciones fundamentales para comprender – y explicar – la evolución del realismo crítico. No se trata de ninguna clase de bizantinismo, sino de una separación real – aunque no fácilmente detectable – que obedece a unos determinados propósitos. Los escritores neorrealistas tienen una intención testimonial a la que añaden una leve carga crítica . . . La práctica de los realistas sociales es, respecto al grupo anterior, sólo una cuestión de grado que supone una intensificación: menosprecio – o poco aprecio – en bastantes casos de la forma y decidido compromiso social hasta los límites de una literatura política de denuncia.[47]

Sanz Villanueva posits the existence of a *real* separation between two groups within the *novela social* trend, but immediately and rather curiously qualifies this by describing it as 'no fácilmente detectable'. If it does exist and obeys certain (again unspecified) 'propósitos', then it seems not to affect the evolution of the *novela social* as a writing practice: despite the division, an early neo-realist phase gives way, in an apparently smooth, seamless fashion, to a later critical realist, politicized phase, the difference being merely one of degree, the later phase simply a more intense version of the earlier one. Is there perhaps a paradox here? On the one hand, Sanz Villanueva seems to argue for a continuity between the realism of his two groups, while at the same time claiming that they are divided by an unexplored 'separación real'. What kind of separation is it? Sanz Villanueva focuses on writing practice and chooses a feature which at the best of times is difficult to quantify: the degree of explicitness of the critical intentionality of a novel. He also appends the widely accepted idea of the lack of concern, in novels of the later, politicized phase, towards formal and aesthetic matters. Whatever the terminology or subdivisions employed, by this or other critics, the end-result always appears to be the same: the cordoning-off of certain early writers from the rest of the trend, i.e. Fernández Santos, Sánchez Ferlosio, and Aldecoa. These are the very writers who tend to be regarded, particularly in literary terms, as the best and most accomplished of the social novelists. They are also the writers who are thus least vulnerable to the sorts of attack and jibe invariably levied at the *novela social*: technically and artistically deficient, aesthetically poverty-stricken, politically ineffective, a waste of time, etc.

The division within the *novela social* between an early and a later phase, characterized by a growing degree of politicization in the novel may not be totally unfounded. It cannot be denied, for example, that writers of the mid- and late 1950s shift their thematic focus from rural poverty and lower-class alienation and begin to deal more overtly in their novels with cases of exploitation, repression, injustice, etc., particularly in the workplace and the home (e.g. *Central Eléctrica* (1958), *La piqueta* (1959) and *La mina* (1960)) reinforcing a certain proletarian tendency within the *novela social*. On a wider plane, though the delay and the connections between one dimension and another are a matter of considerable theoretical as well as historical debate, we cannot detach developments in the novel from those taking place in Spain and outside within the opposition movements of the time: the politicization of the universities, influenced by the circulation of texts on Marxism and writings by Marxists, authorized as well as clandestine, among students and intellectuals; the evolution of the notion of political commitment within the European left, especially from Sartre and in the light of destalinization and anti-colonial struggles; also, within Spain, the role of the P.C.E. in attempting to organize inter-class, popular mobilizations against the regime by way of national strikes (in 1958 and 1959) on the assumptions (radically mistaken) of widespread popular support and the imminent collapse of the regime. Juan Goytisolo usefully captures the mood of the times among opposition writers and intellectuals:

> En el momento en que aparecen las primeras novelas y poemas de la generación del medio siglo, el fin de la guerra fría, el deshielo ideológico del campo socialista alimentan la esperanza de una transformación radical y a corto plazo de la anacrónica sociedad española: este objetivo (irrealizable, lo sabemos hoy) parecía exigir de nosotros la movilización, a su servicio, de todas nuestras energías . . . el quehacer literario se integraba en una lucha más general y ajena a la literatura, en la que ésta actuaba de avanzadilla, y como tal, sujeta a una serie de consideraciones de orden estratégico y táctico. Escribir un poema o una novela tenía entonces (así lo creíamos) el valor de un acto: por un venturoso azar histórico acción y escritura se confundían en un mismo cauce, literatura y vida se identificaban. . .[48]

Nor can we ignore the fact that after the publication of *El Jarama* Sánchez Ferlosio fell silent, Fernández Santos turned his attention to film making and Aldecoa, though continuing to write, seems to have been somewhat marginalized in relation to the writers coming through in the late 1950s. This silence might well indicate early doubts at least in Fernández Santos and Sánchez Ferlosio concerning the use of literature as an instrument to affect or help to transform social reality. There would seem to be something of a case, then, for accepting the politicization of the *novela social*, and because of their relative lack of visibility in the later development of the trend, a certain detachment on the part of the early writers mentioned above. Now whether this is sufficient reason to claim a fundamental separation between two groups within the *novela social* seems to me to be rather dubious. Indeed, the separation, it seems to me, is in part more an effect of the attempt retrospectively to salvage from the *novela social* writers who, after the ignominious demise of the trend, and the resulting accusations and recriminations this provoked, can still be regarded as 'good'. In other words, these are writers who are supposedly untainted by the deleterious effects of trying to write politicized literature, writers who eschew a 'denuncia' in favour *only* of a careful, measured, moderate sprinkling of 'crítica' over their objective testimony.

This supposed separation, as Marfany has argued, is difficult to sustain and distorts a more complex picture.[49] It leaves out of account the existence of censorship, in relation to which any discussion of the explicitness or otherwise of the novel and an author's intentions has to be set. It also passes over the very rationale underlying the writing of the *novela social*: the suppression of the author's views and identity in the interests of the objective rendering of the real, a prerequisite for the collaboration of the reader. Finally, in historical terms, we have to accept that the *novela social* takes a number of different narrative and political routes, especially in the early stages while an aesthetic is being constructed, tried out, and modified according to certain formal and ideological influences and inputs. It is doubtful whether we can speak, in any precise way, of a 'neo-realist' group in the early years (see the early novels of Goytisolo or Aldecoa), although the ideas and prescriptions of Italian neo-realism do play a major role in the formation of a certain writing style and approach. Moreover, in terms of overall purposes and objectives, as Goytisolo points out, even in the early years writers are engaged in developing a political literature, but, I would argue, in different ways and according to varying standpoints and views both on politics and on the degree to which writers should attempt to reflect their positions in the novel. So, while critics, on the outside, have been predominantly concerned with dividing up the *novela social* between politicized and non-politicized writers, on the inside, debates arguably turned on the relation of novel writing to the demands of a particular historical conjuncture as well as on the appropriate combinations and interconnections between aesthetics and politics, between literary and political efficacy, i.e. how to produce a novel which, while as far as possible retaining its artistic integrity, could be successful in raising reader consciousness. Clearly, the formula for the *novela social* would vary according to a complex set of determinations, including matters of political calculation and relatedly, the writer's relationship with his audience. In this connection, the relatively rapid and unexpected success of the *novela social* in the late 1950s prompted questions as to how writers should respond to the nature of their newly emerging readership. Should they, for example, continue to develop a proletarian realism according to the tenets of a socialist realism, or should they concentrate on a critique of the bourgeoisie? Such questions indicate the sort of theoretical debates occurring and also signal the contradictory and paradoxical situation of the radical writer in Spain: writing for radical social change but being read by an almost exclusively bourgeois public. The higher visibility of the anti-bourgeois strain within the *novela social* in the late 1950s perhaps reflects a response to the above questions. That is, writers of predominantly bourgeois extraction increasingly doubt their ability to reflect the reality of a lower class, to which they do not belong or of which they have no direct knowledge. At the same time, they implicitly raise the question of the risk of falling into a voluntaristic and romantic solidarity with the working classes. The sort of debates surrounding these issues were no doubt of major importance in determining the various novelistic responses which go to make up the *novela social* and the pursuit of an effective writing formula. But, as Goytisolo again observes in a rather embittered fashion, this goal was somewhat elusive and, indeed, neither side of the literature-politics equation was satisfied in practice: 'Supeditando el arte a la política, rendíamos un flaco servicio a ambos; políticamente ineficaces nuestras obras eran, para colmo, literariamente mediocres; creyendo hacer literatura política no hacíamos ni una ni otra cosa.'[50]

In an equally hard and disillusioning comment, Curutchet highlights the evident but, for him, naively misplaced political character of what he calls that 'realismo ingenuo' of the 1950s, arguing that writers involved in the trend were victims of:

una doble equivocación: primero, su convicción acerca de la proximidad e inevitabilidad de la caída del régimen, a colaborar con la cual consagraron sus mejores esfuerzos; y por otro lado, la convicción de que a la novela correspondía informar objetiv-amente acerca de una realidad silenciada por la prensa oficial; y también, por último, una convicción acerca de la supuesta descomposición de la burguesía española y su sistema de valores.[51]

Whatever our final judgement on the *novela social* as a literary and political project, the point to be made here is that while a certain case can be made for differentiating between early and later writers and works, the notion of a *real* separation still needs to be more fully substantiated. In the meantime, it is worth retaining the idea of the *novela social* as a broadly definable but variegated trend, rather than one with separate yet linked parts or one consisting of two progressive stages or phases. More importantly, it seems to me that we need to move beyond the limitations and empiricist dilemmas occasioned by the sort of broad, unitary definitions analysed above. We need to move to a recognition of the very real variability and diversity of the *novela social* as a trend and attempt to incorporate that understanding into our view. In short, the problem is not one of definition, but of the considerable gap between current definitions and a socio-literary phenomenon called *novela social*. One possible and fairly obvious way of bridging this gap is to expand the notion of *novela social* from a unity of formal resemblances or a teleologically-based continuity to a more sociological relationship. That is, an historically and contextually informed relationship between a number of different, perhaps even incompatible narrative types and approaches which develop, not in a discrete, linear, cumulative fashion, but contrast, overlap, and even pull in different directions. The *novela social* would then be conceived as a series of diverse attempts to construct or create a politically committed novel. And an appreciation of this variability would seem to be essential for any genuine grasp of the trend's historical character. The *novela social*, then, could be conceived as a broadly definable but internally contradictory phenomenon, a unity in diversity.

If we accept the notion of the *novela social* as a definable class of writing, this seems to take a little while to emerge. Outlining a provisional scenario, we could argue that only in the mid-1950s does the *novela social* begin to distinguish itself as a class. Before then, in novels such as *Los bravos* (1954), *El fulgor y la sangre* (1954) and *Juegos de manos* (1954), what we have are a number of formally rather disparate attempts to develop an early committed literature, by no means unequivocally realist or testimonial but informed by

Sartrian 'engagement' and Italian neo-realism and by a politics based primarily on a set of moral or ethical concerns. Commenting on the work of these and other young writers of the time, Castellet began to observe certain general, common features among them: 'parece evidente', he wrote, 'que esta "última promoción" parece, en principio, más preparada y con mayor empuje que su inmediata antecesora y, especialmente, más compacta, más unida en su ideología e intenciones.'[52]

But, it is arguably only in 1956 and thereafter that the *novela social* actually develops a distinctive identity as a class and begins to make an impact on novel writing. A major factor in this process of formation is undoubtedly the success of *El Jarama* in winning the *Premio Nadal*. This was perhaps the crucial breakthrough which put the new realism on the map and gave it a degree of commercial viability and critical backing. Also, while Sánchez Ferlosio's novel provided writers with formal and technical guidelines and acted as a model for the emerging objective realism, the Nadal prize was no doubt vital in generating a readership for the *novela social*. This was very likely composed, in large part, of students and intellectuals, but would quickly become significant enough for publishers (such as Destino) to incorporate the *novela social* into their promotions and publishing policy. Strictly speaking, a new literary class can be seen as emerging only when there exists a public consciousness about the class and its conventions among readers, writers, critics and publishers. Though difficult to determine with any precision and in relation to the *novela social*, this consciousness only really starts to take shape after 1956, when the *novela social* begins to attract a more sustained, polemical, critical-theoretical input (from Castellet, Goytisolo, etc.), growing interest from publishers (not only in strictly commercial terms, but also politically, e.g. the collection Biblioteca Breve and the promotional assistance of Seix Barral), the use of institutional platforms and cultural activities (e.g. beginning perhaps with the ill-fated *Congreso de Escritores Jovenes* of 1955, and including the *Premio de la Crítica*, awarded to *El Jarama* in 1957 and on whose panel we find a few allies of the *novela social* in Castellet, Antonio Vilanova, and Lorenzo Gomis); nor should we ignore the role of *Acento Cultural*, the *Congreso de Formentor* of 1959, interest from foreign publishers such as Gallimard, and most importantly, as we have seen, a growing readership (though how far this was influential in determining the nature of the class is debatable). What is fairly clear is that by 1959/60, the *novela social* achieves a certain degree of autonomy as a class of writing from other types. This is made very clear in the opposition to it from official publications and reviews of the time, such as *La Estafeta Literaria* and *Correo Literario*. The trend also begins to affect the development of contiguous and other types of writing.[53] For example, writers who up to the mid-1950s may have been seen as rather extraneous to the trend begin to adopt certain of its technical and thematic features and become incorporated in or at least broadly identified with it, e.g. Candel, Lera, Delibes. Other writers whose work also reflects the impact of the *novela social* none the less remain ideologically at the margins of the trend, if not opposed to it, e.g. Zunzunegui, Dolores Medio, Elena Quiroga. Also, there are many writers who simply appear to jump on the bandwaggon, and in particular reflect the growing anti-aestheticism of the trend in the late 1950s. Their work is thus curiously reminiscent, in technique and temperament, of the crude realism of the 1940s, e.g. Tomás Salvador, José María Castillo-Navarro, Ramón Solís, etc. And we should not forget the development of a trend in the novel of the early 1960s, whose practitioners declare their opposition to the *novela social*, i.e. the so-called 'grupo metafísico', linked to Planeta and represented by Manuel García Viñó, Antonio Prieto, Andrés Bosch, Carlos Rojas, etc. In this way, the *novela social* emerges, then, not so much as a retrospective perception of resemblances in the mind of the critic, but as a broadly definable socio-literary reality, which has impacts in various ways on other writers, groups, and narrative types, but which also has its own relative autonomy and particular history.

The above comments are not intended as an explanation of the *novela social*. Rather, they attempt to raise certain questions and problems to do with its analysis and at most provide a provisional outline for work still to be done. Work, that is, which will tease out the many complex mechanisms, relays, and linkages between the texts, writers, readers, and wider socio-literary processes which make up trend. This is not to argue, however, for the indiscriminate contextualization of the trend, where the latter is dissolved back into a wealth of supporting detail, thus losing its definition as a literary phenomenon. Nor is it to underestimate the importance of historical and contextual factors in shaping the *novela social* in various ways. What is needed is an analysis and a resulting definition sensitive to both dimensions. Here, I have suggested that the *novela social* might be usefully seen as a contradictory unity of different narrative types, engaged in the construction of a committed literature. Of course, any more comprehensive definition of the phenomenon would also have to attend to those forms and approaches which seem to develop at its margins as well as those in opposition to it. This sort of focus might help to overcome the easy continuities and evident rigidities of formal models which attribute an exaggerated degree of unity and homogeneity to a class and tend to see it as a basically stable formula with surface variations. As already suggested, variations might be more usefully and historically understood as the result of ideological differences between writers, groups of writers, narrative strategies and the demands of inter as well as extra-literary pressures. But, if the *novela social* is seen as a diverse and variegated class, both historically and as a writing, then this is not to postulate a simple pluralistic coexistence between narrative types. In theory, I suggest that a literary class, once it has formed, will tend to be dominated by a particular narrative type, which acts as a common reference point or defining model for the class as a whole. Though more detailed analysis is required, *El Jarama* seems to provide an example of just such a reference point, not only in technical terms as a formula for objective realism, but also as a significant stimulus to the production of *novela social* and to the reconsideration of novels already written. For example, thanks to the existence and success of *El Jarama*, *Los bravos* seems to be recuperated as a pioneer social novel and is reinserted into the trend. Other examples of such reference points might include García Hortelano's *Nuevas Amistades*, in relation to the anti-bourgeois novel and Goytisolo's *Campos de Níjar*, in connection with the 'libro de viajes'. Conversely, Luis Goytisolo's *Las afueras* arguably represents an option, based vaguely on Lukácsian theories of 'historical realism', which is *not* followed in any significant degree. But this dominance is never total, fixed, or inevitable. It would be better to say that a particular narrative type exerts a degree of hegemony over the class and this has certain implications:

1 Its dominance is relative and always subject to varying degrees of competition and reinforcement from alternative narrative types within the class.

2   Obviously, only by continually adapting and accommodating itself to challenges posed by these alternatives can the dominant form continue to represent the class.

3   This ability to accommodate is limited and thus the dominant will change, as will the internal hierarchies of the class, its outer limits and its main features.

This might be what happens in the case of the anti-bourgeois novel, which seems to challenge yet not supplant the hegemony of the proletarian realism represented by *El Jarama* (and later continued in *La mina* and *La piqueta*). Even so, this leads to the reorganization of the class around a new, competing point of reference. So, the nature and specific form of the dominant narrative type is only intelligible as a product of a shifting balance of forces between a variety of narratives, shifts which also relay extra-literary and extra-class pressures into the sphere of writing. The outer limits of the class then are, in practice, fluid, constantly being recast, however marginally, to include and exclude narrative types. This recasting happens as a result of sets of processes and mechanisms which historically form and re-form over time. In part, these are clearly relations between books, but also relations between people, i.e. writers, critics, editors, booksellers, readers, teachers, etc. Thus differences over the definition of the *novela social* will respond to differences between individuals and groups, over how the class is to be organized and interpreted. Moreover, as we have seen, depending on the dominant definition of the class at any one time, and on the criteria held to be central or marginal in its conception, the class will exert significant influence on what gets written and how.

Chapter Two

WRITING AND OPPOSITION

In broad terms, the *novela social* of the 1950s and 1960s was the outcome of a process of interaction between novel writing and political opposition to the Franco regime. My main concern in this chapter is to explore the ways in which the relations between writing and opposition initially took shape. In other words, what sort of preconditions were necessary for the emergence of the *novela social* and, in particular, how can we account for the development of an oppositional consciousness among writers? On the whole, critical opinion tends to see the *novela social* as the product of a new generation of young writers who, as innocent children, were supposedly scarred by the traumatic effects of the civil war. This argument, first developed by Castellet, can be summarized as follows.

The young writers of the 1950s, the so-called 'Generación del medio siglo', tend to be identified by their common experience of the civil war. Unlike their parents, they did not participate in the war, nor did they have to take sides politically. Rather, as Castellet argues, they suffered the horrors of war as 'espectadores mudos, como víctimas inocentes' experiencing 'hambre, desplazamientos, bombardeos'. Their formative years were also marked by the difficult 1940s, years of rationing, censorship, international isolation, and, for Castellet, 'una situación cultural de total aislamiento y anormalidad'.[1] Because they were children at the time, the civil war is seen as having had a severe, traumatic effect on these

29

youngsters. This, combined with the adverse conditions of the 1940s, gives rise to a broad condemnation of the older generation, which is held responsible for a monstrous, bloody, and ultimately unnecessary conflict and its aftermath. As Martínez Cachero puts it: 'Para todos ellos, la guerra civil y la postguerra y los acontecimientos coincidentes con esta última fueron algo así como el hecho generacional que actúa de eficacísimo revulsivo'.[2] This reaction, as Castellet states, gives rise to 'una actitud de inconformismo', as well as a 'voluntad de superación', which is translated into a generation gap.[3] The latter then finds its literary expression in the *novela social*.

At first sight, the explanation of the rise of the *novela social* in terms of the civil war and its effects on children has a superficial plausibility, confirmed by the early work of Ana María Matute and the odd novel by Juan Goytisolo. However, an obvious difficulty with it is that such novel writing, from the point of view of children caught in a war-time situation or its aftermath, is not found to any significant degree among the social novelists. Moreover, rather than take an historical perspective, the 'trauma' approach presents a rather reductive, vulgar, psychological view, arguing that the *novela social* is somehow a vehicle for the dramatization and purging of childhood anxieties and oedipal struggles. Castellet remarks that 'esta generación (del medio siglo) es dura con sus antecesores y estudia los errores cometidos por los hombres de las generaciones que la precedieron'.[4] This raises one of several basic weaknesses in the argument: the fact that the civil war is seen in the rather abstract terms of emotional and moral outrage as one huge mistake, whose effects are visited upon a whole generation of innocent children. This arguably diverts attention from an historical understanding of the civil war and its implications. As Marfany points out, 'La guerra, com qualsevol altra guerra, no fou pas una absurda i incomprensible explosió de bogeria collectiva: els uns i els altres tingueren poderoses i lògiques raons per fer-la.'[5] In other words, the Spanish civil war was not some abstract orgy of violence and bloodletting, but an historically complex result of certain social, political, regional, and class forces and pressures, which can be explained and which produced a postwar society divided into two opposing camps: winners and losers. It is also arguable that what Castellet takes as a 'voluntad de superar muchas de las actitudes de los bandos contendientes', found among the emerging social novelists, is something of a distortion.[6] Indeed, rather than attempt to transcend the war-time political divisions, the new writers seem to develop an attachment, albeit romantic and voluntaristic in the beginning, to the losing side in the civil war.

Another weakness with the argument lies in its explanation of the 'inconformismo' of the social novelists, the reason for the generation gap, which undoubtedly existed. This need not rely on the idea of a childhood trauma. Indeed, apart from the difficulty of evaluating and verifying the effect of the civil war on children in general and on writers in particular, it is quite possible that the kind of war-time experience supposedly suffered by children also affected grown-ups as much or even more than their offspring. There seems to be no reason therefore to suppose that children were affected more than anyone else. In the case of the *novela social* and the writers associated with it, in its initial stages, the majority of writers are drawn from the middle- and upper-middle-class families of the winning side, who probably coped better than most with the hardships of the civil war and the privations of the 1940s. Also if the horrors of war did have traumatic effects, it is only fair to assume that they affected the majority of writers who were children at that time. Why is it, then, that only the *sociales* supposedly reflect this experience while the *non-sociales* are remarkably unaffected? Those who continue to support the trauma thesis or aspects of it would have to show, for example, that a novelist such as Juan Goytisolo (an undoubted *social*) was affected, and if so, explain why a writer such as García Viñó was not. In this connection, Goytisolo himself seems quite clear. To the question, '¿Qué le llevó a interesarse en su narrativa por la problemática social?' Goytisolo replied: 'Es fácil explicar mi curiosidad. Dejemos aparte mi experiencia de la guerra porque yo era un crío entonces; después de la guerra hasta mi entrada en la Universidad fue un período de ignorancia por lo que a ese campo se refiere.'[7] In other words, while undoubtedly a memory and reference point, Goytisolo's war-time experience seems not to constitute a source of trauma, nor a significant stimulus to his non-conformism and interest in social issues. A question of a rather different order is that Goytisolo, and also Matute, take up the theme of the civil war in their writing as a way of condemning the moral and ethical irresponsibility of the older generation. In so

31

doing, they find a prism through which to project their generational revolt. In other words, the civil war acts as a focus and a legitimation of a generational conflict already in evidence, rather than as its source or motivation.

A third and final point is that at the beginning of the 1950s, signs of a new literature and a new novel begin to appear. That there is a general coincidence between the rise of this new novel and the appearance of a new generation of young writers is fairly obvious. Yet, it would be mistaken to explain the nature of the new writing simply by reference to this chronological coincidence alone. What seems to confer a certain generational identity on the appearance of the *novela social* is thus not so much chronology or the civil war, but the broad direction taken by novel writing up to the 1950s. That is to say, for a whole decade, the 1940s, and despite a few isolated exceptions, literature and the novel in Spain had been the exclusive product of the winning side, whose values and point of view, either directly, indirectly, or by omission, it broadly reflected. Only at the beginning of the 1950s do we see the emergence of a literature which begins to be written from the opposite standpoint, that of the losing side in the civil war. And this is a literature whose emergence corresponds, not to the traumatic effects of the war, but to the first signs of cultural dissent and to the initial formation of an intellectual opposition inside Spain. As Marfany argues, 'Si cal esperar aquesta data, però, no es perquè els joves que aleshores accedeixen a la majoria d'edat estiguin marcats per un trauma infantil, sinò perquè estan nets d'antecedents polítics i només llavors comencen a donar–se les condicions objectives per a la seva organitzatció en intel.lectualitat discrepant.'[8]

Given the fact of political and ideological repression and the resulting general situation of depoliticization, rigorously enforced by the regime, the question arises as to how writers and intellectuals of the new movement move towards 'inconformismo' and arrive at opposition attitudes. Since many of those belonging to the movement, especially in its emergent phase, were the sons and daughters of families of the winning side (in the case of Sánchez Ferlosio, for example, son of an ex-Minister of Franco), the development of opposition attitudes would depend primarily on a process of disenchantment and ideological conversion. This would obviously not happen out of the blue, but would require certain stimuli and a vehicle of some sort. There is a view that sees these requirements being met by Falange, primarily through its youth organizations such as the SEU. In this connection, Martínez Cachero, for example, assigns to Falange a crucial and positive role in the emergence of the movement, while playing down, by implication, the movement's oppositional character.

FALANGE AND IDEOLOGICAL CONVERSION

The writers who belong to the emergent period of the *novela social* were all university students. Martínez Cachero takes as an indication of their affiliation to Falange the fact that some of them began their writing careers in SEU reviews. He points out, 'Quizá sea, también, que no resulte perdonable el hecho de que jóvenes como Aldecoa y Fernández Santos rompieran a publicar en revistas del SEU – como *Juventud*, *La Hora* y *Alcalá* – tan activas y abiertas.'[9] What he omits to mention is that membership of the SEU was compulsory for all Spanish students and that SEU reviews were virtually the only youth publications in existence that, financially and politically, had a chance of survival and that offered outlets to aspiring young writers. Even so, it cannot be denied that, lacking viable alternatives, Falangist organizations and publications did indeed provide certain opportunities for the youth of the winning side to express dissent and to develop towards left opposition attitudes. Here, Martínez Cachero wants to claim some credit on behalf of the SEU reviews, 'tan activas y abiertas', because they happily accommodated discrepant attitudes. In a word, they were liberal, or as Elías Díaz observes 'publicaciones, que por otra parte, admitían manifestaciones de un cierto y no despreciable pluralismo, y a las cuales, es verdad, a su vez aquellos escritores contribuían a transformar.'[10]

The above argument suggests several things: first, SEU publications were relatively open, prepared to tolerate dissent, and thus played a part in the development of left opposition attitudes; second, certain social novelists were initially falangists or closely affiliated, through SEU publications, to Falange; third, in general, Falangismo constituted a source of liberal opinion as well as opposition to the regime for which, as Martínez Cachero seems to argue, it should be given greater recognition, and even credit.

Before dealing with the role of the SEU as a channel for dissent, it is worth making a brief preliminary comment on Martínez Cachero's third point. The idea that falangists are somehow a major source of opposition and liberal opinion in the 1940s is something of a misrepresentation of the historical record and of the term liberal. Let us recall that, in the 1940s, falangists were fascists and that, within the umbrella of the National Movement, Falange was the socio-political instrument adopted by Franco to give ideological direction and organizational solidity to his regime.[11] It was also an unswervingly faithful adherent to the rising of 18 July 1936, an implacable enemy of Communism and political liberalism, and the regime's willing and well-rewarded servant in the Vertical Syndicates, state bureaucracies, youth organizations, media, etc. If Falange, at different times, opposed and was opposed by other groups within the regime's arc of forces, this does not necessarily make it liberal or allow us to infer any general tendency within it towards political pluralism or opposition. Indeed, rather than oppose legislation and policies that thwarted its political ambitions and flagrantly contradicted its ideological outlook (such as the Decree of Unification of 1937, the Law of Succession of 1947, or the Hispano-American economic and military pacts of 1953), Falange willingly accommodated itself to the *Caudillo's* wishes. If this is indicative of the fundamental weakness and subservience of the organization to the dictator, it also shows that Falange had more to lose than it had to gain by being recalcitrant.

So, when critics talk of liberalism in relation to Falange, they can hardly be referring to the broad membership of the *FET y de las JONS*, even less the old guard 'camisas viejas', or the leaders of the *Frente de Juventudes*. In other words, those people who do show a certain tendency towards ideological discrepancy and difference were not falangists in general, but a very small number of falangist academics and intellectuals.[12] That is, people such as Laín, Tovar, Ridruejo, Maravall, etc. – the very people whose task it was during the war years to provide the Nationalist cause with an aggressive, combative, unifying ideology of counter-revolution. Of course, once the war was won, this ideology and its violent, demagogic, pseudo-revolutionary slogans were no longer needed. The postwar situation in Spain demanded a rather different form of dominant ideology, more suited to the requirements of repression and social control and thus, while retaining much of Falange's programme, it drew substantially on Catholic conservatism and traditionalism.

This meant that the revolutionary posturing of Falange was simply surplus to requirements and that its postwar intellectual role, if such a phrase is appropriate, would be limited to working out the theoretical and doctrinal legitimation of the new regime. Given this loss of status and prestige and a largely technical peace-time role, some members – in particular those most highly politicized – would and did harbour feelings of resentment, betrayal and a desire for revolt. For the vast majority of the membership, many in lucrative jobs in the bureaucracy, such feelings would not matter. But for a few writers and intellectuals, this shift to a basically decorative function, as Marfany argues, would be translated 'sobretot, en una reafirmació de l'elevat caràcter ètico-social de l'ofici de l'escriptor'.[13] And one of the first tasks undertaken by some falangist writers and intellectuals after the civil war would be the conditional recuperation of certain outlawed Republican intellectuals.

Figures such as Machado, Unamuno, and Ortega would be recuperated not in terms of their politics – which were vigorously denounced – but purely and exclusively as intellectuals. Thus the notion of falangist liberalism applies only to the extent that a few falangist intellectuals feel a certain affinity or identity with their Republican *confrères* and wish to incorporate them into their elitist concept of an intellectual brotherhood, which transcends political divisions. At the same time, the concept of the intellectual with moral and ethical responsibilities which went beyond the dictates of party dogma had implications for writing. These involved a rejection of literature as a mere game, adornment, or escape; indeed, writing was seen as involving a commitment to telling the truth. As we have already seen, this elevated principle, predicated on revealing 'toda la verdad', was regularly aired in relation to *tremendismo*. However, if in the 1940s such a view of writing had vaguely dissenting connotations, it constituted a type of revolt which, as Marfany argues, 'no s'exercia contra cap objectiu històric concret, sinó que s'esgotava en ella mateixa i es traduïa en un vitalisme irracionalista i cruel – el de *la vida és així* del tremendismo – o en un cristianisme resignat i comprensiu – el d'una certa literatura intimista.'[14] In other words, the high-flown claims for literature advanced by certain falangist intellectuals would be contradicted and unfulfilled in practice. But, paradoxically, where they would be translated into a serious concern with 'life as it is'

35

would be in the social novel of the following decade. This perhaps suggests that some of the writers of the emergent phase of the movement inherit their social and ethical preoccupations from their experience of the SEU and Falange, but develop radical, oppositional views precisely because of their disillusionment with these organizations. Let us consider how well the argument applies to specific cases of writers, beginning with Aldecoa and Fernández Santos.

As regards Aldecoa, it seems clear that in the early stages of his career he had connections with *Juventud, La Hora,* and *Alcalá,* the three SEU reviews mentioned by Martínez Cachero. Whether this indicates an active involvement in them, in any internal, editorial capacity, for example, is not certain. Nevertheless, over the period 1948–55, he published well over a dozen short stories in them, significantly more contributions than any of his colleagues were to publish in the same reviews over the same period. Furthermore, in December 1953, he won the *Premio Juventud* with the short story 'Seguir de pobres' and sat as a member of the panel that adjudicated the prize the following year.[15] At least until the mid-1950s, then, Aldecoa seems to have maintained fairly close ties with these SEU reviews. The strength of these ties is asserted in an open letter of 1954, addressed to Aldecoa from the pages of *Juventud.* Between 1947 and 1954, four of his short stories had appeared in the review, he had won the *Premio Juventud* and had just published his first novel. To commemorate these achievements, the 'Carta a Ignacio Aldecoa' hailed the young novelist as a product of SEU initiative and reminded him that 'Todos tus pasos han sido dados, casi totalmente, en páginas nuestras . . . aquí en este mismo papel.' It also stressed Aldecoa's identification with the SEU, 'Por lo que tienes de hombre de nuestras mismas filas, por lo que tienes de amigo y camarada . . . es natural que en lo tuyo no podamos cumplir ningún papel de meros observadores . . . nosotros también somos parte de tu afán.'[16]

It should be noted, however, that Aldecoa had published widely in other places. At the beginning of 1954, his wife, Josefina Rodríguez, calculated his writing output at approximately sixty short stories, seven short novels and *El fulgor y la sangre.*[17] Most of the short stories had in fact been published in non-SEU reviews, which rather contradicts *Juventud*'s claim to being an indispensable patron. None the less, in the mid-1950s, Aldecoa was still publishing in official reviews such as *Ateneo* and *El Español* and writing in *Arriba*, the falangist daily. He also took part in certain officially sponsored 'jornadas literarias', lecture tours, and also did regular work for the radio station *Voz de la Falange*.[18] However, in June 1962, following his return from the fourth Congress of the European Movement held in Munich, Aldecoa was arrested at Barcelona airport along with many others, being released after interrogation. The Munich meeting had brought together both right- and left-wing political groups from inside Spain and from exile, though the Spanish Communist Party had been excluded. The aim of the meeting had been to approve a common programme relating to the sort of conditions the EEC should lay down for Spanish entry.[19] Aldecoa's presence and involvement in the famous 'contubernio de Munich', as well as his signing of collective letters and petitions against torture and repression in Spain in the early 1960s, would seem to indicate a fairly clear break with the regime. As Gaspar Gómez de la Serna argues, we could regard Aldecoa's case as that of a writer with early falangist connections, yet whose ideological conversion is difficult to establish, let alone date, but which seems to have come late in his career.[20] However, as Fiddian tells us, Aldecoa's alleged falangist background is disputed by his wife and, given the lack of substantive indications of his political leanings, remains unproved.[21]

What is not generally questioned is that Aldecoa shares with the early social novelists the sort of literary and ethical concerns that underlie and motivate the new emergent literature. These are concerns that also coincide with the sort of elevated conception of the writer and of literature enunciated by certain falangist writers and intellectuals in the 1940s, e.g. a social awareness, a literature committed to telling the truth; but these were ideas that, at that time, were being largely channelled into the truculence and diffuse cynicism of *tremendismo*. In a broad sense, the *novela social* could be seen as initially motivated by analogous principles but which are redefined and given a more concrete, social focus, that is, the working-class losers of the war and a more defined ethical or political intention: to create an awareness of oppressive social conditions in order to change them. This is evident in Aldecoa's own preoccupation with the truth, with the hidden realities of Spain, which prompted him to plan several trilogies on Spanish workmen within the framework of what he called 'la épica de los grandes oficios', including fishermen, sailors, miners, and steelworkers. His plan was inspired by an awareness of the situation of poor people in Spain and by 'el convencimiento de que hay una realidad española cruda y tierna a la vez que está casi inédita en nuestra novela . . . Ser escritor es, antes que nada, una actitud en el mundo.'[22] Using the vocabulary typical of the social novelists of the 1950s, Aldecoa here affirms that the very act of bearing witness to that 'realidad . . . inédita' involves the author in a 'toma de posición', the adoption of an 'actitud' or the taking of a position. In other words, an ethical or political stand against poverty and injustice. Yet, despite this outlook, there is still the fact that Aldecoa was later regarded by some of his more committed colleagues with a degree of doubt and suspicion. This might well be explained by the continued links he maintained with the Establishment in the 1950s.

Turning to Fernández Santos, Martínez Cachero is perhaps exaggerating somewhat when he claims that he began his career in the three SEU reviews previously mentioned. In fact, Fernández Santos only ever published in one of them, *La Hora*, and even then, his contributions amounted only to two solitary pieces, nonfictional in nature.[23] In the first of these, he took up the question of social conflict and its representation in North American literature. He began by singling out two main problems in American society: first, the decadence of the middle classes, as a result of which they were failing in their historic role as providers of 'directices espirituales' to the country at large; second, the interconnected problems of social disintegration and racial assimilation produced by America's mixture of different races and ethnic groups. Both of these concerns, focused and expressed in ways strongly reminiscent of falangist attitudes and rhetoric, were seen as being vividly represented in both drama and the novel, 'cuyo carácter fuertemente realista es quizá la nota más dominante en Norte-america'. Impressed by this realism, Fernández Santos also revealed an acquaintance with the works of Dos Passos, Hemingway, and Faulkner, showing special interest in their treatments of 'average' American men. He mentioned O'Neill in connection with the drama of social conflict and the American cinema, in terms of its depiction of racial issues. Though perhaps rather sketchy and superficial, his comments do indicate an incipient and very positive interest in American literature, drama, and film, valued, it seems, for its strongly realist outlook and its more direct, muscular treatment of social problems. In contrast to the first, the second piece was a very simple and general exposition concerning the use of the theme of the sea in Western European drama, with no reference to wider social matters.

Though we cannot infer a great deal from one article, the way Fernández Santos approaches the subject of North American culture, his interest in racial and class tensions and his evident support for their realistic portrayal in different media, suggest the following: a young writer, who seems to be operating within a vague falangist framework ideologically (illustrated perhaps by the repeated use of the word 'yanqui' in the text). But, at the same time, a young writer impatient and dissatisfied with prevailing literary orthodoxies inside Spain, frustrated by Falange's lack of real commitment to social issues and who is looking to American writers for a viable, serious, realist aesthetic. Paradoxically, as Fernández Santos seems to intuit, American realism fulfils a major falangist literary precept, touched upon earlier, the commitment to 'present life as it is'. What his article shows is the attractiveness, both in aesthetic and ideological terms, of the American example and the contradictions, in this regard, in falangist theory and practice.

Fernández Santos attended Madrid University between 1943 and 1948, where he met and became friendly with Aldecoa, Sánchez Ferlosio, and Sastre, as well as Alfonso Paso and Medardo Fraile. He left without finishing his degree and, in 1949, like his colleague Sánchez Ferlosio, enrolled in the newly-created *Escuela Oficial de Cinematografía*. A contemporary of Saura, Bardem, and Berlanga, Fernández Santos graduated in 1952. During his two periods of formal education, there are signs to suggest that he had fairly strong links with the SEU, at least in cultural terms. He was actively involved in the *Teatro Universitario* movement in the late 1940s and directed as well as acted in adaptations of Saroyan and O'Neill for Radio SEU and Radio Madrid.[24] Also, as Herzberger points out, Fernández Santos would develop his interest in American writing and culture in the various literary *tertulias* in Madrid, alongside young colleagues, who would circulate copies of translations of Hemingway, Steinbeck, Faulkner, and dos Passos, etc.[25] In general, in Fernández Santos, we seem to have a case of a young writer with initial falangist affiliations, certainly cultural and perhaps ideological but who becomes distanced from and disaffected with the organization's limitations and empty rhetoric and who is looking for an alternative to fill the gap.

Another case relevant to the question of ideological conversion among writers is that of Sánchez Ferlosio, though we can only infer this from a few scraps of available evidence. As a starting point, there is the fact that he came from a politicized family. He was the son of a prominent falangist politician, Rafael Sánchez Mazas, a true 'blue' militant, who was dismissed in 1940 from Franco's second government (1939–41), after he and other *camisas viejas* failed in their attempt to swing the regime towards a more thorough-going National Syndicalism.[26] It is clear that Sánchez Mazas harboured strong anti-Franco feelings and no doubt the ideas of the *revolución pendiente* and the *revolución traicionada* were kept alive within the family. This is confirmed by his son Miguel, who wrote in 1957:

> Hace unos tres años, mi padre, en uno de los furores antifranquistas a que su sentido de la dignidad humana le llevaba con frecuencia – y espero que le vuelvan, antes del finme decía que si había en España una docena de ciudadanos de honor, procedentes del bando vencedor, capaces de ir a la cárcel por razones morales, más allá de toda exigencia particular y egoista, Franco estaba perdido.[27]

It is legitimate to suppose that Sánchez Ferlosio would be affected by this anti-Francoist family atmosphere and recognize, if not support, the nostalgia as well as the disillusionment of an erstwhile falangist militant like his father. Referring to his son's upbringing and education, Sánchez Mazas confirms this, stating: 'Es una formación muy suya. Pero dentro de un clima muy nuestro. Quiero decir el de nuestra familia.'[28]

Evidence to suggest that Sánchez Ferlosio himself had early falangist leanings is almost non-existent. However, a letter written by him to the student review *Alcalá*, in March 1952, in its choice of language and overtones, is symptomatic of falangist views and sentiments. Launched in January 1952 as a continuation and replacement for *La Hora*, *Alcalá* is viewed by Sánchez Ferlosio as a disappointment in that it lacks vitality and bite, largely because 'el estilo no alimenta'. Something much stronger and more appetizing is required.

Los muchachos esperan una alimentación rica y alegre. Entremeses variados y platos fuertes, guisotes. Pero morirán de inanición o limitarán y empequeñecerán su naturaleza si eternamente les vais a estar dando vuestra sopa de letras Ybarra.... Es preciso que nuestra fauna sea mucho más variada.

Alcalá's rather insipid fare might just keep alive 'cisnes elegantes, pelícanos', but not, as Sánchez Ferlosio tellingly argues 'jabalíes, esos animales maravillosos, esos cerdos violentos, ágiles, agudos, velocísimos, impetuosos y cortantes, luchadores, rompedores de cabeza.' For Sánchez Ferlosio, the challenge is clear:

Escribid para jabalíes. Echadles grasa. Quebrad vuestra austera tipografía. Dadles una tipografía jugosa, rica, inencuadernable, que dure poco, que corra rápida. Que sea como un bulto lanzado al cuerpo – ¡Ahí va eso! – y no como un perfil. Mejor es que se os escape algún que otro mal olorcillo que no oler a nada.[29]

The use of *los muchachos* and the familiar *vosotros*, the extremely clever exploitation of the food and animal metaphors in reference to *Alcalá*'s readership, the demand for a hard-hitting, aggressive typography and for a touch of *mal gusto* or *mal olor* reflect the ingredients of falangist rhetoric, as well as Sánchez Ferlosio's considerable literary skill. So, from a rather detached position, it seems that Sánchez Ferlosio speaks for a more robust, virile, militant sort of Falangismo, which is not being delivered by the new review. This might indicate the author's concern at the lack of impact of Falange, through its youth publications and his adherence to a more assertive brand of falangist thinking. Another apparent sign of Sánchez Ferlosio's links with SEU publications and Falange can be found in a letter, addressed to him from *Juventud*, which congratulated him on winning the Premio Nadal with *El Jarama* in 1956. *Juventud*'s 'Carta a Rafael Sánchez Ferlosio' was a grovelling panegyric, similar in many ways to the treatment accorded to Aldecoa two years earlier. While the letter does not refer to the author as *camarada* or *hombre de nuestras mismas filas*, it places him alongside other writers, such as Aldecoa and Fernández Santos, considered as examples of SEU patronage and initiative.[30]

To sum up, we might regard Sánchez Ferlosio, not as a

41

committed *seuista* but as someone who is aware of the contradictions between Falange's radical programme and its lack of real political influence. Also, his anti-Francoist background and criticism of the elitism of official youth publications would no doubt sharpen that awareness and perhaps open the way towards dissent and a search for political alternatives.

An early indication of this process is suggested by Alfonso Sastre who, talking of *Revista Española*, recalls how he and José María de Quinto (already critically reassessing their own falangismo) 'arrastramos a Ferlosio hasta cierta simpatía por nuestras lucubraciones social-políticas; quizá su cuento "Niño Fuerte" fue una manifestación de esa simpatía.'[31]

Alfonso Sastre states, 'Otro caso, quizá más interesante, puede ser el mío; que no era falangista pero tampoco todo lo contrario.' He regards himself as 'objetivamente promocionado como crítico por una revista oficial del SEU y como autor por un grupo oficial del mismo SEU.'[32] Though he in fact denies any formal connections with Falange, his writings in *La Hora* between 1948 and 1950, especially his theatre criticism, are strongly permeated by falangist nationalism and a dogmatic belief in student elites as the vanguard of cultural renewal. For example, 'El tiempo que vivimos exige un teatro de signo muy distinto al de Benavente . . . un teatro inoportuno que caiga sobre el público como una lluvia de fuego. . . . Este teatro lo puede dar la juventud.'[33] Also, 'los teatros de ensayo españoles significan, en el panorama de nuestra escena, una vergonzosa servidumbre al teatro extranjero. No me interesan nada.' Sastre's solution to foreign domination is 'un teatro de gran proyección social', but one still inspired by falangist corporativism '[un teatro] que una a los españoles en un cauce común de preocupación social'.[34] The verbal radicalism and social concern found in Sastre's writings of this period seem typical of the highly politicized falangist militant. Yet, it is a militancy still dominated by the idea of revolution from above, carried out by educated elites and as yet uninformed by the concept of class. Hence Sastre's advocacy of a socially aware, combative theatre that will supposedly (and paradoxically) try to *unite* all Spaniards.

José María de Quinto, Sastre's colleague, notes how this proposed socially aware theatre, the *Teatro de Agitación Social*, 'sin saberlo ha venido a coincidir con una vieja aspiración falangista que ahora va a llevar a la práctica: imponer en los escenarios españoles el drama social.'[35] That aspiration, ideologically informed by student falangismo, was never fulfilled. Repeatedly blocked by the authorities, the *TAS* never materialized as an active, ongoing theatre group. And no doubt, the unwillingness of SEU bureacrats to encourage and promote innovation in the theatre, especially when seemingly grounded in militant falangismo, would help to push Sastre and company ideologically to the left.

Other examples which illustrate more clearly the falangist experience at work relate to people who come from politicised families and who are active in SEU organizations. This seems to be the case with Manuel Sacristán, not a novelist himself, but closely connected with the social novelists and their intellectual allies in Barcelona. Sacristán, in fact, acknowledges the influence of his family background in his own ideological preferences as well as his active involvement in SEU organizations.[36] He was *jefe político del SEU* in Barcelona's *Instituto Balmes* in the early 1940s and admits to espousing hard-line falangist beliefs at that time. However, he also claims to have undergone an ideological conversion, which he attributes to two main factors: the very strict control imposed on young *seuistas* in Cataluña and also, the crisis of falangist ideology in the universities, which he dates as early as 1943. As a result, Sacristán says he quickly turned to Marxism, though how quickly is not made clear. José María Castellet, critical guru of the *novela social*, is another example of a young intellectual involved with Falange early in his career. As regards family influence, Castellet affirms that 'La actitud de toda mi familia creo que me situaba en un terreno de democracia liberal, con muchas prevenciones respecto a compromisos de tipo extremista.'[37] None the less, he acknowledges that his father signed him up as a *requeté* in 1937 and that as a youngster he belonged to the falangist youth, 'un pelayo de dotze anys'.[38] Though it is not clear that he held any official position, he was certainly on very friendly terms with Sacristán in the *Instituto Balmes* and up to and including his period of collaboration in the official review *Laye* admits to adhering to some form of enlightened national syndicalism. Carlos Barral, a collaborator in *Laye* and close friend, talks of 'los jóvenes pensadores de procedencia más o menos falangista, Manuel Sacristán y José María Castellet', adding 'J.M. desmiente tal hipótesis por lo que a él respecta pero yo tenía esa impresión entonces.'[39] Castellet thus seems to have been influenced by falangist ideology. He dates his ideological conversion at the end of 1953, following a trip abroad financed by the SEU. As with many other young intellectuals, contact with the outside world acts as an important stimulus in ideological reassessment. For Castellet, the trip revealed to him that 'En Europa, se desarrollaban por parte de la gente más inteligente ideas clarísimamente socialistas. Fue al regreso de ese viaje cuando tomé conciencia plenamente de la situación interior.'[40]

At this point, we can make a possible distinction between the cases examined so far. On the one hand, there are those who were or appear to have been active and committed *seuistas*, e.g. Sacristán, Sastre, Quinto, probably Castellet, and quite possibly Aldecoa. This is shown in their background, their SEU connections, and their involvement and collaboration in SEU reviews. On the other, there are the *jóvenes inquietos*, people whose links with Falange and the SEU were perhaps more tenuous and whose contributions to SEU reviews would be minimal. However, as writers, they would be appropriated by certain reviews and identified as products of SEU initiative, e.g. Fernández Santos and Sánchez Ferlosio. For both types, the contradictions and paradoxes of the Falangist experience would be influential in pushing them towards a more critical, radical standpoint and eventually to the opposition.

Turning now to the wider implications of the relations between Falange, the SEU and political dissent, Sacristán makes the useful general observation that Fascism 'se presentó como si su base fuese la juventud, como si ésta fuera una categoría social homogénea.'[41] The attractiveness of fascism for young people lay in its stress on political action and its blatant demagogy, which exploited the ideas of the bankruptcy of the older generation and the privileged role of youth as a new political vanguard. In Franco's Spain, to the *jóvenes inquietos* of bourgeois origin and right-wing family background, i.e. to the sons of the winning side, falangist rhetoric made a similar appeal and fulfilled a crucial requirement. In other words, it was the only ideology available in the 1940s capable of acting as a vehicle for youth revolt. Its attractiveness obviously lay in part in the concepts and slogans woven around the core idea of *revolución*: *la revolución pendiente*, anti-capitalism, violence, nationalism, commitment, social concern, nationalization of the banks, agrarian reform, etc. Of course, for young members who were already highly politicized, an awareness of the incongruities of the falangist programme, coupled with the regime's blatantly non-revolutionary intention to establish a clerical, conservative monarchy as its preferred form of the state, would exacerbate feelings of betrayal and in the end lead to ideological crisis. In the literary sphere, similar contradictions existed, notably between the emphasis on the rebellious stance of the writer, his social concern, and the quest for truth and a conception of literature and literary production as a detached, elitist, Olympian activity. Thus, in the letter to Aldecoa from *Juventud* already referred to, Aldecoa's vocation as a writer, his *afán*, is conceived in strikingly non-revolutionary terms. He is asked to remain pure and unsullied by external distractions, 'un símbolo de este escribir sin claudicaciones'.[42]

For most people involved in SEU activities, the contradictions illustrated above would not present any problem. After all, the SEU was the regime's political school, producing people who would later become administrators and politicans, e.g. Pablo Porta, Rodolfo Martín Villa, Manuel Fraga Iribarne, Adolfo Suárez. It provided the first steps in a political career, a training centre where one learnt the ropes of political life in the regime. However, for a few people, the contradictions had to be overcome. Here, the articulation of disenchantment with *falangismo* was only possible *in real terms*, outside the organization. In terms of practical action, one could not be a *falangista* and be anti-regime; being a *falangista* or *seuista* meant being identified with the regime, like it or not. The Falange of *la revolución pendiente* or what Ridruejo calls *Falange hipotética* was precisely that, a hypothesis, 'algo que históricamente no ha existido jamás'.[43] *Seuistas* thus had to accept Falange in its historically existing form or get out. As we have noted, those most likely to leave Falange and move towards the opposition would be those most active and involved in politics, that is SEU militants. Sacristán confirms this process, stating:

> por los mismos años, entre el 1943 y el 1950, ese abandono de los últimos restos de ideologías fascistas en general y falangista en particular, se produce, que yo sepa, en casi todos los distritos universitarios y principalmente en gente que en el SEU había estado en Prensa o en Formación Política, es decir en los sectores más interesados por asuntos teóricos.[44]

Regarding the direction and ideological content of this

disenchantment, Ridruejo again reminds us that the political education of Spanish youth 'ha estado impregnado temáticamente de conceptos ideológicos revolucionarios – al margen de cualquier consecuencia real'. This has produced 'un gran número (de jóvenes politizados) que deseaba cambiar una revolución falsa – o traicionada – por una revolución auténtica del mismo signo ideológico o de signo opuesto o de signo por inventar.' So, while some militants remain wedded to their theoretical falangismo, others abandon it. But they do not jettison their revolutionary militancy. Rather, they seek out alternative ideologies predicated on the notion of revolution. As Ridruejo says, they seek 'su salida en un absolutismo de significación inversa al que ha constituido su ambiente formativo'.[45] For some disaffected *seuistas*, then, a revolutionary alternative is found in some form of Marxism. Of course, a major feature of the ideological transition from falangismo to Marxism is that the Fascist idea of a revolution from above is replaced by a notion of revolution based on class. Thus, crucial to the process of ideological conversion is the acceptance of a view of society based on class inequalities and class struggle.[46] Though by no means fully articulated and perhaps still responding to the influence of student falangismo, an awareness of class is already vaguely evident in the work of some of the early social novelists, who begin a process of rediscovery of Spain's lower classes and marginal groups. In broader terms, these writers and other *jóvenes inquietos* would realize sooner or later that a solution to the political contradictions of *falangismo* and to the paradox in falangist thinking between literary commitment and the autonomy of the author could only be achieved outside Falange. Equally, the kind of literature they wanted to develop (realistic, committed, *recia*, deeply Spanish) would only be possible outside the ideological and aesthetic co-ordinates they had inherited from the organization.

Of course, we still have to keep in mind that, given its monopoly position, the SEU would provide almost the only platforms for student cultural activities and publishing. These outlets would be both appropriated and re-directed by disaffected *seuistas* as well as infiltrated from outside. As Ridruejo states:

todas las manifestaciones juveniles que han podido significar incomodidades para el gobierno brotaban de las filas del falangismo juvenil o se han servido de plataformas por él administradas. Revistas como *Alférez*, *La Hora*, *Alcalá* y *Juventud*, promovidas por las organizaciones oficiales, fueron ricas en reticencias cuando no en acusaciones.[47]

We might also add the examples of *Laye* and *Acento Cultural*, manipulated by people who did not identify with the regime. This was allowed to happen, however, not through liberalism, blindness, or naiveté on the part of the administrators, but by consciously-made pacts and concessions. The fact is that the success of SEU chiefs in their political careers depended in part on containing the student movement within certain tolerable limits and by showing to their superiors a dynamic youth culture. Unfortunately, the only intellectually and culturally active youth available in the 1950s was in the opposition or in the process of moving towards it. Hence the need on the part of the regime to give tacit recognition and a small degree of manoeuvre to people potentially or actually opposed to the system. Moreover, SEU administrators felt it necessary to claim dissent as part of the success of their own policy, thereby integrating it and presenting the regime as the liberal patron of its very own rebellious youth. Ridruejo talks of 'una calculada reivindicación adulatoria', paraded in many official publications, towards the emergent discrepant intelligentsia. He sees this as a response to the fact that, 'la generación acusadora se ha formado en el encofrado mismo del sistema y era necesario encajar el hecho con palmaditas paternales que disimulasen la ruptura. . . . Absorber, neutralizar, tomar posesión, jactarse de haber engendrado la generación rebelde era, sin duda, operación más hábil que cerrarle el paso.'[48]

In a sense then, Martínez Cachero is right to acknowledge the role of SEU youth publications in the formation of a dissenting intelligentsia. That these reviews did tolerate a degree of ideological divergence is probably true, but this should not be taken as a mark of their inherent liberalism or open-handedness. In any case, the publication of heterodox views would be limited and always subject to negotiation. Also, it would be mistaken to overstate the importance of falangist organizations and regard them as the only vehicle for the development of political deviance. The passage towards opposition attitudes, therefore, does not depend uniquely on the transition from one type of politicization to another, whose ideological foundation has been reversed. There is also a second important channel, which seems to involve a transition from a state of ignorance on political matters and non-activism to one of political awareness. It arises, in general, out of moral, ethical, or religious motives, particularly in the context of a religious education.

POLITICIZATION THROUGH REACTION

Not all young Spaniards in the 1940s passed through falangist organizations. However, most sons and daughters of the bourgeoisie would receive their primary and secondary education in orthodox religious schools, by which I mean Roman Catholic. In these institutions, as well as the imposition of cultural censorship and strong religious pressures, a political education was likely to be minimal. This situation was powerfully reinforced by a particular form of family upbringing. Talking of the students of the early 1950s, Salvador Giner points out that, 'Their parents had no doubt countless times given them the stern advice not to "meddle in politics" – a pattern of socialization not unknown in pre-Civil War Spain but now emphasized by the majority of families.'[49] Ridruejo also states, 'La familia tiene aún en España una fuerte trabazón y por lo tanto ejerce una honda influencia sobre los jóvenes, tanto más cuanto más modestas son las familias. Está claro, sin embargo, que ni las familias ni las instituciones educativas han tenido gran interés en impulsarles al escabroso camino de la política.'[50] In this connection, José María Maravall reminds us that 'Political and ideological allegiance to the regime was compatible with a fear of politics, with politics as a family taboo. The civil war and the Franco regime were seen as a reaction and a safeguard against the abysmal dangers of politics.'[51] The situation of depoliticization, then, engendered through family and school experiences, gives us a second route towards opposition attitudes, which can be illustrated with the following examples.

Carlos Barral, poet as well as patron and publisher of the *novela social*, is a prime case in point. Of traditional bourgeois stock, he recalls his family's belief in the disciplinarian effects of a strict religious training,

en la mesa familiar se hablaba de la estricta educación jesuítica como de algo necesario, algo que me corregiría no sé qué defectos. Yo creo que las gentes que efectivamente se sentían liberadas, la burguesía que había permanecido en zona republicana y para quienes las fuerzas fascistas habían ganado la guerra, tenían la obsesión de enmendar el país, de restaurar quién sabe qué orden arcáico y pensaban que había que entregar a sus hijos inocentes a la tarea de los reformadores.[52]

As a victim of the the reformers' zeal, Barral remembers his religious education in an elite school for its repressive aspects and its obsessive puritanism. The day-to-day compulsory rites and observances of school life, the morning masses, the communions, the collective prayers, spiritual exercises, confessions, religious symbolism, etc., would eventually lead him to reject Catholicism and formal religion. He states, 'Naturalmente, yo no me daba cuenta entonces, pero esa espesa estructuración conventual de la vida escolar, ese abuso de las prácticas religiosas, era una magnífica, casi infalible, vacuna contra el sentimiento religioso.'[53] Barral explains his political evolution as a gradual process, beginning with a simple feeling of revolt against family and schooling. He notes:

El sentimiento de rebeldía que se da en todo niño, si no es completamente estúpido, me opuso a mi familia; entonces, oponerme por oponerme, me oponía al franquismo, por ejemplo, de un primo mío que vivía en casa. O por ejemplo, frente al sentimiento religioso, mi evolución comienza con la rebeldía ante la mojigatería de mi madre o ante su insistencia por las prácticas religiosas o la rebeldía ante el colegio . . . que era un campo de concentración.[54]

In the beginning, Barral sees himself as 'políticamente antifranquista, porque el franquismo significaba para mí el conformismo con una gente que me parecía detestable'. Barral's early revolt seems to take the form of a rather anarchic and indiscriminate reaction against authority, one that still awaits a minimal political or ideological foundation. As he says himself, in those early years, 'mi antifranquismo era despreocupado y cínico, esteticista'.[55] However, running parallel to this desultory rejection of Francoism there seems to be a vague, romantic attachment to the Second Republic and, by implication, to the losing side in the

49

civil war. Though basically ignorant of the Republic, Barral's emotional identification with the political antithesis of the regime would offer him an initial oppositional identity. He states:

En nuestras primeras pasiones políticas no contaban tanto las delgadas ideas como la aversión, una sana y sólida repugnancia, por el mundo que intentaban imponernos. La sordidez de la retórica fascista y la mediocridad de sus mentiras nos hacían irreconciliables enemigos de aquel poder sin prestigio, de aquel órden por la fuerza; y la nostalgia de una República que no habíamos conocido y acerca de la cual no habíamos oído un solo juicio objetivo, nos hacía filomarxistas o anarcoides.[56]

Still, at this stage, Barral is but a rebel, as yet without a concrete ideological alternative to the system he rejects. He does mention, however, that during his university years he was able to clarify his politics through the help of friends and contacts and that he himself actively sought and found an alternative in the forbidden fruit of Marxism, beginning with a reading of certain Marxist texts in the *Colegio de Abogados* in Barcelona.

As in the above case, for many youngsters of bourgeois extraction, a repressive religious education would give rise to what Maravall calls 'cultural deviance', especially in relation to the influence of forbidden reading material. Indeed, the cultural restrictions, obscurantism, and censorship practised in elite religious shools inevitably produced a fascination for prohibited books and a pattern of unorthodox reading, which invariably prompted feelings of cultural superiority, sophistication, and dissent. As regards the sort of material in question, Maravall distinguishes between authors involved in the Second Republic, who generally had a reformist, democratic image in Spanish culture (e.g. Machado, Lorca, Baroja, Unamuno) and those who were unorthodox either from a rigidly Catholic standpoint, such as Gide, or from a left or Marxist perspective, such as Pavese or Sartre. Summing up, he states:

Cultural restrictions made it clear to adolescents that there was in Spain a relationship between culture, religion, ideology, and politics, an interdependence that was underlined by the students' experience of censorship. Cultural deviance, then, was perceived as political deviance. Gide was as subversive as Lenin . . . .

Reading and religion were thus important in the turn towards political dissent of those students who had a politically orthodox family background and had studied in orthodox religious schools.[57]

Clearly, travelling abroad would also be important in providing opportunities for exposure to deviant ideologies, through foreign books and personal contacts, for people hitherto limited to the highly restricted cultural panorama of the dictatorship.

Also, given the situation of depoliticization produced by a repressive family background and an orthodox religious education, contact with *la otra España*, that is with working-class misery, would also act as a stimulus to ideological deviance. This seems to be the case with Juan Goytisolo, who states, 'Vivía en una familia burguesa, se me educó tradicionalmente, en fin no tenía la menor idea de que existían suburbios, clase obrera ni problemas sociales.' Like Barral, Goytisolo rejected his family upbringing and education, but without a set of ideas on which to hang that disaffection. As he says 'a partir de los 16 años, cuando perdí mi fe católica, estaba en contra de la educación recibida, pero sin pasar de ahí; era un malestar cuya fundamentación ideológica vendría después; me refiero a su proyección social.' What gave focus and substance to Goytisolo's already evident rejection of his background and its values was an awareness of class differences. Seemingly, the chance discovery of the *chabolas* on the outskirts of Barcelona had a very powerful effect on the young Goytisolo: 'me fascinó y me horrorizó a la vez. Mi descontento con la clase social a la que pertenecía mi familia, mi radicalización política – la visión negativa del régimen que había permitido tal estado de cosas – parten de ahí. Contaba entonces con 22 años.'[58]

From the above discussion, a tentative picture emerges of the ways in which writers and intellectuals of the early period of the movement of social novelists evolve towards opposition attitudes. Initially, there seem to be two main routes.

First, that provided by falangist youth organizations, principally the SEU and which seems to involve two sorts of people: on the one hand, those who were active and committed *seuistas*, e.g. Castellet, Sacristán, Sastre, Quinto, López Pacheco, and possibly Aldecoa; on the other, those who were not SEU militants, but came from falangist families and are initially identified with the

SEU, e.g. Sánchez Ferlosio and Fernández Santos. These people all receive a minimal political education, permeated by falangist notions of revolution, nationalism, commitment, social reform, etc., and which, unlike the vast majority of students, they seem to take seriously. Yet, given the subordination and weakness of Falange under Franco and the lack of practical outlets for those who uphold its radical claims, disillusionment with the organization and its values leads to ideological deviancy. In some cases, usually among those most involved in politics, this is translated into an ideological *volte face* in which, having jettisoned falangist principles, their remaining revolutionary militancy is newly attached to some form of Marxism. This seems to happen in the cases of Sacristán, Sastre, Quinto, López Pacheco, and probably Castellet, though it is far less clear in the cases of Sánchez Ferlosio, Aldecoa, or Fernández Santos. In the early 1950s, the latter seem to adhere to a vague anti-Francoism, but one which has not quite detached itself from a socially-aware falangismo.

Secondly, there is the transition from a situation of depoliticization to one of political awareness. This mainly involves people from the non-politicized families of the Francoist bourgeoisie. Here, the combination of a particular family upbringing, which places a taboo on politics, as well as a repressive, orthodox, religious education, seems to provoke an initial revolt against authority. This gives way to ideological deviancy, which develops through a mixture of influences, including exposure to forbidden reading material, visits abroad, and contacts with lower-class poverty. Examples here include Barral and Juan Goytisolo, and almost certainly his brothers Luis and José Agustín.[59]

Later, the movement of social novelists is joined by writers of a rather different background, giving us a third possible route to opposition attitudes. This involves the lower-middle and working-class families of the losing side, the 'resistance' families that would pass on their anti-Francoism to their offspring. They would also hand down an identity of belonging to the defeated as well as a feeling of solidarity with the working class. As regards relevant writers, these seem to fall into two categories: on the one hand, those who have a university education and a professional background, working as teachers, civil servants etc., e.g. Juan García Hortelano, Alfonso Grosso and José María Caballero Bonald; on the other, those non-university, working-class people, who have passed through a series of different jobs or at best have received some technical or industrial training, but in literary terms, consider themselves largely autodidacts, e.g. Antonio Ferres, Armando López Salinas, Juan Marsé, Francisco Candel.

Of course, some names are missing from the above analysis and no doubt there will be specific experiences that do not coincide with those outlined. However, I have not attempted to be exhaustive and the omissions need not invalidate what is no more than a tentative typology, based on often very patchy and fragmentary evidence, to illustrate how writers of the movement reach opposition attitudes. The main emphasis has been placed on the initial period of the movement, which explains the amount of space devoted to Falange, a topic that perhaps deserves even more detailed investigation. On the whole, what seems to emerge is a picture of radical, opposition politics in Spain in the 1950s led mainly by the well-heeled offspring of the upper-middle classes of the winning side. That this is the case should not be so surprising. Let us recall that the working classes in postwar Spain were in no position, at least until the early 1960s, seriously to challenge the dictatorship, given their massive defeat in the civil war, the excessive degree of repression suffered in the 1940s and 1950s and the sheer amount of time needed by the opposition parties to rebuild the working-class movement. It was thus from the ranks of the victorious bourgeoisie for whom, as Barral says, Franco had won the war, that we find the first splits and defections, principally among those too young to have been actively involved in the civil war and affected by its political divisions. These were the students of the late 1940s and early 1950s, the first protagonists of intellectual and cultural dissent under Franco. That opposition student politics was for some people a romantic, voluntaristic, even frivolous affair, which attracted more than a few armchair revolutionaries, is no doubt the case. That an ideological attachment to working-class struggle against the regime gave rise to untold contradictions between their radical politics and class origins is also true. That the penalties for student dissent were as nothing compared to the sort of treatment meted out to clandestine opposition party workers is again quite clear. But it was the same activism and dissent of these bourgeois *jóvenes inquietos* which was seen as important and which was gradually appropriated by the real opposition parties, particularly the Communist Party, and channelled into a broad, democratic opposition front against the regime. This was nothing new, of course, given the way left parties have traditionally recruited many of their militants from the disaffected members of the ruling class. As regards the writers of the emergent phase of the social novel movement, initially drawn from this ruling-class sector, if they do engage at all in a rejection of the older generation based on an ethical condemnation of the civil war, they do not stop there. Rather, they seem to take up positions, informed by a concept of class, that support the losing side in the civil war. This does not necessarily mean the defeated Republican government or the exiled parties, but rather Spain's working classes. Talking of the offspring of the Francoist bourgeoisie, Ridruejo points out, 'del seno de la misma burguesía, brota un torrente de disgusto por las formas y situaciones creadas bajo su predicamento y una apetencia de descubrir pueblo como quien descubre tierra.'[60]

Chapter Three

A MOVEMENT IN THE MAKING

In the early 1950s in Spain, in the context of the emergence of an opposition intelligentsia, two reviews act as important focal points in the formation of the movement of social novelists. These are *Laye* and *Revista Española*, published in Madrid and Barcelona, respectively.[1] On the one hand, *Laye*, principally in the writings of Manuel Sacristán and José María Castellet, provides some of the initial theoretical groundwork for the notions of literary commitment and the role of the intellectual, that will guide the aims and programmatic assumptions of the movement. On the other, *Revista Española* publishes work by the main pioneering members of the movement, such as Aldecoa, Sánchez Ferlosio, Fernández Santos, Sastre, and other colleagues and gives early indications of the sort of aesthetic options and writing practices that make up the initial development of the *novela social*. At the same time, both reviews tend to differ from official student publications such as *Juventud*, *La Hora* and *Alcalá* and it is in this difference that their importance also lies. In the SEU publications, we certainly find people writing who come to form part of the movement. But as contributors and dissenting student intellectuals, they appear dispersed and disconnected, merely a set of individuals who, with the exception of Sastre and Aldecoa, publish only occasionally. In *Laye* and *Revista Española*, however, the young contributors are no longer scattered individuals. We now see them coming together and forming groups which, in the case of *Laye*, for example, will later be linked to Seix Barral Publishers and to the important Biblioteca Breve series. Though not quite coinciding chronologically and very different in aims, contributors, materials, and outlook, both reviews none the less parallel each other in the existence and formation of their respective 'teams'. They also illustrate the ways in which disaffected young writers and intellectuals attempt to rise above the drabness of university life and the mediocrity of official cultural forms through friendships and by taking refuge in their own, often quite esoteric and elitist, literary 'ambiente'.

LAYE

Laye first appeared in March 1950 and was supported financially by the *Ministerio de Educación Nacional* and the *Movimiento*. It was an official publication, whose main objective was to act as a bridge between the *Delegación del Distrito de Educación Nacional de Cataluña y Baleares* and school teachers in the state sector. It was thus partly conceived as a forum for dealing with the professional concerns of teachers and as a means of defending and promoting their interests. However, it was more than simply a professional journal; indeed, its other half-title described it as a 'boletín cultural'. And it is this label which is perhaps a more accurate indicator of what the review initially aspired to and without doubt what it would later become. At the local level, ultimate responsibility for the review lay with Eugenio Fuentes Martín, nominal editor and *delegado provincial de Educación* in Barcelona. However, the real job of collecting and preparing material for publication was the responsibility of Francisco Farreras, a falangist, head of the *Seminario de Estudios Políticos* in Barcelona and SEU bureaucrat. In this task and in shaping *Laye*'s political outlook, he would be supported by Ramón Viladás. Both of them, according to Barral, 'constituían entonces el misterioso motor de inspiración política de la publicación'.[2]

Regarding *Laye*'s editorial team, many of its occasional contributors had previously met at Barcelona University in the mid- and late 1940s and already constituted the group that Farreras would call upon to help in launching the review. The group included Castellet, Sacristán, the Ferrater brothers, Gil de Biedma, Ferrán, Oliart, and Costafreda. Barral points out, however, that they were not especially close knit on a personal level:

las afinidades selectivas dividían aquel partido del ocio literario en fracciones poco acumulables. . . . Oliart y Gil de Biedma se apreciaban poco. Costafreda no congeniaba ni con uno ni con otro. Castellet y Sacristán sólo se producían en sesiones magistrales y a partir de la existencia de *Laye* en las de la redacción de la revista, lo mismo que los Ferrater . . . o los últimos llegados, los Goytisolo.[3]

Despite these divisions, what Barral also calls the 'grumoso grupo que formábamos', 'una fratría de pensionado',[4] shared a common class and student background as well as a mixture of contempt and indifference for the depressing limitations of their university education. Unhindered by life's more pressing problems, they would all to some degree adopt the pose of the *déraciné* intellectual, holding court in the Faculty bar, impressing each other with their latest readings and clandestine acquisitions, trying to outdo each other in discussion, etc. Indeed, the endless and now forgotten debates in bars and flats would act as a bonding element as well as a form of therapy, fostering a shared sense of sophistication and purpose in their learning which the desolate cultural milieu around them tended to negate. All this would create a certain group identity, to a large extent autonomous and hermetic, at odds with the outside world. In particular, an awareness of the backwardness of their common cultural milieu, of the essential anti-intellectualism and narrow nationalism of the regime, as well as a constant desire to explore alternative cultural developments beyond the Pyrenees, reinforced their self-image as an embattled intellectual elite and made them vaguely anti-regime.

The local and unifying elements in the group were Sacristán and Castellet, who already had connections with official cultural life through the SEU. But it was principally Farreras and Viladás who would provide the political inspiration behind the gradual take-over of *Laye*. It was they who would able to effect the shift towards a more enlightened, critical stance precisely because of the fact that they were already politicized. But, if the politicized founders of *Laye* created the conditions for a relatively liberal, heterodox review, it was the mainly non-politicized contributors among the new entrants who transformed *Laye* into a predominantly cultural publication, at odds with the backward intellectual climate of postwar Spain.

However, despite its modernizing, dynamic, critical outlook on cultural matters, *Laye*'s political stance was far more ambiguous and contradictory. This is best exemplified by the fact that the review decided to publish a series of articles by the official religious spokesman, José Montagut Roca, which condemned the divisiveness of regionalism and separatism and attacked Catalan nationalism with particular venom.[5] So, if *Laye* did become a fairly sophisticated, specialist cultural review, it remained politically wedded to a sort of enlightened falangist syndicalism, in the process of revision to be sure, but still limited and still fundamentally hostile to Catalanist sympathies. None the less, *Laye* consistently criticized the narrow nationalism, appalling amateurism, and suffocating isolationism of contemporary Spanish culture. And in reaction, apart from inadvertently helping to rehabilitate 'enemy' poets, such as Hernández, it developed an increasingly European and non-Castillian cultural perspective. This can be seen in Barral's obsessive interest in Rilke, and Joan Ferrater's commitment to the modernist writings of Joyce (of whom he translated chapter XIX of *Stephen Hero*) and Eliot (of whom he published *in Catalan* a full translation of *The Waste Land*). Ferrater also and rather exceptionally paid some attention to Catalan literature, including Pla's *El carrer estret*, Riba's *Elegies de Bierville*, Blai Bonet's *Cant Espiritual*, and Joan Vinyoli's *Les hores retrobades*.[6] However, in so far as *Laye* put forward any alternative aesthetic prescriptions of its own, these seem very far from those that would characterize the *literatura social* of the 1950s. Indeed, in terms of its literary and cultural concerns, *Laye* adopts a fairly elitist, vanguardist, neo-Orteguian attitude, committed more to the autonomy of the art object than to its location and role in wider cultural and political processes. Manuel Sacristán, for example, published a highly complex and celebratory reading of Sánchez Ferlosio's *Alfanhuí*, stressing the novel's remarkable formal qualities and the notion that 'la naturaleza del arte es el artificio'.[7] In a similar vein, Barral's important essay 'Poesía no es comunicación' opposes the traditional primacy given to message over medium, as exemplified at the time in Carlos Bousoño's poetics, and demands greater recognition of the purely formal, de-subjectivized nature of the poetic function, as found in Mallarmé or Rilke: 'La teoría de la poesía como comunicación constituye, cuando se formula científicamente, una simplificación peligrosa del proceso y del hecho poético, simplificación que desconoce la autonomía del momento.'[8]

A similar emphasis on the formal, self-reflexive, non-representational, anti-humanist view of artistic creation can be found in Gabriel Ferrater's writings on art criticism and history. In them, he calls for a more rigorous, scientifically-based art criticism, committed to exploring the materiality of the art object as form and function; moreover, in defending abstract painting, Ferrater sees his mission as one of rescuing present-day painters from 'la peligrosa borrachera del sensualismo y de la fácil copia fotográfica'.[9] Like his brother, Joan Ferrater is equally critical of the primacy given to the author and to literary mimesis; as Bonet points out, 'como respuesta, propone, en la mejor línea intelectualista de *Laye*, un autonomismo del texto literario frente a las peripecias del escritor que permita, a la par, una mayor participación mental del lector.'[10] In this regard, Ferrater's essay 'Aspectos de la obra de arte' is symptomatic of a new interest in the reader and in the reception of the art object.[11] Indeed, in line with ideas already being developed by Castellet, Ferrater adopts a vaguely Sartrian framework for his view of the relationship between artist and receiver, explaining the artwork in terms of *propuesta* and *operación* and stressing the crucial moment of its reception. However, in contrast to the dominant formalism and anti-representationalism of *Laye*'s literary and cultural critics, Juan Goytisolo published a short article on the Italian novelist Guido Piovene. In it, he showed a positive appreciation of Piovene's existentialist view of man's disorientation in the modern world, seen through the prism of Italy's fascist past; also, and rather exceptionally, he expressed support for the author's attempts at objective narration, which he linked to the critical, testimonial writing of Malraux.[12]

On the whole, in the light of the above indications and despite Goytisolo's tenuous adherence to an existentialist realism, *Laye* might well appear an odd and extremely unlikely source for the sort of ideas that would guide the movement of social novelists in its early stages. But, in two important respects, the review does seem to make a significant contribution to the movement's aesthetic and intellectual development. The first of these has to do with the question of *engagement*. In *Laye*'s first three numbers, we find a series of articles concerned with what Sacristán calls 'el traído y llevado asunto del alistamiento de los intelectuales bajo banderas políticas'.[13] The debate turned primarily on the social and moral responsibilities of the intellectual and whether active political involvement in a cause or organization compromised his independence and ability to discover the truth. While some argued for political involvement, notably the falangist militants among the contributors, others adopted a more cautious, distanced perspective, relatively independent of official ideology and dogma and curiously reminiscent of the sorts of misgiving voiced by Sartre himself concerning the relationship between the intellectual and the PCF in the late 1940s. The link with Sartre is developed, if only discreetly, in a lengthy footnote to an article by Sacristán in number 3 of the review. Proclaiming a critical, active, interventionist role for the intellectual, Sacristán argues – significantly – that the intellectual can consider himself committed by fulfilling the task of revealing reality, a task in which 'no es que haga coro en un concierto destinado a acallar todo ruido que no sea el de la lucha por la substancia vegetativa, sino que le informe al ciudadano cómo son los cielos y cuántos.' If the intellectual can inform, reveal, demystify, while remaining above the pressures of party politics, then '¿ no se enrola a diario, de insuperable manera?' Sacristán seems to take his view of the intellectual's 'ethical' commitment straight from Sartre, in whom 'es difícil encontrar algo que fundamente el postulado de la colaboración política'.[14] Yet, this is a version of Sartre that, for obvious reasons, is unable to incorporate the complexities and contradictions pertaining to the historically-determined relationships between intellectual and left-wing parties in postwar France. If Sacristán's understanding of Sartre's position is perhaps simplistic, it none the less recognizes the fact that *engagement* has a special relationship to the question of revolution. And here, Sacristán seems to appreciate the role Sartre outlines for the revolutionary philosopher, which is to make explicit the essential directions and underlying trends in revolutionary activity. But, he can only do so by actually placing himself within the movement responsible for those trends. Hence, a notion of intellectual *engagement* as active, interventionist, and politically motivated. So, while *Laye*'s own political limitations and Sacristán's residual falangism prevent him from adopting a more nuanced, more historically-informed position in relation to Sartre, it none the less provides him with a crucial stimulus for reassessing notions of commitment and revolution, bequeathed by his *falangismo*. It also foregrounds a view of *engagement* which seems to underpin the emergent *novela social* and which is seen in terms of an ethical responsibility to reveal the truth of the real world in a critical manner in order to change it.

A corollary of the above and also of major importance in the construction of a new literary–critical discourse are Castellet's writings on literature and on broader socio-cultural themes. As well as occasional notes and book reviews, Castellet's output in *Laye* included three major pieces devoted to questions of narrative technique and the relationships between author and reader. These three articles could be seen as raising the sort of aesthetic and ideological questions which would be taken up by the movement of social novelists. They are: 'Técnicas de la literatura sin autor', 'Notas sobre la situación actual del escritor en España' and 'El tiempo del lector'.[15] The first and the third of these would later be collected in Castellet's primer on narrative technique *La hora del lector*, published in 1957, in the collection *Biblioteca Breve*, which was administered by ex-members of the *Laye* group. The second, alongside other articles and reviews which had appeared in *Revista* and *Alcalá*, would be reproduced in his *Notas sobre literatura española contemporánea* (1955), published under the auspices of *Laye*. Interestingly, since these early articles were reprinted without substantial revision or additions, we can perhaps assume that during the time of his collaboration in *Laye*, Castellet had already elaborated the views and positions that would soon distinguish him as the major theoretician and propagandist for the *realismo social* of the 1950s.

In general terms, what characterizes all of Castellet's writings, in the early as well as the late 1950s, is a profound awareness of the backwardness and poverty of Spanish literature and culture and the absolute necessity of a process of revitalization and modernization. This vital task is held back, however, by a censorship system which, according to Castellet, 'es causa directa de una literatura neutra, aséptica, que nace muerta, abortada.'[16] Moreover, in the face of a general official indifference to cultural matters, Castellet adopts the role of cultural critic and dissenting voice, consistently denouncing an anachronistic and depressingly mediocre official cultural scene. At the same time, he is the mouthpiece for what is modern, a missionary engaged in bringing to public attention a whole range of new, different, up-to-date, superior, and invariably

61

foreign ideas and writings. His impatience and campaigning zeal around this time seem to reflect the outlook of the young falangist intellectual, convinced of his historic role in a process of cultural renewal. A 'divulgador' *par excellence*, Castellet makes it clear that he wishes to reach not only the producers of art and literature, but also the consumers; indeed, in much of his writing, there is a deep concern to develop and improve the cultural 'formación' of an already existing readership and, by doing so, to encourage and propitiate a new, more extensive one. His writings are thus permeated by a strong pedagogical intention; in fact, their earnestness and occasional rigidity of ideas reflect a rather lofty, arrogant cultural elitism, tempered by a desire to inform, elucidate, 'spread the word' concerning a cultural storehouse unknown or simply ignored inside Spain. Castellet's main role and the one for which his work of the 1950s will be remembered, is that of mediator or conduit, recycling and popularizing ideas already well-documented or sedimented in Europe but largely prevented from crossing the Pyrenees. In more specific terms, by drawing on mainly American and European examples of novel writing and especially on developments in modern narrative technique, Castellet sets out to help liberate the Spanish novel from its dependence on outdated and exhausted forms and conventions. Yet, at the same time, while promoting the requirement to modernise, Castellet also proclaims the need for the writer to be fully aware of his own national traditions: 'Un escritor consciente . . . debe conocer a fondo la tradición literaria de su lengua y estar al corriente de las técnicas literarias. Eso cuando menos. Sin tradición y sin técnica, nunca podrá un escritor producir otra cosa que obras inocuas, impersonales e ineficaces.'[17] Castellet's modernizing, radical stand is thus complemented by a respect for tradition, but a tradition, as we have seen, reconstructed according to a trajectory involving realism, testimony, and social critique.

Most important of all then, and certainly most relevant to the formation of the movement of social novelists, Castellet espouses the idea of ideological commitment in the novel and a notion of the novelist as active participant in the process of social and political change. On the role he assigns to the writer, he states, 'por su condición de revelador de la verdad y de miembro dinámico del proceso histórico, es un revolucionario nato que propone al público lector . . . el perfeccionamiento de su libertad personal, muchas veces contra dogmas y sistemas.'[18] Faithful as always to the Sartre of *Qu'est-ce que la littérature?*, Castellet proposes a view of the modern writer as a demystifier of ideology and a revealer of truth; writing is conceived in Sartrian terms as a secondary mode of political action, indeed, an act that has revolutionary implications. Of course, the nature of that truth and its mode of representation in writing are left vague, but, given the dictatorship conditions in which Castellet is writing, are implicitly understood as critical, realist, and anti-regime. Paradoxically perhaps, and in contrast to the active, revolutionary role assigned to the writer, Castellet's articles propose a writing practice that relegates the figure of the author and his presence in the text to a secondary, almost minimal level. What matters is the accurate reproduction of the real, whose rendering, in historical terms, as Castellet reminds us, has been achieved by means of those 'técnicas de la literatura sin autor', i.e. first-person narration, interior monologue, and objective narration. Castellet thus registers the shift, in the modern critical paradigm, from author–text to text–reader relations and, in a sense, following his mentor Sartre, stands as a pioneering proponent of what we would now refer to as 'reader theory' or 'reception aesthetics', or what he himself called in the 1950s 'el tiempo del lector'. Once again showing his indebtedness to Sartre, he formulates the new relation in the following way:

> El arte literario ya no es un simple acto creador del escritor, sino ante todo una doble operación que se realizará según el siguiente esquema: el escritor crea para el lector una obra que éste acepta como una propia tarea a realizar. Concretamente, en el caso de la novela, él revelará un mundo que el lector se comprometerá a poblar activamente.[19]

Castellet is rather vague on how the reading process is to be carried out and says nothing regarding the prior competences and experience of the reader and how these shape the text–reader encounter. Hence a rather superficial, dehistoricized approach to the relationship. Yet, in line with the phenomenology of Roman Ingarden, Castellet shares the view of the text as a structure concretized by the reader; and from Sartre, he takes the notion of reading as a contract, willingly entered into by both author and reader, in which the author's proposed revelation of the real is incorporated into the reader's experience and consciousness of the world. In these early pieces, it is clear that Castellet is rather too absorbed in his own foreign sources, too engaged by their difference and novelty; hence an often uncritical adaptation of new ideas and concepts. The impression is given, in these articles, of a young intellectual who has seized upon a set of potentially radical ideas, at least for his time, but which are yet to be adequately elaborated and their implications fully worked out. But exposure to such foreign sources and, indeed, Castellet's reaction to them and his subsequent role as a channel of diffusion, are symptomatic of a certain historical situation in Spain and a rapid and superficial assimilation of what Bonet has termed a 'sentimiento europeo'. In other words, a number of university students in the late 1940s and early 1950s, through readings, trips to Paris, Heidelberg, Rome, etc. and foreign contacts, experience a cultural 'other', enticing and radical, and, as Bonet puts it, 'todo ello fruto todavía exótico, por no decir prohibido, en una España aislada, decrépita e históricamente congelada'.[20] *Laye* reflects in many ways the results of these cultural encounters.

By the final numbers, it became clear that *Laye*'s increasingly critical and heterodox outlook was proving troublesome to the authorities. Castellet states, 'el tó progressiu d'inconformisme que va a caracteritzar els darrers números de *Laye*, va despertar el recels d'alguns dels elements oficials que la finançaven.' And despite the intervention of Fuentes Martín and even Ruiz Giménez himself, it was Arias Salgado who 'va exigir que *Laye* passés a règim de publicació no oficial i que, en conseqüencia, s'atengués a les normes de censura prèvia.'[21] The editorial board refused to be bound by external controls and, rather than give way, decided to close down the review with number 24, whose cover was significantly framed by a black border. In the manner of a valediction, the final number carried a well-known line by Garcilaso: *Laye* was disappearing 'sufriendo aquello que decir no puedo'.[22]

After the closure of the review, the *Laye* group continued to be active and became directly involved in the *Instituto de Estudios Hispánicos* in Barcelona, something of a cultural bridgehead whose infiltration broadly coincided with that of *Laye*. As Barral explains, 'La apropiación de la revista *Laye* . . . venía a ser estrictamente paralela de la ocupación del Instituto de Estudios Hispánicos de Barcelona, filial bastante autónoma de la casa grande madrileña.'[23]

The *Instituto* was formally run by a couple of SEU administrators, one of whom was 'el futuro sociólogo Marsal . . . en aquel entonces venenosamente fascista', according to Barral, but after twenty years in the USA, a fervent democrat.[24] The activities of the *Instituto* focused above all on seminars: politics, led by Farreras; social sciences, by Juan Eugenio Blanco; economics, by J. Alba Aroca and the seminario Boscán, organized by the poets of the *Laye* group. Such seminars acted as meeting-places for a number of people not directly related to *Laye*, such as Ana María Matute and Mario Lacruz, among others.

By way of conclusion to this section, several points seem relevant. First, *Laye* gives us an example of the way an official publication was gradually taken over and increasingly used for critical and vaguely oppositionist ends. This was possible, as we have seen, because the review had been founded by falangists of proven militancy, but whose ideological contradictions and disenchantment with the regime led to a process of ideological reassessment. It was they who were responsible for incorporating into the review a group of people, the majority of whom were not politicized but who did have a certain amount of experience of working in an official publication. These, with the support of the founders, would be responsible for turning *Laye* into an ambitious, sophisticated, cosmopolitan, critical, but also a specialist and elitist, cultural journal, addressed to a select university audience. So, by the end of the process, *Laye*'s cultural front would dominate and virtually displace its official and primary function as a professional bulletin.

Second, though the process is not linear or directly cumulative, the attacks and polemics experienced by the review would help sharpen its critical edge and make it more willing to publish potentially heterodox pieces. At the same time, however, we must take account of the fact that, even allowing for its secondary character, the educational front in *Laye* was always a feature and thus always a limitation, however minimal, on its cultural activities.

Third, *Laye* offers no coherent ideological position, unless we include here its consistent hostility to the massive presence of the Catholic Church in the education sphere. Nor does it really offer a glimpse of a solid left-wing alternative, despite its occasionally sympathetic attitude to Sartre, existentialism, neo-realism, etc. Censorship is obviously a factor in this lack of definition. What we find, rather, as Barral tells us, is a situation of transition in which the team of contributors, having rejected the status quo, are in the process of searching for alternative ideas and political frameworks. The review thus acts as something of a testing ground for new and different political and cultural options, which are rapidly and perhaps badly digested initially, given the situation of cultural backwardness. In the cultural sphere, a similar incoherence obtains in that we find a reverence for the autonomy of the art object and a New Critical emphasis on form cohabiting with a view of the text as instrument of consciousness-raising and political action. These two strands of thinking are not totally divorced, however, since Castellet seems to take from the poets and art critics their de-emphasis on the irrational, subjective, expressive notions of authorship as well as their focus on the text–receiver relationship. But they do differ substantially in that, for all its alleged modernity, Castellet's commitment to objective narration and the novel as faithful recording of the real also appears rather dated, when compared with developments taking place in Europe in the 1950s. And it is contradicted by those, like Barral, who are committed to a non-communicative view of the art object or literary text, who recognize that the novel is not merely a reproduction of a given real, but a construction in its own right. So, in *Laye* we find different sets of tensions, for example, between Sacristán's Germanic rationalism and Ruiz's or Farreras' falangism; or, in the aesthetic area, between Sartrian *engagement* and Anglo-American autonomy theory, suffused with Orteguian elitism; hence a series of strands and influences which seem to pull in different directions and in which the anti-realist outlook tends to dominate. None the less, *Laye* constitutes an important outlet and platform for new ideas and for a set of young intellectuals, some of whom are in ideological transition and who would play an important role in working out the precepts and rationale of the *novela social*.

REVISTA ESPANOLA

Coinciding almost exactly with the closure of *Laye* in Barcelona, there appeared in Madrid a new literary magazine which, despite its ephemeral existence, constituted an important focal point and publishing outlet for those writers who form the initial thrust of the movement of social novelists. *Revista Española* came into being as a result of the contact between these writers and Antonio Rodríguez Moñino, teacher, scholar, and at that time director of Castalia Publishers. The idea for the magazine seems to have arisen in Madrid's Café Lyon during one of Rodríguez Moñino's regular literary *tertulias*, attended both by friends and colleagues and by many aspiring young writers. From among the latter, Aldecoa, Sánchez Ferlosio, and Sastre were chosen to administer and edit the magazine, while Rodríguez Moñino provided the finance and Castalia's printing facilities. *Revista Española*, 'publicación bimestral de creación y crítica', would concern itself mainly with the publication of short stories and literary and art criticism, offering a regular and much needed publishing outlet for largely unknown talents.

Among the latter, we find a number of writers who constitute a clearly defined and relatively coherent group, linked as much by friendship as by common literary concerns and which Alfonso Sastre refers to as the review's 'frente literario': 'Pero su "frente literario" fue mucho más que un grupo literario con alguna coherencia; fue un grupo de amigos entrañables y sensibles, abierto a todo lo bello y verdadero.'[25] The group, from among whose number the review's editorial team had been selected, had all met previously at university. Carmen Martín Gaite – who would soon marry Sánchez Ferlosio – had known Aldecoa at Salamanca University before they both transferred to Madrid to finish their degrees. In Madrid, Josefina Rodríguez – who married Aldecoa – recalls how Fernández Santos, Sánchez Ferlosio, Sastre, Quinto, Martín Gaite, and Aldecoa 'como otros muchos de la misma generación en Barcelona o en otros lugares de España, formábamos un bloque de amistad y camaradería absolutamente ebrio de literatura.'[26] As with similar groups in other cities, their group identity, underpinned by their passion for literature, would develop through the many contacts made with other individuals and groups in the capital's numerous literary *tertulias*. In cafés such as the Lyon, Gijón and the Gambrinus, they would meet up with Luis Martín Santos, Juan Benet, Miguel Sánchez Mazas, Eva Forest – who would later marry Sastre – and many other young writers and intellectuals. Indeed, reflecting the experience of the *Laye* group in Barcelona, the literary education of many of these youngsters would be forged, not in the university, but in the bars and cafés, in discussions, debates, exchanges of books, and readings, etc.

The main importance, then, of *Revista Española* and the reason why we need to take it into account is that, like *Laye*, it shows how the members of the emergent phase of the *novela social* come together and form a fairly compact group. And as its valedictory note suggests, the review was motivated by a set of concerns that make it an important site in the early development of 1950s realism. *Revista Española* set out to:

> brindar estímulo a la creación literaria que hasta ahora no había encontrado acomodo en otra parte; ofrecer a los lectores de habla española un repertorio de ensayos y obras breves, nacidas con plena independencia y sumisas solamente a la inspiración que les dio vida; y, en suma, llevar a todos el convencimiento de que es posible afrontar las realidades que nos asedian y darles expresión artística.[27]

The most obvious indication of the neo-realist stimulus in *Revista Española* was, of course, the publication in the very first number of part one of Zavattini's 'Totó', translated by Sánchez Ferlosio. The appearance of the story happened to coincide with the *Segunda Semana de Cine Italiano* held in Madrid, the presence of Zavattini himself in the capital as invited guest and the launching of the new and controversial film review *Objetivo*, whose first number paid homage to Zavattini and unequivocally nailed its colours to the neo-realist mast. However, the publication of Zavattini's story (as well as the plot synopsis for de Sica's *Mirácolo a Milano*)[28] is rather less crucial here than his reputation and his influence as an advocate for neo-realism and the Italian left. In fact, 'Totó el bueno' (first published in Italian in 1943), was far from being a representative example of objective narration. Conceived and written as a story for children, but also aimed at the adult reader, it deals with the shack-dwellers of a mythical place called Bamba, who are led by the virtuous Totó in their struggle against eviction by the wicked capitalist Mobic. Part-fable, part-allegory and drawing on the conventions of folk and fairy tale, the story cleverly integrates the precise and convincing observation of detail with the free play of fantasy and imagination, filtered through a very engaging yet overtly intrusive narratorial voice. In this, it may be justifiably compared to Sánchez Ferlosio's own *Alfanhuí*, with which it has many similarities, including its third-person narration, imagery, humour, and nostalgia for childhood innocence. But perhaps the main attraction of Zavattini's realist fantasy lies in the way it elevates to the level of legend the absolutely banal and inconsequential lives of its characters, turning them into heroic protagonists of an epic tale. At the same time, just below the allegory, the story offers a powerful satire of capitalist exploitation and maintains a solid grip on the sort of real, day-to-day difficulties faced by the poor and dispossessed of any major city.

A further indication of the neo-realist outlook in *Revista Española* can be seen in Fernando Namora's short story 'Días de viento'.[29] Namora was among the leading figures of the neo-realist movement in Portugal during the 1940s and 1950s, though as in the case of Zavattini's contribution, his tale of the encounter between a liberal-minded doctor and the son of a starving gypsy family is not given a fully objectivist treatment. Rather, it conforms to Castellet's injunction to explore techniques of authorial suppression, being largely narrated in the first person, from the point of view of the doctor. The story turns on the clash between the concerned professional, in solidarity with the poor, and his difficulties in overcoming the gulf of suspicion and fierce independence, embodied in the gypsy boy. In certain respects, especially in terms of the always problematic relation between the professional (i.e. the doctor) and the representatives of the 'pueblo', the story invites comparison with *Los bravos*.

As Carmen Martín Gaite has pointed out, *Revista Española's* principal role was that of a workshop where, before embarking on the writing of novels, the members of her group served an apprenticeship in the short story. This required, above all, the writer's keen awareness of the realities around him, both visual and verbal, and the ability accurately to document them: 'Aprendimos a escribir ensayando un género que tenía entidad por sí misma, que a muchos nos marcó para siempre y que requería, antes que otras pretensiones, una mirada atenta y unos oídos finos para incorporar las conversaciones y escenas de nuestro entorno y registrarlas.'[30] If *Revista Española* reveals some of the groundwork out of which the *novela social* will emerge, it also shows a group of writers keen to explore a variety of narrative modes and technical resources, not all of them by any means leading directly to the famous objectivism of the *novela social*. Indeed, we have to be careful not to regard the latter as a completed, available writing practice, based on an already developed and unchanging technical option, but as a series of variations, a process involving different narrative choices as to how best to convey the illusion of a particular reality. Moreover, we should not assume that the writings of the 'frente literario' in *Revista Española* are simply a link in a process which evolves, neatly and unproblematically, into the realism attributed, say, to *El Jarama*. Perhaps it would be better to regard the output of the 'frente literario', during this period of transition and testing, as the exploration of a varied set of options and strategies aimed at capturing, in different ways, a verifiable, external reality; and as a corollary, the search for ways of motivating the reader to look beyond the textual surface to the 'unsaid' of the disclosure, the reality implicitly addressed between the lines.

The contributions of Sánchez Ferlosio illustrate particularly well this phase of transition, experimentation, and the testing of options. His first published story, 'Niño fuerte', seems clearly indebted to Zavattini and stands much closer to the realist fantasy of *Alfanhuí* than to the sober realism of *El Jarama*.[31] The story concerns a poor couple, whose unique ambition is to produce a healthy child, a 'niño fuerte', against all expectations. But, because of their wretched circumstances, their son Eustaquio is born weak and under weight; and it is only through their constant care and attention that the youngster reaches adolescence, finally winning a struggle for survival, against massive odds. As Darío Villanueva has correctly observed, 'Todo el cuento es la idealización de una serie de hechos cotidianos; los que jalonan el crecimiento de Eustaquio ante la mirada amorosa y atenta de sus padres.'[32] However, if the representation of the real is intensified by means of the use of fantasy, in technical terms, we are still some way off from the sort of austere, objective testimony found in *El Jarama*. Despite indications at the end of the story of the author's skill in rendering natural dialogue, 'Niño fuerte' is none the less dominated by a powerful, intrusive, though sympathetic narrator, whose language too often draws more attention to itself than to the reality it purports to reflect. In fact, the exploitation of a range of rhetorical devices reveals a linguistic virtuosity which harks back to *Alfanhuí*: for example, the use of repetition and accumulation emphasizes the grinding poverty of the *barrio* (40–1); we also find a widespread predilection for anthropomorphism, by which houses breathe and windows sweat, and rats are 'adultas y severas, republicanas, inteligentes, suaves y espeluznantes'(43). All in all, rather than a straight, unadorned, realistic representation, we have a poetic, aestheticized depiction, rich in image and symbol.

'Hermanos', the only other story published by Sánchez Ferlosio in *Revista Española*,[33] contrasts sharply in style and technique with 'Niño fuerte', abandoning the latter's intrusive narrator, its reality–fantasy opposition and its excessive 'ternura' and opting for a much simpler, more economical, more detached mode of narration. The story concerns a family feud, involving two sets of brothers from different social classes. It is thus readable as an analogue or microcosm of the civil war, from a largely non-partisan perspective and seems to suggest that attempts to suspend confrontation and seek a non-violent solution to the conflict are undermined by the prejudices and inflexibility of both sides. Technically, the story is less self-consciously literary than the earlier one, and by using a first-person plural narratorial position at some points, Sánchez Ferlosio appears to invite the reader to identify with young protagonist's demand that the point of view of the other side should be heard.

Ignacio Aldecoa had two stories published: 'A ti no te enterramos' and 'Muy de mañana', both of which reflect some of the main stylistic and thematic features of his later novels and which confirm a view of life he found admirably expressed in Alfonso Sastre's play *Escuadra hacia la muerte*: 'la incertidumbre y la desesperanza del hombre de hoy'.[34] 'A ti' concerns Valentín, eldest son of a peasant family, whose worsening tuberculosis prevents him from working and taking over the role of head of family from his ageing and exhausted father. He journeys to the city to look for work, but has nothing to show after nine days of searching: 'No sabía lo que pasaba en la ciudad; se sentía extraño a ella.'[35] Overcome by despair, Valentín is trapped in a *situation limite*; at this crisis point he decides to return home, wilfully deceiving himself that he will manage to work for his keep.

The main thrust of the story concerns one man's futile search for work in a hostile environment and the uncomfortable realization that his place is finally and inevitably on the land. 'A ti' thus explores the difficulties of rural migration which, in relation to Valentín's dilemma, are given a vaguely existentialist treatment. Technically, the story is structured according to a feature that will be widely exploited by the practitioners of the *novela social*, i.e. the simultaneity of scenes or episodes. This can be seen, for example, in Part I, as the male members of the family set off at dawn to work their respective 'parcelas'. On the whole, the story keeps to a chronologically linear development, though Aldecoa does intercalate instances of retrospection and anticipation. However, except for a few isolated instances of interior monologue, character action and motivation are filtered and interpreted through the discourse of the narrator.

In 'Muy de mañana', Aldecoa again deals with the themes of loneliness and isolation. The story concerns an old melon vendor, at the end of the fruit season, whose solitude is tragically reimposed when his only companion in the world, his dog Cartucho, is accidentally run over by a car. The story reflects Aldecoa's interest in society's marginal types and his lasting fascination for the uncertainty and cruel paradoxes of existence. In technical terms, Aldecoa's narrator still maintains firm control over events and characters; also, the very rapid scene changes marked by the word 'Ahora' indicate another dominant device in Aldecoa's writing: that of repetition or *iteratio*, appropriately exploited within the story's overall circular structure.

The themes of illness and isolation, seen in Aldecoa's contributions, are also explored in Fernández Santos' first published story 'Cabeza Rapada'.[36] This time, however, they are treated from the perspective of orphaned children who are trying to survive the misery, malnutrition, disease, and abandonment faced particularly by the lower-class losers in Spain's difficult postwar years. The story focuses on Cabeza Rapada, hardly ten years old, and his vain attempts – supported by an unnamed companion who acts as internal narrator of the story – to secure medical help for his already advanced pneumonia. The story is symmetrical in shape, beginning and ending in the same lugubrious, windswept avenue at night. However, the use of flashback allows Fernández Santos to widen his temporal and spatial focus to include events of the previous day, such as a visit by the two protagonists first to a hospital and afterwards to a bar. This introduces a wider community of lower-class figures, who are condemned to the same sort of deprivation, official indifference, and lack of professional medical care as Cabeza Rapada. On top of this, the imagery of light and darkness evokes an ominous environment in the city suburbs and the sad, ashen faces of the hospital patients add to the general atmosphere of unrelieved gloom and hopelessness. By portraying children as innocent victims of a concrete historical situation, the author is able to exploit a powerful, emotive symbol which condenses the specific problem of abandoned children and, more generally, the difficulties experienced by the losers of the civil war. By implication, then, Fernández Santos points an accusing finger at the negligence and irresponsibility of the victors, by showing their indifference to the needs of those least able to defend themselves.

In 'Hombres', his second published story, Fernández Santos uses a young boy to recount the life and death of Miguel, a Portuguese migrant worker, who decides to settle down in an isolated mountain village, after finishing work on a road building scheme in León.[37] In a scene that bears some similarities to Pascual Duarte's seemingly unmotivated murder of his dog, Miguel is finally killed by a workmate under the midday sun, after a quarrel. Like the death of Lucita in *El Jarama*, the incident is given no narrative prominence; indeed, the cool, detached, innocent manner in which it is reported by the young narrator simply serves to heighten its absurdity and pointlessness. Here, death is divested of any transcendent significance; it is reduced almost to a commonplace, to one more trivial event in the predictable lifecycle of the village. In the author's third and final story published in *Revista Española*, 'El Sargento',[38] Fernández Santos again uses the technique of first-person narration, thus allowing the sergeant in question, stationed in Cuba during the Spanish–American War, to communicate directly to the reader his experience of war and his agonizing illness after contracting malaria. Exploring an important moment in Spain's recent historical past, through using it as an analogue for more recent wars, the story deals with the gradual erosion of the protagonist's dreams of heroism on the battlefield as he becomes aware of the death and disease suffered by his colleagues at the front and behind the lines. His fantasies of honour and glory are finally undercut by his own malaria infection and the certainty of a slow, painful death.

Where previous contributions draw their subject matter mainly from the daily lives of the rural and urban poor, those of the female members of the 'frente literario', Carmen Martín Gaite and Josefina Rodríguez, shift the focus of attention to the middle and lower-middle classes. Dealing with such topics as the alienating effects of routine, the indifference of the wealthy to lower-class suffering, the oppressive nature of petit-bourgeois respectability, these stories anticipate, to some extent, the sub-trend in the *novela social*, known as the anti-bourgeois novel.

In 'Un día de libertad', her only contribution to *Revista Española*, Carmen Martín Gaite explores the contradictory moods of freedom and fear, self-confidence and self-doubt, which are released by one man's fleeting revolt against conformity.[39] Presented through the consciousness of the narrator–protagonist, a cultivated but lowly-paid office worker, the story begins *in medias res*, at the moment he arrives home after having engineered his own dismissal at work. The story is unusual for its use of first-person narration in the perfect tense, not unlike Pedro's initial monologue in *Tiempo de silencio*, which gives the reader the illusion of direct access to the protagonist's anguished thought-processes. However, despite the protagonist's momentary subversion of the status quo, the story focuses mainly on the difficulty or impossibility of breaking with routine and established patterns of existence. Out of love for his wife and fear at upsetting her banal, conformist life-style, the protagonist finally determines to tell her nothing of his unique day of freedom and to ask for his job back: 'Sí, sí. Lo arreglaré. Volver al cauce, al sueño. . . . Pero mañana mismo. A primera hora. Lo tengo que arreglar, Dios mío. Lo tengo que arreglar.'[40]

Problems of conformity, the inability to communicate one's feelings and, indeed, the fear of freedom itself, lie at the heart of Josefina Rodríguez's first published story, 'Voces Amigas', perhaps one of the most accomplished pieces in the whole review.[41] The title refers to a radio programme playing record dedications, of mainly foreign singers, broadcast on a Sunday. The story concerns Luisa, a refined, sensitive but lonely spinster, probably in her forties, who lives by herself in a slightly run-down flat and works in a flower shop. On her birthday, in order to ease her oppressive loneliness, she has 'Voces Amigas' play her three records, corresponding to two previous sweethearts and her present employer, Sr Díaz – all of which she arranges herself. Simply structured and lacking in any substantive action, the story is presented both through a third person voice and by means of Luisa's own brief snatches of interior monologue; apart from the radio, no other character voice is represented on the page. Luisa's isolation and lack of contact with other voices and people are cleverly conveyed in a conversation in Part II, in which questions to which she responds are not enunciated in the text but have to be inferred. Above all, she is denied a voice of her own by the still powerful voice of patriarchal authority invested in her dead father whose influence, symbolized in the portrait, seems to extend well beyond the grave.

Rodríguez's second story, 'Transbordo en Sol', also takes up the problem of lack of communication, this time following a woman's suicide in the Madrid underground, to which a middle-class boy, on his way to school, has been a direct witness.[42] Desperate to tell his parents of the event, Carlitos is coldly reassured by his mother: '¿Qué historia es ésa del Metro, hijo? Tú no te preocupes de esas cosas. Son asuntos de personas mayores. Qué te importa a ti lo que le suceda a cualquier desgraciada. Dame un beso y vete a cenar.'[43] The story turns on the boy's day-long 'toma de conciencia' after the suicide, which results in nausea, guilt feelings, and lack of concentration at school. Against this background, the insensitivity and indifference of the parents seem all the more brutal and reprehensible.

The final, though perhaps tangential, member of *Revista Española*'s 'frente literario' to be considered is José María de Quinto. Better known for his work as a dramatist and theatre critic, alongside Sastre, he was nevertheless a writer of short stories and intimately connected with the movement of social novelists. In *Revista Española*, he published three stories in all, whose thematic concerns broadly coincide with those of his colleagues, but whose ideological outlook is expressed rather more forcefully and explicitly. This is nowhere more evident than in 'Noviembre en los huesos', in which the child protagonist, 'el Rubiales' loses his job as a lift attendant at a large cement company for sleeping during working hours.[44] His arbitrary and unfair dismissal not only brings him closer emotionally to his consumptive mother, but also quickens his coming of age and inspires a feeling of solidarity with his community of *chabolistas*.

The story is very much an amalgam of features already noted in other stories of the group: focus on lower-class poverty through a marginal grouping, the *chabolistas*; child protagonist; extreme situation; illness; inevitability of death; gap between rich and poor and class oppression; 'toma de conciencia'; class solidarity, etc. However, unlike other stories which tend to allow the reader to infer the reasons for injustice and harsh social conditions, Quinto's narrator insistently poses the problem of responsibilities through direct questions. His second piece, 'Atardecer sin tabernas', could almost represent a continuation of the previous story.[45] It deals with the inhabitants of one of Madrid's poor quarters who wreak spectacular collective revenge on a black marketeer. Once again, using techniques of repetition and accumulation, the narrator's outrage at the conditions suffered by the poor is made abundantly clear:

> Era el hambre de la postguerra. Y alguien, un día, murió en una cama sin sábanas. Y alguien, otro día, desapareció del barrio en una ambulancia. . . . Y un niño se levantó y pidió pan. Y toda una familia se acostó una noche sin cenar y con los ojos llorosos de hambre. . . . Y se prostituyeron las muchachas. . . . Ay, sí, Dios de los pobres; era el tiempo de la postguerra.[46]

In his third contribution, 'Noche de agosto', which deals with a destitute unmarried mother driven to a mercy killing of her syphilitic baby, Quinto's wearisome, heavy-handed moralizing is replaced by a less emotive, more sober, detached presentation.[47] Here, apart from a sympathetic portrait of the mother, Quinto's critique of the clergy and the medical profession, his denunciation of their hypocrisy, negligence and indifference to the protagonist's dilemma are handled in a more subtle, nuanced, and finally more effective fashion.

Having briefly surveyed the creative output of the 'frente literario', we can now draw some provisional conclusions. First, in broad terms, their stories certainly seem to confirm the stated aims of *Revista Española*, in particular that of giving artistic expression to 'las realidades que nos asedian'. In fact, the stories consistently engage with aspects of the everyday reality of a hidden, unreported Spain, predominantly the Spain of lower-class poverty and social injustice, the forgotten, voiceless Spain of the losers of the civil war, and the casualties of the postwar dictatorship. This is immediately evident in the choice of protagonists: poor peasants; migrant workers; the casually employed; the urban poor; *chabolistas*; unmarried mothers; abandoned children, etc. It is also apparent in the types of setting used: the 'pueblo perdido'; the isolated farm or village; the city outskirts; the 'barrio pobre'; the *chabola*; the street corner, etc. It is most obviously seen in the sorts of theme that dominate the stories: the tedium of daily existence and the lack of horizons, exploitation at work, family, generational, and class oppression, the struggle to survive in the face of loneliness, alienation, abandonment, poverty, illness, and death.

Second, though the stories are readable at many levels, their subject matter and thematic reference points do draw substantially on historically verifiable social and economic phenomena of the period. However, in the process of literary mediation, such trends and aspects are inflected and dealt with in ways that go beyond the bounds of a simple repertorial realism. For example, a frequently visited topic is that of the 'campo–ciudad' opposition, encompassing the questions of migrant labour ('Hombres') and migration to the cities in search of work ('A ti'). Here, Aldecoa's story is in many ways an admirable and sensitive treatment of the dilemmas faced by the migrant worker, surplus to requirements in both city and country. But, at the same time, the story illustrates a tendency found among other writers of the 'frente literario' to identify a little too closely with their subjects and perhaps overstate their case, out of solidarity with the victims. In the case of 'A ti', while Aldecoa convincingly portrays the alienating effects of an outsider's first contact with the city, his version of the rural life is less persuasive. Hard, exhausting, unforgiving it may be, but it is also sustaining, wholesome, and masculine, in contrast to the softening, 'feminizing' effects of the city. Hence, Valentín's dilemma at being unable to fulfil his masculine role on the farm and his decision to leave. There is a also a degree of romanticizing sentimentality in Aldecoa's picture of the peasant family, notably in Berta, the mother, who is always honest, even-handed, self-sacrificing, even-tempered, a wonderful cook, and totally virtuous. Here then, an author's quite legitimate admiration for the underdog seems to slip into literary idealization. This tendency can also be seen in the stories dealing with immigrant families, recently arrived in the cities. While they correctly stress the desperate living conditions of the inhabitants and their exploitation as cheap labour ('Niño fuerte', 'Noviembre en los huesos', 'Atardecer sin tabernas'), they tend to present too simple and optimistic a picture of collective resolve in the face of hardship and threat. In short, for quite understandable reasons and perhaps at times inadvertently, some writers overplay the virtues of their subjects, the strength of lower-class solidarity and end up transforming their resistance to oppression into a rather romanticized heroism.

Third, many of the stories, directly or indirectly, deal with or dramatize the process of consciousness raising. On some occasions, the process is enacted within the boundaries of the story by a character or narrator–protagonist; at other times, mediating figures are set aside in favour of external narratorial commentary or the verbal testimony of characters. On the whole, apart from Quinto's more positive, optimistic endings, a new awareness of misery, oppression, numbing routine, or lower-class despair is rarely translated into any form of action, resistance, or a search for alternatives, at least within the boundaries of fiction. In fact, while many stories implicitly invoke the need for corrective action, the situation they deal with is presented as fundamentally unalterable: in 'A tí', Valentín is forced back to the farm; in 'Hermanos', the drive to close ranks and refuse to dialogue is aggressively asserted and further entrenched; in 'Muy de mañana', Roque's isolation is reimposed; in 'Cabeza Rapada', the youngster is destined to die; in 'Un día de libertad', the rebellion against routine and conformity cannot be sustained; in 'Voces Amigas', Luisa remains trapped in her world of silence and isolation; and in 'Transbordo en Sol', the youngster's 'toma de conciencia' is simply ignored by his mother. Clearly, by stressing the situation of stasis, entrapment, circularity and lack of tangible solutions within the fiction, the stories invite the reader not only to engage in his own 'toma de conciencia', but also to infer the reasons and historical determinants underlying this social stagnation.

Fourth, one of the devices frequently employed to mediate between the reader and the represented reality of the stories is the child protagonist. In *Revista Española*, the latter seems to be used in two main ways: first, as a casualty of postwar conditions, an innocent victim of lower-class misery, who also represents the wider community of the poor and constitutes an indictment of the regime's attitude towards the losers of the war ('Cabeza Rapada', 'Noviembre en los huesos'); second, as direct witness and mediating voice of poverty and misery and their effects ('Cabeza Rapada', 'Transbordo en Sol', 'Noviembre en los huesos'). What this approach might lack in terms of narrator flexibility and reliability, i.e. in terms of the constraints imposed by working through a child's subjectivity, it more than makes up for in its potential for emotive impact on the reader and indeed, in its role as the latter's conscience inside the story.

Finally, there is the matter of narrative technique. This varies considerably from one story to the next, although certain patterns of similarity and difference do emerge. In structural terms, many of the stories are circular or symmetrical in shape, returning to the point of departure, thus suggesting inevitability, closure, and lack of outlets. They also tend towards linear chronology, with little fragmentation or rearranging of the temporal order of events; however, there is widespread use of both retrospective and prospective sequences, allowing for the introduction of a wider historical or psychological perspective. At times, these insertions are used to clarify the causality of the narrative; at others, they serve to generalize the effects or consequences of the particular theme in focus. In some cases ('Niño fuerte', 'A ti.', 'El sargento', 'Un día de libertad'), we find significant amounts of reported detail, not all of which is necessary to the movement of the story; rather, it is used to enhance the story's 'reality effect' and extend the reader's knowledge of character motivation or social context.

As regards modes of narration, some writers are clearly more interested in the portrayal of interiority and subjectivity as a way of approaching the rendering of the real. They thus tend to resort to the use of interior monologue to represent the consciousness of their characters or narrator–protagonists ('Cabeza Rapada', 'Un día de libertad'). Other writers, like Sánchez Ferlosio, prefer to mediate their fiction through a dominant, third-person narrator, frequently combining this with direct mimesis through character dialogue. However, as we have seen, dominant narrator figures, making frequent and explicit incursions into the text, do seem to undercut the features used to authorize the credibility of the story (i.e. individualized characters, narrative objectivity, repertorial detail, character dialogue, motivated causality, etc.). But on the whole, we find a broad mixture of narrative perspectives, with perhaps the first-person narrative mode dominating the series. Only in a couple of instances ('Niño fuerte', 'Un día de libertad') do we find fantasy, dream, non-realistic backgrounds being exploited in juxtaposition to the real, in order to reinforce and naturalize the representation as 'life as it is'.

In most cases, the stories provide fairly convincing and realistic portrayals of their subject matter, drawing on the sorts of feature noted above to sustain their credibility. Of course, at times, their artifice can be quite overt on the page, ranging from structural symmetry and the use of simultaneity of episodes to imagery, metaphor, *iteratio*, and narratorial moralizing which, as in the case of Quinto, tend to undercut the illusion of verisimilitude. In general, then, we are still at some distance from the final goal of linguistic transparency, still experimenting with techniques of authorial suppression, still searching for the narrative formula with which to allow Spain's voiceless 'others' to tell their story in their own way. Also, more work is required at this stage in the construction of positions for the reader from which he or she can experience the narration directly rather than be lectured or told, at second hand, of events, without other forms of corroboration. None the less, *Revista Española*'s literary team do seem to be experimenting with certain non-authorial modes of address, a sign perhaps of a growing concern for a figure in the literary communication whose time, according to Castellet, had now arrived.

Sastre seems to be right, then, in talking of a 'frente literario' in *Revista Española*. By all appearances, we seem to have a group of writers who are basically agreed as to what they want to do and why. But it would clearly be wrong to give the impression that broadly-shared aims at the level of writing practice, within the 'frente literario', corresponded to an identity of ideological motives. As Sastre also points out, 'Nuestro grupo de los años cincuenta era más y menos que un grupo. Por una literatura "social", estábamos Quinto y yo y de alguna forma, arrastramos a Ferlosio hasta cierta simpatía por nuestras lucubraciones social-políticas: quizá su cuento "Niño fuerte" fue una manifestación de esa simpatía.'[48] In the context of the early 1950s, what Sastre seems to understand by a 'literatura social' is a writing that fairly directly expresses the standpoint and politics of the author. It would be fair to say that such an attitude does not emerge from the work of Aldecoa, Fernández Santos, Martín Gaite, Rodríguez, or Sánchez Ferlosio. The latter tend to write in ways that do not make their viewpoints explicit. What is interesting, however, is that the sort of emphasis Sastre places on making one's commitment more explicit in writing is an indication of the division, set up afterwards by the critics, between early and later social novelists, between the 'sociales' and the 'politizados'. Rather than posit the existence of a division, it might be historically more accurate to talk in terms of a difference of emphasis among writers. That is to say, while some choose to express their politics more directly in their writing, others prefer to let the writing speak for itself, less encumbered by authorial judgements, asides, or other forms of commentary. This seems to be the posture adopted by the majority of members of the 'frente literario'.

To conclude, both *Laye* and *Revista Española* constitute important sources for the early formation of the movement of social novelists. But, as well as their specific contribution, they are also symptomatic of the intellectual and artistic trends emerging within a certain historical and cultural moment in Spain in the early 1950s.

In specific terms, as we have seen, they illustrate how, for the first time, members of the movement begin to form relatively compact groups. If group cohesion and identity exist more at the personal than the political level at this stage, the respective groups still seem to share certain common intellectual and artistic concerns. Dominant among the latter are an acute awareness of Spain's cultural backwardness, exacerbated by the regime, and a demand for cultural and literary modernization. In *Laye*, this is translated into an increasingly critical, heterodox, dissenting attitude combined with a cultural eclecticism, 'Europeanism', and patrician elitism. It also finds expression in the debates over the role of the intellectual and the tension between those who proclaim the autonomy of the art object and those, like Castellet, who advocate an active, interventionist role for art and literature in social and political change. In *Revista Española*, which certainly reflects *Laye*'s cosmopolitanism and elitism in the cultural field, the creative work of the 'frente literario' seems to view art and literature above all as communication, revelation, testimony etc. This happens, paradoxical though it may seem, quite independently of the sort of ideas being advanced by Castellet in *Laye*. Also, contained within the title *Revista Española*, we appear to have two contradictory but, in the end, complementary tendencies: on the one hand, the promotion of creative work by native Spanish writers and, on the other, an appetite for and openness towards all things foreign. Both reviews show an obvious interest in European and Anglo-American creative and critical writing, but while the main initial stimulus behind *Revista Española* is undoubtedly Italian neo-realism, in *Laye* it is a mixture of French, German and Anglo-American work, especially Sartre, Rilke and Eliot.

At the same time, the reviews differ markedly in their origins, patronage, financing, editorial policy, contributions and general purpose. *Laye* was an official publication, linked to the Ministry of Education while *Revista Española* was independent, inspired if anything by the altruism of its founder. Also, while in *Laye* we find evidence of a 'takeover' by its politicized editorial board, but mainly by its non-politicized team of contributors, in *Revista Española* such a struggle was absent. In the latter, there was little question of having to deceive the editor or of dismissing contributors (as seems to have happened in the case of Joan Ferrater).[49] In *Laye*, however, its official links did give rise to a certain atmosphere of intrigue and infiltration, no doubt exploited and enjoyed by the young contributors. This perhaps partly accounts for the different orientations in the reviews towards art and literature. For example, its official role, the politicized nature of its founders and its regime of internal supervision make *Laye* potentially more open to political radicalism and to seek ideological support, not only in José Antonio but also in Sartre. Also, for the young poets and art critics of *Laye*, anxious to defend modernism and proclaim the separation of art and politics (or at least falangist politics), the reverential attitude of the regime's official spokesmen towards traditional notions of realism provided a ready-made target. On the other hand, *Revista Española* refuses the separation advocated in *Laye* and under the influence of neo-realism, ratifies a powerful interest in favour of realism. We thus have a curious situation in which the sort of precepts originally advocated by Sartre and restated by Castellet are implicitly and indirectly being worked through by the 'frente literario' and under the impulse of a different set of determinants. In the end, almost independently of each other, the two reviews are beginning to make the sort of interconnections between theory and writing practice that will soon give rise to the *novela social*.

Finally, both reviews are symptomatic of a broader period of cultural transition and renewal, promoted by a generation of young writers and intellectuals at odds with the regime and searching for the means to express their disillusionment and rejection. *Laye* illustrates a growing disenchantment both with institutionalized *falangismo* and its vacuous rhetoric and with a cultural panorama characterized by its poverty and official indifference. *Revista Española*, reflecting the openness of its founder and the tastes of its editorial team, is indicative of a trend in which young creative writers are anxious to break into the field and re-shape its boundaries and practices. Above all, and despite its evident limited appeal, through the medium of fictional writing, they seek to put the case for the losers of the civil war, in particular to give a voice to Spain's postwar underclass. Separately, though not disconnectedly, these two reviews illustrate the theoretical debates and the sort of writing practices that feed into Spain's home-grown version of committed literature.

Chapter Four

COMMITMENT, NEO-REALISM, AND PRACTICES

Given the adverse cultural climate in Spain in the 1950s, it should not surprise us that the social novelists, as well as other writers and intellectuals, were acutely predisposed to the reception of trends and influences originating from beyond the Pyrenees and Censura's *cordon sanitaire*. This appetite for things foreign obviously responded in part to a desire to sample the forbidden fruits of European and Anglo-American culture; it also reflected an intense dissatisfaction with the backwardness and conservatism of official cultural forms. Of course, the social novelists were receptive to some trends and not to others since they were already looking for something, and vaguely aware of the role they wanted their literature to play. This, broadly speaking, was a political role, one of critically contesting the dominant definitions of the real by revealing another social reality that had been systematically distorted or simply ignored by the regime. In so doing, the *novela social*, like other artistic forms, was no doubt taking upon itself some of the functions normally discharged by the press in a democratic society.

Though their impact was certainly felt more widely, we can identify three main foreign influences which operated on the movement of social novelists during its formative period: (i) Sartre's ideas on *engagement* and the notion of a committed literature; (ii) Italian neo-realism, in literature but particularly in film; (iii) The American realist novel of the inter-war period. The effects of these three influences began to be felt at roughly the same time and this chronological coincidence would have repercussions on the ways in which they were received. Quite simply, they were not taken up independently of one another, but substantially overlapped and tended to reinforce each other. So, while it is intended to examine them separately and establish their distinctive modes of reception, it is worth recognizing that they cannot always be separated in their effects.

SARTRE AND *ENGAGEMENT*

That Sartre was an important source of theoretical and programmatic inspiration for the movement is undeniable. For example, when writers and critics, especially during the 1950s, refer to the *novela social* as a 'literatura de compromiso' or 'literatura testimonial', when they define the purpose of writing in terms of effecting a 'toma de conciencia' or 'toma de posición', or when they claim that 'ser escritor es una actitud en el mundo', etc, they are using a phraseology that is directly informed by Sartre's writings of the 1940s on literary commitment. Perhaps more than any other work, it was Sartre's *Qu'est-ce que la littérature?* (1948), in the Losada translation of 1950, which would become the movement's source of reference on commitment and the role of the writer.[1] It was this text that, circulating clandestinely, would provide critics such as Castellet and Goytisolo with the concepts and the rationale for an indigenous, committed, realist novel. By way of preparing the ground for an examination of how Sartre's ideas were received in Spain, it seems appropriate to review briefly the main features of his argument.

L'action par dévoilement

For Sartre, the fundamental obligation facing the committed writer was that of revealing to the reader his situation in the world and his freedom (and ability) to change it. By disclosing a situation to the reader (and thus by changing the nature of the reader's relationship to that situation), the writer invited the reader to effect a critical judgement, a *prise de conscience*, in order to transcend that situation (i.e. achieve a 'dépassement') and bring about its transformation. Literature thus operated on the reader by converting a non-reflexive awareness of the world into a reflexive, self-conscious awareness, after which the reader could no longer take the world for granted. So, by naming and revealing the world, the business of literature was to make the reader responsible for changing it.

As regards its medium, the job of revealing and changing the world required the transparency of prose, in which words are regarded as referential, direct, transitive bearers of unitary meaning. Poetry, argued Sartre, at least in 1947/8, was of little practical use to the committed writer, since for the poet, words have the opacity of objects, not the transparency of the prose sign and embody a multiple *sens* rather than a single *signification*. Prose was seen as essentially instrumental, 'utilitaire par essence'(26), and capable of responding to Sartre's imperative of simplicity of designation. Thus, in the very act of writing, the prose writer was seen as someone who had adopted 'un certain mode d'action secondaire qu'on pourrait nommer l'action par dévoilement' (29–30). Moreover, the revelation of a situation, argued Sartre, necessarily implied an intention to change it: 'L'écrivain engagé sait que la parole est action; il sait que dévoiler c'est changer et qu'on ne peut dévoiler qu'en projettant de changer' (30).

Il n'y a d'art que pour et par autrui (55)

With this now famous dictum, Sartre pointed to the crucial and indispensable role of the reader in completing the literary work, arguing that without his participation, 'L'acte créateur n'est qu'un moment incomplet et abstrait de la production d'une oeuvre' (54–5). The reader was seen as perfectly entitled to ignore the work, but if he chose to open it, he was considered as having assumed a certain responsibility for it. And far from being a mere act of passive consumption, the work became 'une tâche à remplir', requiring the reader's active, productive involvement which had to be freely undertaken. Reading was thus conceived as an act of generosity on the part of the reader, something that the writer had to respect and constantly encourage. As a 'relation dialectique', this collaborative effort had as its source and its end the pursuit of freedom. Summing up, Sartre states, 'Ecrire, c'est donc à la fois dévoiler le monde et le proposer comme une tâche à remplir à la générosité du lecteur'(76).

The notion of freedom is clearly the key concept which connects

Sartre's thinking on aesthetics and politics. For Sartre, all art is potentially liberating, all art depends on an unfettered imagination and imagination is seen as synonymous with the freedom of human consciousness. Art, literature, etc. thus depend on and work to foment human emancipation. This perhaps explains Sartre's mistrust of excessively emotive, partisan writing and his horror of propaganda, or propaganda masquerading as art. Hence his insistence that the writer should be careful not to alienate the reader by telling him what to think or involving him in an enforced participation. This not only put the reader's freedom in jeopardy but also threatened the artistic integrity of the work and its effectiveness as a communication: 'Dans la passion la liberté est aliénée. . . . De là, ce caractère de pure présentation qui paraît essentielle à l'oeuvre d'art; le lecteur doit disposer d'un certain recul esthétique' (62). Sartre thus signalled the need for a degree of detachment in novel writing, an aesthetic distance between author and reader capable of facilitating the act of communication and predisposing the reader towards the substance, rather than the form of the revelation. In Genet's words, this aesthetic withdrawal constituted 'la politesse de l'auteur envers le lecteur'(63), a reminder to the reader that this was a work of literature and not a pamphlet. In terms of writing practice, Sartre's insistence on the need for aesthetic distance seems to imply the abandonment of the omniscient author and the adoption of more objective modes of narration, in keeping with his requirement of 'pure présentation'. Of course, by presenting the world more objectively, the writer chose to leave many things unsaid and unexplained; writing would tend towards ellipsis, becoming opaque, complex, and obscure. This, however, was the price to be paid for reinstalling the reader as co-creator and in the end for respecting the reader's freedom and generosity in taking up the work, the reward for which ultimately lay in personal liberation.

Contribuer à l'avènement futur de la société concrète des fins (331)

If, as Sartre argued, it was the task of the committed writer to reveal injustices in an imaginary form and involve the reader in an imaginary commitment, aimed at bringing about change, it was up to the reader to take responsibility for such injustices and become committed to their abolition in the real world: 'Ecrire, c'est faire appel au lecteur pour qu'il fasse passer à l'existence objective le dévoilement que j'ai entrepris par le moyen du langage' (59). For Sartre, however, *engagement* was not simply an abstract moral commitment to justice and freedom but something more concretely political. If art depended on man's freedom and operated to extend that freedom, then the writer, argued Sartre, was bound to work towards some form of democratic society in which all men and women would be free to read and to take the sort of action suggested by committed works. Moreover, the divorce between the writer's real public (bourgeois and reactionary) and his virtual public (working-class and progressive), would only be overcome in a classless society of the future. As Sartre declared, 'nous devons dans nos écrits militer en faveur de la liberté de la personne et de la revolution socialiste' (322) and thus 'Il incombe à l'écrivain de juger les moyens, non du point de vue d'une morale abstraite, mais dans les perspectives d'un but précis qui est la réalisation d'une democratie socialiste' (348).

In the real world of a class society, however, the committed writer was without a public. One role open to him was that of critic and 'fossoyeur' of the bourgeoisie, reflecting its decadence and 'mauvaise conscience' in his work. But a rather more important matter was how to encourage and capture the 'virtual public', i.e. the working classes which 'pourrait aujourdhui comme fit la bourgeoisie de 1780, constituer pour l'écrivain un public révolutionnaire' as well as 'le sujet par excellence d'une littérature de la praxis' (303), the very subject matter of a new revolutionary literature. However, between the committed writer and the working classes stood the single party. In the context of postwar France, Sartre's attitude towards the political expression of the working classes, i.e. the PCF, was unequivocal: 'la politique du communisme stalinien est incompatible avec l'exercice honnête du métier littéraire' (307–8). Indeed, party affiliation, especially to the conservative and opportunist PCF, was seen as inimical to the activity of the enlightened bourgeois intellectual, from whose ranks the committed writer was drawn. Affiliation posed the danger for the intellectual of being exploited by the party, of being associated with its mistakes and of having the revolutionary impulse of a committed literature vitiated by a non-revolutionary party. Also, party membership for the working classes was seen as equally negative in that, given the party's claim to and monopoly over the truth of Marxist ideology, it set them beyond the reach of effective communication from the committed writer.

Enemy of the PCF and critic of the bourgeoisie, the committed writer was thus isolated, writing against everybody and moreover, still without a public. From this position of excommunication, as Sartre called it, the writer had to begin to transform a virtual into a real public, not by vulgarizing literature, but by exploiting the mass media: 'ce sont les vraies ressources dont nous disposons pour conquérir le public virtuel: journal, radio, cinéma' (322); the writer had to learn to use their codes and discourses: 'il faut apprendre à parler en images, à transposer les idées de nos livres dans ces nouveaux langages' (322). The exploitation of popular forms and conventions thus had a pedagogical function and, in the end, was aimed at revealing to the potential public, 'ses exigences propres et de l'élever, petit à petit, jusqu'à ce qu'il ait besoin de lire' (323).

Qu'est-ce que la littérature? is full of attractive, optimistic assertions and portentous claims for the role of literature in the transformation of social consciousness. Yet, Sartre's discourse leaves serious issues only vaguely explored and represses others. In France, though always hugely influential as a writer and thinker, Sartre's ideas on literary commitment were not directly incorporated into a consistent body or school of literary production. Indeed, developments in the novel, such as the nouveau roman of the 1950s, seem to move in almost the opposite direction, expressing a profound disquiet over the ability of the prose sign faithfully to reflect social reality. In Spain, however, in a very different, rarefied, and highly receptive political and cultural context, Sartre's ideas were welcomed by an emerging literary and cultural opposition. On the one hand, they gave guidance for the creation of a committed, realist novel and on the other, they provided an example to the young Spaniards of a politically committed writer, long experienced in the problematic relationships between the intellectual, the working classes, and the Communist Party. This sort of experience would help Spanish colleagues pose the problem of their own political position and function within the opposition forces inside Spain.

On 30 October 1948, by special decree emanating from the Holy Office in Rome, all of Sartre's works were placed on the Index of Prohibited Books. A few months previously, the staging of Les Mains sales in Helsinki had prompted the Soviet government to ask its Finnish counterpart to have the play banned, considering it as propaganda hostile to the USSR. By the end of 1948, therefore, Sartre had brought off the almost impossible trick of alienating not only the nerve centre of orthodox Communism but also the spiritual guardians of anti-Communism. It was the reverberations of these events that acted as a catalyst in the passage of Sartre's ideas and works into postwar Spain, despite the complete ban imposed upon them.

Before 1948, it is safe to say that Sartre was scarcely known inside Spain and only very occasionally written about or referred to.[2] With his condemnation by the Catholic Church, however, the situation changed dramatically; he very quickly attracted attention, with his atheism and radicalism proving easy targets for falangist and Catholic militants, eager to defend Spain's innocent masses from moral and spiritual contagion. As we might expect, none of Sartre's most vocal critics tried to explain existentialism to the unprotected reader or, as one writer put it, 'si en Francia el concepto del existencialismo sirve para sugestionar turistas, en España peligraba por la ignorancia de su contenido.'[3] But this did not prevent the regime's servants from equating Sartre with world Communism: 'la tontería internacional tiene muy bien organizada su quinta columna' or global subversion: 'La obra de Jean Paul Sartre, afortunadamente poco conocida en España, entra de lleno en el campo de la subversión mundial y nos complace en extremo el que la Iglesia la haya sancionado para prohibirla.'[4] Communist, atheist, fifth columnist, corruptor of morals, subverter of Western Christian values, tool of Stalin, evil incarnate, etc., were among the many amusing and picturesque epithets ritually heaped on Sartre. For the regime's spokesmen, then, he was the intellectual bogeyman, a dangerous, threatening figure, all the more so since hardly anyone seemed to know, let alone understand, his ideas.

The rantings and ravings of the regime's hacks towards Sartre elicited precisely the opposite reaction from the young, dissenting writers and intellectuals of the new generation. Indeed, official hostility to foreign ideas was almost bound to foster an admiration and a rather uncritical appropriation of the French master. This was all the more so in a situation where textual sources were scarce, readings desultory, and ideas frequently simplified into catchphrases and slogans. In chronological terms, Sartre's ideas on literary commitment first began to surface, in a minimally serious and consistent fashion, in Alfonso Sastre's early writings on the theatre.[5] Sastre was the first of the younger dramatists to make contact with Sartre and this may well be related to his falangist background and to the fact that Sartre's ideas connected directly with the concerns of a socially aware, militant falangism, now in crisis, and receptive to alternative ideological support.

In the process, Sastre's concern over questions of aesthetic distance and his rejection of propaganda literature are overidden by Sastre's own combativity and anti-aestheticism. Indeed, in his early plays of 'agitación social', such as *Escuadra hacia la muerte* (1953), Sastre uses a number of formal elements and preachy, discursive passages which are clearly at odds with Sartre's recommendations. None the less, at this stage, Sastre seems to regard the representation of human anguish, defeat, entrapment, etc. as an effective counter to the established theatre and conducive to arousing public indignation over social issues.

Though Sartre's *Qu'est-ce que la littérature?* was frequently mentioned in intellectual circles in the early and mid-1950s in Spain, it seems to have been less widely read. We can infer this from the fact that it was subject to a major process of secondary diffusion and commentary, principally in the writings of Castellet. Indeed, Castellet became both the disciple and 'divulgador' *par excellence* of Sartre's ideas, which were variously glossed and recycled in his *Notas sobre literatura española contemporánea* (1955) and *La hora del lector* (1957).[6]

Notas consisted of a miscellaneous collection of articles and book reviews previously published in *Laye*, *Revista*, and *Alcalá*. Blending polemic with what Castellet called 'sociología literaria', they dealt with the situation of the writer in Spain and Cataluña and variously attacked or denounced the irresponsibility of Spanish novelists, the disorienting effects of a para-official criticism, and the pernicious influence of literary prizes on the quality of novel writing. For Castellet, *Notas* brought together in one volume a set of pieces which, when taken as a whole, might help to stimulate the sort of non-conformism and dissenting debate he saw as lacking in Spain. His main cause for concern was the staggering lack of preparation of both writers and critics, especially the latter. The writer in Spain, argued Castellet, faced a number of daunting handicaps: ignorance and lack of access to the contemporary literatures of other cultures; severe limitations on the choice of novelizable subject matter; a literary field dominated by para-official 'pseudo-escritores', 'grafómanos' and assorted aficionados; censorship, economic hardship, and a situation in which 'la lectura es un lujo que pocos desean y muchos no pueden pagarse'.[7] As regards a serious, professional, impartial, and responsible literary criticism, it was simply absent in Spain; what passed for criticism displayed a 'terrible vaciedad teórica' and resulted in 'la total desorientación del lector'.[8] At the same time, argued Castellet, the increasing number of literary prizes seemed not to have significantly improved the overall standard of novel writing nor helped to generate a better prepared, more discriminating reading public. In fact, as Castellet argued, using certain by now familiar terms, if a good novel was one which set out to 'revelar el mundo de su tiempo y de proponerle ese mundo al lector como experiencia propia...',[9] then literary prizes had dramatically failed to encourage good writing.

Here, as in many other instances throughout his notes, we see Sartre's concepts adopted as a measure of the modernity, authenticity, and effectiveness of the literary work. Indeed, in article after article, Castellet works into his critical discourse the notions of 'revelación y propuesta', 'tarea a realizar', etc., which become overriding criteria of value. Such is their pervasive and determining force that even Salvador Espriu's complex, hermetic poetry is transformed into a progressive modern writing whose obscurity – like that of the modern novel – is but an invitation to the creative intervention of the reader.[10] Such a categorical critical outlook is more visible in Castellet's review of Cela's La colmena. Here, in line with Sartre's recommendation that the modern writer learn to 'parler en images', Castellet hints at the sort of objectivism he regards as the final stage in the collapse of the omniscient author. That is, he compares the activity and role of the modern author to the operation of a cine-camera; however, 'no se trata de un behaviourismo llevado a punto de espada, sino de una objetividad no forzada, ya que tampoco es cuestión de engañarnos: el autor existe, sólo que se le niega cualquier jerarquía'. What is curious, however, is that Castellet regards Cela's novel as an exemplary instance of a cinema-style objective narration, contrasting his 'normalista objetividad narrativa' with 'las frecuentes interpelaciones del autor al lector' in Baroja. (Even more curious still is the fact that when dealing with the same point, Juan Goytisolo presents Baroja as the objectivist in comparison to Unamuno's authorial control of the reader.) As for the issue of the exploitation of the media in general, unlike Sartre, Castellet regards writers who work in other media as engaging in a perhaps necessary but ultimately mistaken diversion of time from the central task of writing. At this stage at least, and for obvious reasons, Castellet does not tackle the question of how the use of other media might raise general levels of literacy or help transform Sartre's notion of a virtual into a real public.

Castellet regarded his *Notas* as motivated by a non-conformism, a constructive pessimism, and a desire for wider debate. Though fairly bleak, his conclusions were not altogether negative. Amid a welter of criticism and attacks, one slightly more optimistic note was struck. He generously referred to the novels of Goytisolo, Fernández Santos, Aldecoa, Sánchez Ferlosio, Ana María Matute, and Mario Lacruz as showing signs of the type of literature implicitly advocated by Sartre:

> [estas obras] parecen adelantar las mínimas condiciones requeridas para delatar la presencia del escritor exigente consigo mismo y capaz de emprender la construcción de un mundo propio que sea a la vez revelador de la situación de una sociedad – la suya – y que se ofrezca como tarea común de investigación y crítica al lector.

So apart from *La colmena*, Castellet saw in at least a few writers of the younger generation (based in Madrid and Barcelona) the vague glimmer of an indigenous literature, on the way to becoming committed. Moreover, in comparison to their predecessors, Castellet noted in these writers a greater degree of preparation, drive and ideological cohesion: 'esta última promoción parece, en principio, más preparada y con mayor empuje que su inmediata antecesora y especialmente, más compacta, más unida en su ideología e intenciones'.[12]

Castellet's major contribution to the divulgation of Sartre's theories in Spain was, of course, *La hora del lector* (1957), essentially a continuation but also a re-elaboration of articles previously published in *Laye* and *Notas*. In the introduction to *La hora del lector*, Castellet reiterated his long-standing objective: 'subrayar la importancia que el lector adquire ... como activo creador de la

93

obra literaria'.[13] Also, he was now willing to tackle an issue raised by Sartre but which, so far, had been left out of account: the 'curiosa paradoja' of a 'literatura sin autor' which offers the reader a productive, creative role in the reading process but which cannot attract a reading public. And like Sartre, Castellet was anxious to suggest ways of overcoming this separation. Thus, *La hora del lector* was not, nor did it purport to be, a considered and researched theory of the novel. Rather, it was a collection of prescriptive, programmatic articles, whose main function was essentially *didactic*; it was less a poetics of novel writing than an educational primer for Spanish writers and intellectuals on the major changes in modern literary technique, badly known inside Spain, and their social and political implications.

Apart from the opening 'Justificación', the volume consisted of four essays, a conclusion, and a lengthy appendix, comprising extracts from both literary and non-literary sources, which illustrated the changes in narrative procedures analysed in the text. The first two essays, 'Las técnicas de la literatura sin autor' and 'La hora del lector' had already appeared in *Laye*; the other two, 'Una literatura sin lectores' and 'Hacia la literatura del futuro' were hitherto unpublished pieces but obviously based on material which had already appeared in *Revista* and Castellet's own *Notas*. Compared to the original version, 'Las técnicas' had been substantially re-written; 'La hora del lector', on the other hand, was an almost faithful reprint of 'El tiempo del lector'. The most obvious new structural feature of 'Las técnicas' lay in its organization; it now consisted of seven sub-titled sections, with each devoted to examining one of the technical developments that marked the author's progressive self-effacement from his work, e.g. first-person narration, interior monologue, and objective description. Castellet also made even greater use of previously exploited authoritative sources, such as Ingarden and Magny, providing long, clarificatory quotations and footnote references. But perhaps the most notable new feature was the increased and more overt reference to Sartre. This was apparent in Castellet's more detailed historical analysis of the shifts in authorial perspectives and narrative procedures since the Middle Ages. It was also noticeable in the way he linked changes in the history of literary technique to political and ideological changes, this being a dimension which had hitherto been absent. Inspired by Sartre's revolutionary optimism, but lacking his more subtle and sophisticated reasoning, Castellet unequivocally linked the omniscient author of nineteenth-century realism and his serene mastery of his fictional world to the security and arrogant self-confidence of the bourgeoisie: 'la consecuencia era una literatura analítica que respondía perfectamente a una concepción burguesa de la vida'.[14] To the 'autor dios' of the age of bourgeois ascendancy, whom Castellet accused of having sided with injustice and not progress, the reader was merely a passive consumer of a perfect, finished product. However, the appearance of first-person narration in the novel signalled the beginning of the author's abandonment of his exalted, absolute point of view and the further development of interior monologue was symptomatic of a growing crisis in bourgeois indentity: 'el monólogo interior entraña el abandono de la seguridad y del orden social-burgués a los que sustituye por la inestabilidad y la soledad individuales.'[15] These modern 'técnicas de la literatura sin autor' also aimed at teaching the reader something new, refusing to allow the comfortable assurance of a stable interpretation of a stable world. Under the influence of the cinema, a new stage was reached in the process of the author's progressive self-effacement from the text. Offering images without comment, the modern writer strove to reproduce faithfully 'lo que es pura exteriorización de una conducta humana en una situación dada',[16] Objective narration thus required the active intervention of the reader, allowing the production of the reader's own meaning and the recreation of character psychology and inner states from external data. In general, Castellet related the gradual disappearance of the author from the text to the decline and fragmentation of bourgeois ideology; authorial self-elimination was therefore seen as a rejection of the dominant ideology and thus politically progressive; also, in political terms, the most radical stance was associated with objective narration.

It goes without saying that Castellet's correlations between changes in literary technique and historical shifts in politics and ideology are rather naive and simplistic. They recall to some extent Sartre's own apparent confusion between literary and historical processes, literature, and revolutionary action and echo his faith in the essentially progressive nature of all art and its inevitable forward march towards a political utopia. Castellet also engages in a clearly tendentious account of nineteenth-century realism, using an inflated notion of the 'autor dios' as a foil in order to show up the progressive features of authorial self-effacement. This is just as misleading as his naive assumption that realism, especially in its cinematic form, simply reflects a pre-existing reality more or less truthfully. Besides, there is more than a hint of a teleology at work in Castellet's account of the development of literary techniques, which all seem to move inexorably forward towards objective narration.

In 'La hora del lector' – virtually a reprint of the *Laye* original, except for a section devoted to poetry – Castellet now used Sartre far more explicitly in direct textual quotation, reiterating the well-known coupling of the author–reader engaged in a 'doble operación'. Also, ignoring Sartre's reservations on the matter and incorporating declarations from Barral, Gil de Biedma and Valverde, he saw poetry in terms of 'la misma creación doble' which characterized the novel. However, he was careful not to claim that poetry could function as a communication in the same way as the novel, but did not discount the possibility that it could help to modify the reader's consciousness of reality. Overall, Castellet wished to emphasize the essentially egalitarian, democratic relationship between author (referred to, significantly, as 'un obrero cualquiera') and the reader (willing to re-read and exhaust the text's possibilities), seeing both as pursuing the same truth and the same desire for freedom. This optimism was tempered, however, by the recognition of the modern text's increasing obscurity and complexity, which tended to alienate rather than attract readers.

In 'Una literatura sin lectores', Castellet addressed this very problem, which Sartre had already outlined in the final part of *Qu'est-ce que la littérature?*: 'au moment même où nous découvrons l'importance de la praxis, au moment où nous entrevoyons ce que pourrait être une littérature *totale*, notre public s'effond et disparaît, nous ne savons plus à la lettre, pour qui écrire' (290). Unlike Sartre, and for obvious reasons, Castellet did not propose the exploitation of the media as a means of overcoming the divide between writer and reader through the formation of a new reading public. Rather, for Castellet, a reconciliation had to be based on the much more modest injunction of ' un doble acto de humildad'. By this he meant, on the one hand, that the author should propose a mature novelistic revelation to the reader which was 'completa, sin fisuras, totalmente apta para ser asumida'[17] and which avoided unnecessary complication or gratuitous experimentation. At the same time, and again following Sartre, Castellet warned that the author should guard against subverting the work's artistic and moral integrity by making it 'fácil y asequible para un público amplio' or by trying to harangue the reader. The latter, for his part, hitherto unaware that the modern literary work relied on him 'como miembro dinámico del proceso de creación', had to approach it with 'una humilde y laboriosa disposición de ánimo'.[18] In other words, he had to relinquish the notion of reading as an easy pleasure or escape in favour of reading as a serious business, a 'tarea a realizar', a task to fulfil, requiring effort and patience. In a word, reading as work, which allowed Castellet to construct an identity between both author and reader as 'workers'. However, as he clearly recognized, in his final essay 'Hacia la literatura del futuro', there still remained the paradox that 'la hora del lector se ha convertido en el tiempo de divorcio entre autor y público'.[19]

Having almost argued himself into a corner with this dispiriting conclusion, Castellet none the less drew strength from apparent defeat by looking to the future: 'Si un viejo orden de cosas está dejando su puesto, como parece, a otro nuevo, la literatura debe mirar al porvenir con los ojos de este nuevo mundo por cuyos caminos nos adentramos.' A literature of the future, and one which would overcome the author–public divide, argued Castellet, 'consistirá en abrir a la literatura de par en par, las puertas de nuestra existencia de cada día, es decir, hacer que los temas que definitivamente adopte sean nuestros problemas, nuestras inquietudes, nuestras insatisfacciones y nuestros deseos.'[20] In other words, a committed literature had to deal honestly with the problems and aspirations of real people in the real world in ways attuned to the modern sensibility. Among other things, this meant rejecting an ineffective and discredited socialist realism as a model, as well as the subject matter and narrative procedures of an antiquated bourgeois realism. Only by dealing with new themes and opening up new horizons would a committed literature play an effective role in transforming consciousness and (by implication) in working towards a socialist revolution. Indeed, Sartre had asserted that the fate of literature, its very survival as a genre, was ultimately bound up with the establishment of a socialist Europe. Castellet closed his essay on a similarly millenarian note, though for obvious reasons, generalizing the categories: 'su destino está ligada a la humanidad entera de la que, tanto el mundo occidental, como Europa, como la literatura misma, si quieren persistir, han de sentirse solidarios.'[21]

In these last two essays, Castellet again remains fairly faithful to Sartre, acknowledging the serious paradoxes and contradictions so eloquently raised by the master and still maintaining the latter's unshakeable optimism. Yet, beneath Castellet's borrowed faith in the inevitability of social, political, and artistic change, there lurks a certain hesitancy, even a doubt as to the possibility of constructing a committed literature. Behind the grandiose rhetoric and eloquent phrases concerning co-creation between author and reader, there is little specific guidance as to the nature of the encounter or its outcome. The proposed solution to the divorce between author and reader/reading public, 'un doble acto de humildad', is more of a moral imperative, it seems, than a practical suggestion. And though aware of the difficulties, Castellet never quite confronts the problem of how to encourage or propitiate a readership in Spain for a new, obscure, demanding fiction. Also, in his injunctions to the writer to avoid both over-complication and over-simplification, in the name of artistic integrity and authenticity, he asks the Spanish writer to carry out an extremely difficult balancing act between modes of non-authorial narration and the need to make the text intelligible enough for the willing reader. Given these demands, it is surprising to find that Castellet's notion of the sort of text required by the new, humble, committed reader, i.e. 'completa, sin fisuras', stands uncomfortably close to what he seemed to be criticizing in the bourgeois novel of analysis. In the end, like his mentor, Castellet's discourse falls back on pious hopes and moral exhortations rather than practical suggestions, though this may simply reflect the point reached in his thinking and the difficulties of proposing anything more concrete in a context characterized by censorship and cultural underdevelopment. What is clear, none the less, is that Castellet equates objective narration with left-wing commitment and that, like Sartre, he believes that the revelation of reality in an objective fashion is a politically-motivated act, one intended to change reality.

In *Problemas de la novela* (1959), a collection of essays previously published in *Destino* and a work very much in the same mould as *La hora del lector*, Juan Goytisolo emphatically endorsed Castellet's advocacy of an objective, behaviourist narrative aesthetic.[22] In doing so, he implicitly acknowledged the importance and impact of Sartre's ideas on 'engagement'. Making his well-known distinction between 'showing' and 'telling' in the novel (referred to as 'las dos vertientes de la obra literaria'), Goytisolo championed non-intrusive modes of narration as the most appropriate means of encouraging the reader's creative participation in the text–reader encounter.

He thus favoured Baroja over Unamuno; while the latter intervened in the text to express his own ideas and to limit the reader's freedom of manoeuvre Baroja 'como todo novelista verdadero, deja al lector la responsabilidad de enjuiciar a sus critaturas... con la intacta libertad del que contempla'.[23] (As noted previously, Castellet took a different view on this point and criticized Baroja for doing the very thing Goytisolo found so objectionable in Unamuno. Here, perhaps, Goytisolo's enthusiasm for the new objectivism clouds his critical judgement.)

Also, like Castellet, but in far more strident terms, Goytisolo rejected the bourgeois novel of analysis, the psychological novel, as he called it; among its major limitations was the fact that it failed to deal with characters other than the articulate or intellectually cultivated. In one of many sweeping generalizations, Goytisolo asserted that the Spanish novel of the previous thirty years had been totally dominated by such works, which dealt only with a 'minoría selecta', the middle and upper classes. Oblivious to the impact of the cinema on narrative technique and ignorant of the technical revolution in the American novel, Spanish writers simply lacked the preparation effectively to represent in the novel a wider cross-section of society. In particular, they had left out of account: 'esos otros sectores menos favorecidos, cuyo descubrimiento constituye el mérito fundamental de obras como El Jarama, Los bravos o La colmena'.[24] For Goytisolo, these rather exceptional examples 'nos dan una poderosa sensación de realidad, que no hubiera logrado el más sagaz o profundo análisis psicológico de sus conciencias'.[25] And they do so, argues Goytisolo, because of their adoption of 'el método objetivo del comportamiento externo', i.e. the abandonment of the intrusive narrator, the objective description of characters and the faithful transcription of their words.

Again, Goytisolo is guilty of superficiality, exaggeration, and overstatement, not only in his specific view of the novels he cites, but also in his naive acceptance of the transparency of novelistic representation. None the less, he is clearly echoing Sartre's precepts when he argues that: 'Narrar es tomar una posición . . . sobre lo que se narra.'[26] He uses this to defend *El Jarama* against the charge of being devoid of ideas: 'Su intención radica precisamente en el empleo de su técnica . . . su realismo – insisto – está como bebido de intención.'[27] In other words, Sánchez Ferlosio's objectivist representation of his proletarian characters is by no means neutral or unmotivated; like Cela or Fernández Santos, he offers the reader 'una visión de la realidad, abandonándonos al cuidado de tomar – o no tomar – partido frente a ella'.[28] So as well as being the most appropriate technical means of rendering the reality of working-classs existence, the objective behaviourist method presupposes an implicit (political) intention and allows the writer to establish a new relationship with the reader: 'un lector activo que conserva la libertad de emitir un juicio moral respecto a la realidad presentada por el escritor-novelista.'[29] Freed by the writer to exercise his creative freedom, stated Goytisolo, it was up to the reader, just as Sartre had argued, to take a stand in relation to the revelation of reality offered in the novel. Acknowledging Castellet's role in publicizing these ideas, Goytisolo concluded that 'El tiempo del método objetivo, como decía muy bien José María Castellet es, asimismo, el tiempo del lector.'[30]

In Goytisolo's writings, as can be easily appreciated, we find Sartre's careful and subtle reasoning (which Castellet had attempted to follow to a large degree), reduced to a few basic slogans and radical-sounding phrases. In the process, more than thirty years of Spanish literature are brutally over-simplified, Baroja and Unamuno interpreted in the most curious, reductionist fashion and literary history recast to suit the needs of polemic. But it is precisely because it is such a crude and dogmatic work that *Problemas* is so illustrative of the basic tenets commonly ascribed to the *novela social*: proletarian characters, objective narration, rejection of psychological analysis, and of course an 'intención', all the more evident precisely because it is only implicit.

Among other novelists of the movement, who did not leave us any theoretical writings, Sartre's influence is less easily detectable and perhaps more diffuse. As noted earlier, however, it is not difficult to find clear echoes of Sartre's key concepts of *dévoilement*, *témoignage, prise de conscience, prise de position*, etc., in the occasional statements and declarations made by these writers concerning their own role and the function of their literature. Needless to say, commitment among the writers of the movement, be it in terms of their writing practice, their politics or their public lives, would vary in direction, degree of intensity, and application. Initially, as Sastre's example illustrates, it seems that Sartrian 'engagement' is appropriated as a negation of the status quo in political terms. Later, as critics such as Castellet become more familiar with the theory, it provides a set of prescriptions for the roles of author and reader and recommendations on the sort of narrative procedures best adapted to rendering working-class experience in the novel. However, matters of form and writing practice are not extensively debated. So that while Sartre is a major source of advice on what the writer and reader *should* be doing and what a committed literature *ought* to look like, actual practical guidance on narrative technique – while hinted at in Goytisolo and Castellet – seems to come from elsewhere.

ITALIAN NEO-REALISM

When we talk of the influence of Italian neo-realism on the *novela social* and on the emergence of the movement of social novelists, we usually refer to the neo-realist cinema, examples of which entered Spain in the early 1950s. Though the literary side of the Italian trend is inseparable from its filmic counterpart and though it became known inside Spain at about the same time, only later did it emerge as a focus for debate among writers and critics of the movement.[31] In other words, my main concern here is with the film side of the Italian trend.

Before we can talk about Italian film neo-realism in Spain, we obviously require some general idea of the nature of the trend in its country of origin.[32] This is still an extremely difficult and contentious area, not least because the term 'neo-realism' itself is too often used as a vague, inclusive label in ways that evade or resist substantive definition. The term is customarily related to a set of recurring formal and production features: use of non-professional actors (and the encouragement of spontaneity and naturalness in their performance); exterior locations rather than studio sets; hand-held camera work; continuity editing; minimal scripts; soundtrack composed of 'natural' sounds; grainy film stock; and perhaps most importantly, a sense of documentary actuality

101

and newsreel authenticity. However, despite the many debates and conferences held on neo-realism in Italy in the late 1940s and the 1950s, it cannot be regarded as an organized, coherent, and fully self-conscious film aesthetic. The topographical features outlined above give no indication of the possible mixes and variations to which they are subjected in different films usually covered by the neo-realist label. Nor are such features wholly or even substantially in evidence in any one film example, including the most famous cases, such as Rossellini's *Roma cittá apertá*, which used professional actors in the main character roles. It is thus difficult and historically misleading to try to establish an inclusive, normative definition of neo-realism, according to a check-list of formal features, against which each film example can be read off. At the same time, it is now widely recognized that directors such as Rossellini, Visconti, de Sica, de Santis, etc., worked in different ways, within the neo-realist remit.

Having said this, we can none the less assert reasonably confidently that the principal aim of neo-realism, notwithstanding variations and historical shifts, was to create a totally convincing illusion of reality, to render a filmically constructed world as real, natural, and unconstructed. This structural emphasis on rendering the real implied a deliberate masking of the ways in which meanings were produced. By effacing its signifying activity, neo-realism thus tried to convince us of the universal validity of its significations. As Rossellini put it in 1953:

> Neo-realism is the greatest possible curiosity about individuals: a need, appropriate to modern man, to speak of things as they are, to be aware of reality in an absolutely concrete manner . . . a reality, whatever it is, in order to attain an understanding of things. . . . For me, it is nothing less than the artistic form of truth. . . . Briefly, neo-realism poses problems for us and for itself in an attempt to make people think.[33]

In retrospect and perhaps paradoxically, films such as de Sica's *Ladri di biciclette*, for many years one of the paradigm cases of neo-realism, now appears rather contrived in its plot and development and unacceptably sentimental; it can still be seen as a protest film, but one centred, not on social or collective issues, but on the plight of the individual main protagonist. Indeed, rather than explore social problems, the film seems to assert the unmistakeably

Christian principle of the need for friendship and solidarity against loneliness. Similarly, *Roma città aperta*, perhaps the pioneering film of the whole trend and one which cleared the way for others, was far from being a politically radical or left-wing film. Rather, it was one that emphasized the value of unity through the alliance between a Communist Party militant and a Catholic priest. In fact, *Roma* portrayed Communists as Catholics at heart, but misguided by their materialism, which is equated in the film with their physicality and sexual transgressions. Italian neo-realism cannot be seen, then, as a predominantly left-wing movement or aesthetic outlook. It was more than anything a shifting alliance of Marxists, Socialists, and liberal Catholics and, reflecting the ambiguities and contradictions of postwar alliance politics, fell prey to similar divisions and internal conflicts.[34] By the mid-1950s, neo-realism as a movement was moribund, if not dead, though the debates over realism continued, revitalized somewhat by the appearance in Italy of translations of some of Lukács's early work.

Regarding the relationships between the neo-realist movements in Italy and Spain, Esteban Soler makes the general point that the conditions giving rise to both movements in their respective countries were historically similar.[35] In strict terms, and if we date the effective emergence of neo-realism as a film movement immediately after the ending of hostilities, i.e. in a democratic society in which fascism had just been defeated by the anti-fascist resistance, then Esteban Soler is mistaken. In Spain, conditions were hardly comparable. Indeed, a junior partner of the fascisms of the 1930s was still in power, consolidated moreover by the period of international ostracism of 1946–8 and by the *rapprochement* of the Allied Powers in the early 1950s. Still, Esteban Soler is substantially correct to indicate that the aims of Italian neo-realism were, on the whole, closely bound up with those of the Resistance, as were its achievements as well as its limitations. In Spain, too, neo-realism was assimilated largely into the intellectual opposition and the resistance to Francoism, though its realist outlook and social concerns made it amenable to appropriation by falangist militants, inspired by their theoretical obligations to the proletariat. Also, though Esteban Soler makes no mention of this, in Spain in the early 1950s, the PCE policy of securing alliances with other anti-Francoist, democratic forces and of constructing a national democratic front has obvious parallels with the situation of the PCI obtaining in Italy during and after the war. As already mentioned, by the time Italian neo-realism began to filter into Spain, it was already in terminal decline, in part as a result of the difficulties and contradictions inherent in the pursuit of such a broad front policy. Yet in Spain, that very same policy of forging alliances against fascism still made powerful sense in political terms, given the entrenched position of the dictatorship and the weakness of the political opposition. Hence the obvious attraction for Spain's emerging dissident intelligentsia of a trend so closely identified with the struggles and values of anti-fascism. Moreover, Italian neo-realism introduced a whiff of history and 'real life' into an otherwise lifeless, sterile, cultural environment. It offered a serious (but, in retrospect, overvalued) challenge to Hollywood filmic models and conventions and was viewed in certain circles as a radical alternative to the status quo, a film counter-culture, whose example demanded emulation in Spain.

Alfonso García Seguí notes the influence of neo-realism in a number of Spanish films of the 1950s including Bardem's *Cómicos* (1954), *Muerte de un ciclista* (1955), *Calle Mayor* (1956), and *La venganza* (1957), Berlanga's *Calabuch* (1956), Antonio del Amo's *Sierra maldita* (1954), and Marco Ferreri's *El pisito* (1958).[36] It is also the case that Bardem and Berlanga, for example, in some of their occasional statements of the late 1940s and early 1950s, did not hesitate to acknowledge the value and importance of Italian neo-realism as an alternative aesthetic and set of film codes, offering, as Bardem put it: 'una pureza de lenguaje, una sobriedad narrativa, una desintoxicación de toda manifestación teatral y literaria' and above all 'la presencia de la realidad, la realidad total de su país'.[37] Yet, as Ricardo Muñoz Suay argues, we need to be rather cautious in talking of the existence of a specific, relatively coherent neo-realist movement in the Spanish cinema. Perhaps, as he says, what we find in the Spanish case are merely 'elementos neorrealistas' in a certain number of films.[38] Also, it is by no means clear that directors such as Bardem and Berlanga, usually credited with pioneering a new Spanish film realism, were unconditional supporters of the Italian trend. Indeed, Berlanga's own admiration for its challenging, documentary aesthetic was tempered by certain political reservations: 'el neorrealismo italiano ha conquistado el mundo por lo que tiene de audaz y sobre todo de documento vivo de una época en descomposición'; however, 'tiene una cierta posición ideológica un poco podrida, de un sector político italiano', by which he meant the Communist Party.[39] Berlanga's view was symptomatic of the widespread attitude that Italian neo-realism was Communist-inspired. Given Berlanga's own falangist background, this is perhaps understandable. But, as Overby points out, in historical terms it is a distortion:

> Although a large number of directors and scriptwriters were leftist in sentiment, few of them were either Marxist or Communist. The attacks on neo-realism as being 'Communist-inspired' and the emphasis by many critics on Soviet cinematic 'realism' as an influence on the movement were wide of the mark. Neo-realist films never really approached Marxist solutions to problems.[40]

Turning now to the actual extent of the penetration and circulation of Italian neo-realist films in Spain, it goes without saying that those films that entered the country in the early 1950s were fairly small in number and hardly representative of the most acclaimed or politically most significant examples of the trend. Relatively few films were given a commercial screening and those that were suffered heavily from pre-censorship. Others, which escaped official interference, were exhibited in private, non-commercial venues, before small, select audiences, usually under the aegis of the Italian cultural office in Madrid. This seems to have been the case with Rossellini's *Roma città aperta* which, according to the specialists, arrived in Madrid 'por valija diplomática' in 1950 and was shown in private sessions to the students of the official *Instituto de Investigaciones y Experiencias Cinematográficas* in the capital's Italian Institute.[41]

Apart from Rossellini's film, which is said to have made an enormous impact on its student public, perhaps the most significant event of 1950 in the entry of Italian neo-realism was the commercial screening in Madrid and Barcelona of Vittorio de Sica's *Ladri di biciclette*. Of interest to us here are ways in which the film was received and its meanings variously inflected. A common strategy, as we have already seen, was virtually to dismiss the film by invoking its alleged Communist affiliations. A commentator in *Revista*, for example, referred to *Ladri* as 'tanto un acto de contricción como un modelo de ese realismo socialista' and emphasized its 'desesperación sin límites'.[42] Other critics tended to emphasize the film's Christian, moral outlook while playing down its thematics (the fact that it deals with urban unemployment) in favour of its 'poetización, partiendo de elementos de los cotidiano', as one critic wrote.[43] From a left-wing standpoint, Eduardo Ducay, in *Insula*, excitedly referred to *Ladri* as 'un film asombroso y revolucionario, una obra extraordinaria, fruto de una inspiración excepcional'.[44] His evident hyperbole and overreaction may well have been tactical; such reactions were not uncommon among left-wing advocates of the Italian trend in Spain, anxious to generate support and solidarity for a Spanish counterpart. Yet, Ducay's astonishment might well indicate a genuine belief in the radical potential of neo-realism's documentary, testimonial features in a country like Spain.

In November 1951, Unitalia Films (Italy's official film promotion and export agency) organized the first major public screening of Italian cinema in postwar Spain. Held in Madrid and well attended by the capital's young writers, intellectuals, and film students, its programme included, among other items, *E Primavera* by Renato Castellani, *Cronaca di un amore* by Antonioni and de Sica's *Mirácolo a Milano*, perhaps the major exhibit of the week. In general, the programme was rather limited and uninspiring, presenting none of the most representative films of the neo-realist movement: *Roma città aperta*, *Paisá*, *Germannia ano zero*, *Caccia Tragica*, *La terra trema*, etc. Yet, despite its limitations, it seems to have been influential among young directors and film students. Gubern talks of:

> el tremendo impacto que causó la Primera Semana de Cine Italiano, celebrada en Madrid, entre algunos miembros de la primera promoción de la Escuela Oficial de Cinematografía, fundada en 1947, como eran Bardem y Berlanga. Significó, según ha decalarado despúes Bardem: 'una ventana abierta al cine europeo . . . de golpe conocimos a los cineastas italianos, a Zavattini, a Lattuada, el neorrealismo . . . En fin, una verdadera revelación.[45]

Gubern's observation reminds us of the need to distinguish between the sort of Italian cinema seen by young intellectuals, like Bardem and Berlanga (who could also travel to other countries) and their view of neo-realism; and that seen by the general public. In other words, knowledge of and access to the Italian trend was limited and very much the preserve of a minority intellectual audience. This was still the case with the follow up to the *Primera Semana*. La *Segunda Semana de Cine Italiano*, jointly organized by Unitalia Films and Madrid's *Instituto Italiano de Cultura*, was held in March 1953. Far more ambitious and better organized than the first, the *Segunda Semana* consisted of seven daily sessions, with each opening with a short or documentary and being followed by a full-length feature film. Among the main exhibits of the week were Castellani's *Due soldi di speranza*, Zampa's *Processo alla città*, Germi's *Il cammino della speranza*, de Sica's *Umberto D*, Visconti's *Bellísima*, and Lattuada's *Il cappotto*. At the same time, there were two retrospective sessions in the *Instituto Italiano* during which Rossellini's *Paisá* and Visconti's *Ossessione* were screened. Also significant was the fact that a number of famous names had been invited to the week to introduce and comment on their films, e.g. de Sica, Zavattini, Zampa, Lattuada. On the whole, the week's offerings were rather more representative of the neo-realist movement as well as being more varied, combining social document (*Paisá* and *Il cammino della speranza*), detective thriller (*Processo alla città*), psychological drama (*Umberto D*), and a critical exposé of the star system (*Bellísima*). As before, critical reactions polarized along familiar lines. On the falangist right, Angel del Campo in *Revista* saw the week in terms of: 'Personajes angusti-ados, soledad, decepción y vicio sin pecado y pecado sin vicio.' In *Juventud*, reminding us that in Italy neo-realist films were 'en franca decadencia', but conceding that in Spain neo-realism 'llegó como si fuera la fórmula salvadora y definitiva' for the film industry, the reviewer criticized the trend on account of its predictable pessimism and defeatism: 'El público no quiere un cine cosmo-polita ni depresiva para su patria: neorrealistas derrotistas.'[46]

On the left, Ducay and Muñoz Suay in *Indice* were positive and enthusiastic about the week, noting that it was more important than the first and provided better ammunition with which to counter the stale, escapist film panorama in Spain. Italian neo-realism showed that a society's hidden realities, its voiceless majority, their problems and lives, could be effectively transposed into cinematic form. This was a style whose naturalism, document-ary basis, and 'shock effect' could move as well as inform the spectator. It thus paralleled and confirmed Sartre's notion of action by disclosure, i.e. the manner in which a documentalist representation of reality could be used to raise the consciousness of the reader/spectator, through the expressive power of its illusionism, the 'authenticity' of its depictions. It was thus taken up in opposition circles as both a polemical device and tool of political struggle, engaged in contesting dominant cultural forms and definitions and in the construction of a dissident intellectual front. This is apparent in two significant developments which arose directly out of the *Semana*.

The first of these was the appearance, in Madrid, in July 1953, of the new film review *Objetivo*. It was very much a Spanish offshoot of the Italian review *Cinema Nuovo*, edited by the Marxist critic Guido Aristarco, from whom *Objetivo* took many of its ideas and positions. This can be seen, for example, in its support of directors backed by Aristarco (Visconti, Antonioni) and its reservations towards those criticized by him (de Sica, Rossellini). In general, as Guarner points out, *Objetivo* was important in providing a platform for a new generation of film critics, in 'internationalizing' Spain's film culture (e.g. Muñoz Suay collaborated in *Cinema Nuovo*; Bardem became a jury member at Cannes) and sharpening the divisions between an official and an oppositional film criticism.[47] *Objetivo* was also important in that many of the positions and proposals it publicized, by drawing on native and foreign contributors, run almost parallel to those being developed around the notion of a socially responsible, realist literature. We thus find a significant interplay and set of interconnections between the newly emerging literary and film movements of the early 1950s.

Number 1 of *Objetivo* coincided with the publication of the first number of *Revista Española* and like its literary cousin, chose to pay homage to Cesare Zavattini. Glossing ideas which closely coincide with the aims which animated *Revista Española*, Eduardo Ducay wrote of Zavattini: 'ha comprendido que todo lo que se hace evadiéndose de la realidad es una traición, que la necesidad de evasión es una falta de valor, es miedo'. As a scriptwriter, his work: 'trae la revolucionaria novedad: la de un cinema de técnica literaria . . . que abre la posibilidad de observar lo cotidiano.'[48] Zavattini was regarded as almost the paradigm case of the intersection between literary and film aesthetics, a combination devoted to stripping away unnecessary rhetoric in order to reveal the real. By transposing these categories into literary terms, i.e. by positing a literature constructed according to cinematic principles, we could easily apply them to a novel such as Sánchez Ferlosio's *El Jarama*, which admirably reflects Zavattini's own maximum cinematic goal: that of creating a 90-minute film in which nothing happens: 'la busca del tiempo vulgar'. Here we see the interpenetration between novel and film: on the one hand, Zavattini's belief that effective cinema requires firm literary foundations; on the other, as in *El Jarama*, the exploitation of cinematic techniques to better render 'lo cotidiano'. In number 2 of *Objetivo* (which published an original script by Zavattini, much in the same way that *Revista Española* published his 'Totó il buono' and the plot summary for *Mirácolo a Milano*), Aristarco's ideas on the role of film critic as 'testigo de nuestro tiempo' were prominently featured; they coincided closely with what Castellet had been saying in *Laye*, particularly regarding the critic's role as non-conformist.[49] In number 3, glossing conclusions reached at the Parma Cinema Congress of 1953 and which Muñoz Suay had attended, the editorial emphasized the importance of the links between Spain's literary traditions – or a certain version of them – and film making:

A nuestro cine sólo le puede salvar – con independencia de su estructura industrial y comercial, que es otra cosa – su capacidad de asimilación de nuestro pasado intelectual y artístico. De cara a un realismo – en nuestro cine, neorrealismo – que ha sido la tradición de nuestras mejores artes, de nuestras mejores letras.[50]

Here we see yet another example of how left-wing critics attempted to appropriate Spain's artistic and literary traditions for realism and how a film neo-realism apparently required the legitimizing stamp of a literary, rather than a specifically filmic, tradition. The editorial goes on to demand that the cinema, like literature, must humanize itself, putting people at the very centre of its activity: 'Esto lo conseguirá nuestro cinema, no sólo con el análisis de la realidad sino entrando en ella, empapándose en ella. E influyendo luego en ella y transformándola si fuera preciso.'[51] Here, once again, and coinciding with what Sartre had prescribed for the novel, we find the identification made between the revelation of reality in film and its role as a tool in transforming consciousness. As Bardem points out, for the young directors of the early 1950s, the view of the cinema as an instrument of revolutionary transformation was readily and naively assumed: 'Yo en aquellos momentos pensaba en el cine como arma política en España y en la posibilidad de que el público lograra a entender, a pesar de que le hablasen en un lenguaje un poco en clave, si le dabas unos ciertos datos.'[52] In number 5 of *Objetivo*, this radical optimism received an important reinforcement in an article by the Marxist Carlo Lizzani on the history of neo-realism and its political significance. Lizzani regarded what he called the 'explosion' of neo-realism after the war as inaugurating a profound re-examination of a reality that had been hidden by fascism. Neo-realism thus took part in an anti-fascist process of re-discovery, but just as importantly played a role in a 'revolución nunca cumplida', an attempt to transform Italian society which failed. The novel was also involved in this heroic failure, with Moravia, Vittorini, Pavese, and Pratolini all engaged in uncovering hidden realities through the novelized chronicle: 'Italia se narraba a sí misma su ambición renovadora y no sus propias retóricas . . . inspirando verdadera curiosidad por los hechos verdaderos de su casa.'[53] Lizzani thus connected neo-realism with an unfulfilled revolutionary role – a revolution that historically was never on the agenda – calling indirectly on Spain's young opposition intelligentsia to complete the unfinished task.

A second development arising directly from the Italian film weeks and the existence of *Objetivo* was, of course, the *Conversaciones Cinematográficas Nacionales*, held in Salamanca in May 1955. According to Gubern, the idea of holding a public debate on the Spanish cinema emerged from the *Objetivo* team who, it is suggested, wished to emulate the Parma Congress on Realism of 1953, organized by their Italian colleagues.[54] The Spanish *Conversaciones* were accompanied by a *Llamamiento* which, couched in vaguely Sartrian phraseology, set the radical tone for the conference. Among its injunctions, we find a call to Spanish intellectuals to 'engage' with the realities of their own country: 'Creemos que el intelectual está comprometido con su propio país, fuente inagotable de creación artística. Sólo atendiendo a la realidad, los intelectuales y hombres de letras pueden satisfacer este compromiso.'[55] The *Objetivo* team undoubtedly regarded Salamanca as a potential meeting-place to extend a dissenting cultural front and to turn an official event to their advantage. However, it was the *Cine Club del SEU de Salamanca* which acted as *Objetivo*'s official passport to the *Conversaciones*, since without some sort of official backing, the presence of the *Objetivo* team at an official event, not to say the event itself, would have been unthinkable. After much negotiation – including the decision to allow Aristarco to attend, but not the French left-wing critic Georges Sadoul – the *Conversaciones* were given official approval. They thus took place as a result of pacts, concessions, and a temporary tactical alliance among various tendencies, founded on a broadly agreed rejection of the existing Spanish cinema, but clearly divided as to the solutions required. Also, in official circles, there existed the inevitable suspicion that the event was nothing more than an opposition manoeuvre to gain a public platform. But, in order to present the *Conversaciones* as a major, national SEU initiative and to take the credit for any positive outcome, official attempts were made to incorporate and thus deflect the force of dissident voices.

The series of 'ponencias' at Salamanca were decidedly pluralistic in approach and argument, embracing falangist, Catholic, and vaguely concealed Marxist positions, the latter predicated on Italian neo-realism. All 'ponentes' were in general agreement on the need to reform the censorship system, to overhaul the system of financial support to the film industry, and to set up a more rational and effective means of promoting and selling Spanish films internally and abroad. There was also a broad consensus over the desirability of a realist Spanish cinema, but opinions differed radically over the meaning of the term realism. Falangist speakers, calling for a revolutionary national cinema of realist inspiration, emphasized the importance of rural themes that would exalt, for example, the role of the *Instituto Nacional de Colonización* in promoting 'concentración parcelaria'. By contrast, Muñoz Suay, returning to a demand consistently canvassed in *Objetivo*, argued that a new realist cinema should nationalize itself, exploiting to the full the resources of Spain's great literary and artistic traditions. Letting slip his indebtedness to the Gramscian notion of the 'national popular', Muñoz Suay's traditions were not unexpectedly selective, including the names of Velázquez, Ribera, Goya, even Alberti and works such as *La Celestina*, *El Quijote*, *Fuenteovejuna*, and rather significantly *Los bravos*, another sign of the interplay between the literary and the cinematic movements of the early 1950s.[56] The *Conversaciones* closed to the discharge of Bardem's now famous diagnosis of the state of the Spanish cinema: 'Políticamente ineficaz. Socialmente falso. Intelectualmente ínfimo. Estéticamente nulo. Industrialmente raquítico.'[57] While Bardem's conclusions were generally accepted by the conference, not everyone understood them in the same way. That they concealed some underhand, subversive intention was brought out in subsequent official reactions to the conference.

The always tense tactical alliance which had made the event possible fractured immediately afterwards and revealed its differences. Though they claimed the *Conversaciones* as a victory for SEU initiative, official spokesmen began talking of 'un engaño', alleging that Salamanca had been infiltrated. Reflecting on the event, García Escudero recalls:

> a algunos el cine les interesaba sólo relativamente como medio, no como fin . . . El proceder de algunos hace pensar inevitablemente en la táctica sutil y en definitiva subterránea . . . de la que se han ufanado después los que, bajo el fascismo, convirtieron al *Centro Sperimentale* [de Roma] y demás órganos oficiales del cine en 'plantel de anti-fascistas', que es como a sí mismo se llama un marxista como Lizzani, de quien tomo la cita, y que de esa manera se convierten – tácticamente se entiende – en defensores de la libertad.[58]

García Escudero's diagnosis, by no means inexact, suggests that beneath the rhetoric of unanimity in denouncing a false Spanish cinema, the motivations of the speakers at Salamanca were roughly divisible into the same ideological camps as those of 1936. It also shows that, as in the comparison made with fascist Italy, Salamanca was an act of infiltration, and a significant victory for a dissenting, Marxist-inspired intelligentsia. The fact of having successfully denounced in public an important cultural arm of the state by actually infiltrating and exploiting an official event would have fairly rapid repercussions on other sectors of Spain's intellectual opposition.

Undoubtedly inspired by the example of the Salamanca victory, whose importance as an organizational and political precedent was crucial, plans were made to hold the *Congreso Universitario de Escritores Jovenes*, scheduled for November 1955. It is worth remembering that the original call, as well as the provisional agenda for the conference, had emanated from the pages of *Objetivo* in August 1954, yet another sign of the interrelations between a

112

radical film movement and its counterpart in literature.[59] However, as we have seen, the *Congreso* was finally suppressed by the authorities. Also, coinciding with the date planned for its staging, *Objetivo* was closed down after number 9 (September–October 1955), with many of its staff being arrested. Obviously, having been outwitted once at Salamanca, the regime and the SEU were determined not to fall for the same trick a second time. It is clear that the young anti-Franco writers were attempting to repeat the success of their cinema colleagues at Salamanca. This is so obvious that the authorities were aware of the similarities and thus banned the event and arrested the organizers.[60]

In dealing with *Objetivo* and the conference at Salamanca, I have tried to show how ideas drawn from Italian neo-realism permeate both the filmic and the literary realms in Spain. I have also tried to illustrate how these areas not only paralleled each other in their development but were intimately interconnected, in a relationship in which developments in film and film aesthetics became the dominant partner and set the parameters for literary realism and the novel. Moreover, as Sanz Villanueva has pointed out, there existed close links between the social novelists, film directors, and the world of the cinema.[61] We know, for example, that in 1950 Fernández Santos studied alongside Carlos Saura on 'cursos de dirección', run by the *Escuela Oficial de Cinematografía*; also, after writing *Los bravos*, he devoted himself to film-making for virtually a decade. Sánchez Ferlosio was also a film student, taking directors' courses in 1951 but failing to complete them due to the interruption caused by military service. Some evidence indicating the assumption of neo-realist ideas among early writers of the movement of social novelists can in fact be found in Sánchez Ferlosio's review of *Los bravos*.[62]

Sánchez Ferlosio greatly admired *Los bravos*. Commenting on the opening scene of the novel, he remarked how the unadorned presentation of an apparently trivial event was capable of making a powerful impact on the reader's sensibility: 'Un hecho casi cotidiano, contado con la mayor sencillez, una mano herida en la poda, ha sido capaz de introducirse casi agresivamente en el terreno de nuestra emoción.' Sánchez Ferlosio thus links *Los bravos* to one of the basic aims of neo-realism: the attempt to provide the receiver with unrestricted access to the fictional representation, through authorial self-effacement and formal transparency, i.e.

113

allowing the 'facts to speak for themselves'. As he again says of *Los bravos*: 'El autor ha querido hacerse mudo, frente al sagrado mutismo del pueblo que nos revela; se ha colocado detrás de él y lo ha dejado expresarse.' The reader is given a place in the fictional world as observer or witness and as Sartre had advised, is able to judge for himself rather than be told what to think. Sánchez Ferlosio was also impressed by the manner of the novel's construction, its exploitation of film-editing devices, such as the gradual assemblage of fragmentary, though simultaneous scenes and their contrastive possibilities. Indeed, in *Los bravos*, Sánchez Ferlosio found a certain conception of the novel which, as Darío Villanueva points out: 'llevará a la práctica en *El Jarama*, donde también se narran hechos vulgares, en un lenguaje coloquial y con una estructura muy semejante a la utilizada en *Los bravos*.'[63]

Summing up this section, and not wishing to overstate the case, it seems clear that Italian neo-realism represented a powerful, even crucial, stimulus to the construction of a literary realism in Spain. At the most basic level, it revealed to young writers in the early 1950s that even the most unpromising novelistic subject matter, the most banal aspects of everyday working-class existence, could constitute the subject of literary activity. In transposing the lessons of film into literature, however, the trick would consist of suppressing as far as possible the marks of the narrator/enunciating source or sources, and allowing the characters, in their own words, behaviour, looks, and gestures to establish direct contact with the receiver. What was required was a seamless transparency, a perfect fit between image and world which would preserve the credibility and authenticity of the representation, the aim being to pass off an artistic construction as the 'truth itself', to evoke in the receiver the idea that one cannot argue with 'facts like that'. In short, in aesthetic terms, Italian neo-realism was mainly appropriated for its documentary-style mode of presentation; it posed the challenge to the social novelists of capturing in the novel the sort of visual impact and emotional identifications of a filmed narration. In political terms, Italian neo-realism was seen as confirming Sartre's claim that the revelation of reality necessarily implied an intention to change it. As film director Javier Aguirre recalls: 'Yo he sido de la generación que creía que con el neorrealismo ibas a cambiar el país a través del cine. Yo he vivido la época en que nadie dudaba que a través de *Ladrón de bicicletas* se iba a cambiar la faz del mundo.'[64] The transformative possibilities of a realist cinema, however romantically and naively assumed, would inevitably permeate the ranks of dissenting writers, who would also wish their writing to perform a similiar function.

THE NORTH AMERICAN NOVEL

In terms of its reception in postwar Spain, we would probably expect the American realist novel of the so-called 'lost generation' to be given a more radical, progressive, even left-wing reading than would have otherwise been the case. This general mode of reception has obvious historical parallels in those European countries that experienced a fascist regime in the inter-war period or during the Second World War. It is well known, for example, that the American realist novel was of great interest and importance to liberal-left writers and intellectuals in Italy during the fascist period and in France during and after the occupation.[65] Not only did it seem to contest the very foundations of the traditional bourgeois novel of ideas, but its supposed frankness, directness, stark realism, stylistic modernity, etc. challenged the escapism, rhetorical vacuity, and mediocrity of fascist culture. Such traditions and experiences would be of obvious relevance to Spain's dissenting writers and intellectuals in their own particular encounter with American fiction.

As regards the availability of the American novel in Spain, it is worth recalling that, prior to the civil war, certain American authors were identified with anti-fascism and translations of their work were promoted by left-oriented publishers. This was the case with Cénit publishers, for example, under the direction of Juan de Andrade. Among the titles then available were *Manhattan Transfer* by Dos Passos as well as *Babbit*, *Main Street*, *Elmer Gantry*, and *Dr Arrowsmith* by Sinclair Lewis. Also significant in the pre-war period (and perhaps deserving closer scrutiny), was the role of Antonio de Marichalar in diffusing the American novel and in introducing Spanish readers to Faulkner, whose *Sanctuary* (among other novels) was published in 1933 in the collection *Hechos Sociales*, promoted by Espasa Calpe.[66] In addition, and despite much mythification of their roles, we should not forget the links of writers such as Hemingway and Dos Passos with Republican Spain. These may have been influential among opposition writers of the 1950s in

115

cementing the identification of the American realists with the struggles and cause of anti-fascism.

After the civil war, it was the publishing house Caralt which first began to re-introduce the American realists, promoting Lewis's *The Prodigal Parents* in 1944. But it was only after 1947 that a significant expansion in translations of the Americans took place, corresponding to a surge in the translation market. By 1953, for example, eight novels by Sinclair Lewis were available, including *Main Street* and *Babbit*; we also find *As I Lay Dying* by Faulkner, *The Three Soldiers* by Dos Passos, *The Sun also Rises* by Hemingway, and *The Wayward Bus* and *The Pearl* by Steinbeck. During this period, Caralt, closely followed by Janés, dominated the translation market, putting out between them more than twenty American titles. But, between 1953 and 1957, Caralt's predominance was displaced by the expanding activities of other publishing houses such as Plaza, Planeta, and Gerplá, the latter two strongly promoting younger writers such as Capote and old masters such as Hammett. In just over three years, for example, (1954–7), ten of Hammett's novels were published, including *The Maltese Falcon*, *The Glass Key*, and *A Man Called Spade*. Publication also continued of Faulkner's *Go Down Moses*, Hemingway's *A Farewell to Arms*, Caldwell's *A Place Called Estherville*, and for the first time a novel greatly admired by Sartre, Richard Wright's *Blackblood*.

Overall, the catalogues show that by the late 1950s, a small but significant amount of American realist fiction was commercially available in authorized versions. This is not to say that there were not notable absences due to censorship: Hemingway's *Death in the Afternoon* and *For Whom the Bell Tolls*; Steinbeck's *Tobacco Road* and *The Grapes of Wrath*; Dos Passos's *Manhattan Transfer* and *USA*; Faulkner's *Sanctuary*; and Lewis's *Elmer Gantry*, among others.[67]

The above bibliographical notes suggest the following: first, the fact that many of these novels were published by Caralt, very much a man of the regime, as well as by strictly commercial publishers such as Planeta and Plaza, seems to indicate that the Americans were not immediately perceived as suspect, subversive, or conveying a politically radical message. Second and relatedly, the publication of the American writers must be seen in the wider context of a general boom in foreign translations, which perhaps partly explains why the potentially 'difficult' character of some of the Americans was generally overlooked. Thirdly, though works unavailable in native Spanish editions were frequently read in South American editions or in French translations, the importance and the curious paradox of the American novel lie precisely in the fact of its relative availability. By comparison, French and Italian novels, more directly associated with the historical movements and specific tenets of *engagement* or neo-realism (and indeed, theoretical works to do with these ideas) were not so easily available. So, despite the apparent anachronism, a novel originating in the USA in the 1920s and 1930s constituted, for Spain in the early and mid-1950s, the nearest practical example of the theories of realism circulating within and around the movement of social novelists. Their readings and reception of the American novel would receive additional guidance in some of those theoretical sources (Sartre, Magny, Pavese, etc.); readings would also be made in the light of the known sympathies and links of some writers with the Republic, the obvious case being Hemingway.

As regards the critical reception of the American realist novel, before 1950 Spain's literary journals and youth reviews contained very little relevant material. Something of a turning-point came, however, with the award of the Nobel Prize to William Faulkner in November 1950. Having received the Howell's Medal for Fiction from the American Academy the previous May, Faulkner was big literary news, as well as an international celebrity. In Spain, this prompted a respectful but, in the circumstances, fairly lukewarm and unenthusiastic critical response. None the less, the job of re-introducing American literature, particularly Faulkner, to a basically ill-informed, if not completely ignorant Spanish reading public was carried out by three professional critics who were not official spokesmen, but neither did they have any apparent links with the new social literature. These were Ricardo Gullón and Francisco Ynduráin in *Insula*, and Antonio Vilanova in *Destino* (who would later become a strong supporter of the *novela social*).[68] Unlike Sartre then, Faulkner was never subjected to any sort of official campaign of denigration or rejection, although certain reactions are symptomatic of the dominant, official, critical preoccupations current at the time. For example, Vilanova slotted Faulkner into the category of *tremendismo*, underlining his distorted vision of a brutal, backward society, a vision characterized by its crudity, truculence, sexual obsessions, tragedy, and fatalism; Faulkner was the epitome of a 'tremendismo naturalista norteamericano'.[69]

Gullón agreed, but argued that in spite of their crudity and materialism, Faulkner and the American novel in general were just as concerned with spiritual values: 'Esta literatura, originada en buena parte por el sentimiento de protesta, es predominantemente espiritualista. Aun en los casos del naturalismo más crudo, conserva fe en los valores espirituales.'[70] Ynduráin disagreed, highlighting the predominance of the Americans' direct, documentary-style realism, but regarding it as a serious short-coming: 'los libros americanos han interesado como documento más que como obras de arte.' Their 'estilo desnudo', though superficially attractive was also essentially anachronistic, outmoded, irrevocably trapped 'en la situación en que la novela europea estaba en la época del realismo y costumbrismo'.[71] Though reasonably detached and informative, the comments of Ynduráin and company betray a certain distaste for the Americans' gritty realism and stylistic brashness. Perhaps because of this, they make no explicit connection between the American novel and the construction of a native Spanish novelistic realism.

On the other hand, and notwithstanding their reservations, the same critics pointed to those elements in Faulkner which would soon be attracting the attention of the social novelists. In alluding to them, it is perhaps paradoxical that they tended to use, quite inadvertently, the sort of phrases and coded language that would characterize the social realist movement. For example, Gullón states: 'Esta generación de realistas se lanzó sobre las tierras europeas, infiltrando en ellas pasión de verdad y sustancia de problemas sociales. . .nos sentimos en contacto con las cosas tal cual con . . . con los problemas de la vida.' Talking of the difficulties of Faulkner's style and technique, Gullón also remarks: 'da por supuesto que el lector adivina hechos importantes sin necesidad de que él explícitamente las refiera.'[72] 'Pasión de verdad', 'Las cosas tal cual son', elliptical texts, an active reader; here Gullón unwittingly anticipates the sort of concerns that Castellet, Goytisolo and others would regard as central to a new realist novel in Spain. Vilanova's reading of Faulkner would also be echoed within the movement. Faulkner's novelistic world, argued Vilanova, was a cruel and socially divided one in which the author took the side of the oppressed, a stand evident in *Light in August*: 'Faulkner ha encarnado en la figura del mulato . . . la tragedia de una raza oprimida que soporta su libertad como un martirio, sujeto a una esclavitud moral que convierte su vida en un infierno.' In a later work, *Go down Moses*, Vilanova saw Faulkner's alleged moral nihilism being superseded by 'la más honda interpretación del alma negra. . . una honda preocupación social. . . y unanhelo de esperanza y justicia'.[73]

In their initial encounter with the American novel then, the above critics maintain a respectful distance and an ambivalent attitude. They are sympathetic to the Americans' social concerns for the poor and downtrodden, but this is offset by reservations towards their truculent realism and lack of aesthetic refinement. Paradoxically, these are precisely the features that will be of interest to the new social realist movement, even though there is no sign of critical connections being made at this stage. So, almost by accident, this initial critical reception marks out the terrain and erects the signposts for further and contrary appropriations. A crucial element informing these encounters, particularly in the writings of Castellet and Goytisolo, would be Claude-Edmonde Magny's classic study of the American novel, *L'Âge du roman américain* (1948).[74] It forms an important link in the chain of reception of the American novel and thus deserves a brief commentary.

Magny singles out two fundamental innovations in the cinema that have had powerful repercussions on the novel: first, an objective, neutral, camera-eye mode of narration; and second the facility to vary the point of view thanks to the cutting and editing process, which makes possible a far more complex and pluri-dimensional view of things in their totality. Again, certain of the American realists are seen as exemplifying the practical application of these techniques in the novel. Some, like Hemingway, exploited the objectivist mode of narration which, based on the philosophical premises of behaviourism, offers only external data on event, character, and scene and obliges the reader to infer motivation from character speech, resulting in an almost stenographic recording of words and actions. Such a narrating stance not only strengthens the novel's mimetic effect through the use of dialogue; it also allows the novel to deal with characters and themes drawn from a much wider cross-section of society, thus uniquely enlarging the scope of novelizable material.

With these comments in mind, Magny proceeds to compare the French and the American novel, drawing comparisons that

Castellet and Goytisolo would make all too familiar. Indeed, without disguising her loyalties and prejudices, Magny regards the French novel as written predominantly by intellectuals, dealing with characters who are also intellectuals and in which the reader's role is generally usurped by the over-zealous, self-indulgent intervention of the authorial narrator. By contrast, the American novel is seen as the product of mainly autodidacts, whose ability to broaden the field of subject matter and character and involve the reader creatively in producing the text is made possible only through the adoption of more neutral, non-authorial narrating techniques. Moreover, for Magny, the self-elimination of the authorial narrator from the text, the reduction of his or her role to that of observer, allows the narration of bare facts to achieve potentially far more striking effects on the reader's sensibility: 'Toute interprétation, tout commentaire d'un fait brutal tend à affaiblir le choc sur notre sensibilité.'[75] In short:

> La grande leçon que le roman américain a appris du cinéma: que moins on en dit, mieux cela vaut; que les effets esthétiques les plus saisissantes naissent du choc de deux images, sans commentaire aucun et que le roman, pas plus qu'aucun art, n'a intérêt à se faire bavard – cette leçon que Hemingway, Faulkner, Steinbeck ont si bien compris.[76]

Because of what Magny calls 'cet impératif esthétique de discrétion et de taciturnité', which directly recalls Sartre's comments on aesthetic distance, she concludes that the novel, like the cinema, is essentially an art of ellipsis. This, she argues, not only increases the possibility of achieving striking effects when emotionally-charged events are presented directly, with the minimum of commentary. Such aesthetic withdrawal also ensures the veracity of the depiction, its artistic integrity and 'ce parti-pris d'honnêteté qui oblige le romancier à ne représenter que les faits qu'a pu atteindre sa caméra sans tricher, bref à respecter les conventions qui définissent son art'.[77] Thus, for Magny, the author's responsibility to play fair with the truth is safeguarded through the adoption of an objectivist narrative standpoint, presenting events, not as God might have seen them, but only as a given spectator might have witnessed them. She also recognizes, of course, that the aesthetics of discretion are only achieved at the expense of clarity. Indeed, an art of ellipsis is one that makes a virtue of the meaning potential of gaps and absences; and by simply placing 'the bare facts' before the reader, the writer cannot avoid ambiguities, omissions and silences, rather he or she deliberately intends them. Hence, the reader's crucial intervention in completing the text, closing the gaps, filling the silences, reading 'between the lines'.

The reception of Magny's work in Spain particularly in the writings of Castellet, broadly establishes the ground on which the American realist novel would be discussed within and around the movement of social novelists. For Castellet, the American realist novel, though dated, could still provide useful lessons to Spanish writers in the construction of a new realism. It broadly fulfilled the demands of objectivity, social criticism, portrayal of the lower classes, and 'reader power'. His early critical work on the Americans, begun in *Laye*, constituted one of the main mediations for their reception among writers of the movement of social novelists. And just as he did with Sartre, he drew extremely freely on Magny's ideas, particularly the consecration of Faulkner as the reader's writer, and once again in a fairly uncritical fashion.

After the *Laye* incursions, Castellet produced a series of articles for *Revista* in which, still faithful to Magny, he reiterated Faulkner's status as a model absent author but also made a more explicit identification between the American novel and a committed literature: 'Faulkner, mejor que nadie, nos da en sus obras el más profundo sentido del acto de leer. El nos dice que el buen lector de buenas obras nunca lee para distraerse o evadirse. El lector debe ejercer su función como trabajo purificador: función catártica que busca la libertad.'[78] Castellet even went as far as claiming that Faulkner was concerned with novelizing the class struggle: 'En sus obras, la vieja aristocracia lucha a muerte con el proletariado en ascenso y la población es rodeada e inundada por la creciente marea de la población negra.'[79] Again, Castellet is perhaps a little sweeping in his assertions, offering an arguably idiosyncratic and reductionist reading of Faulkner and rather too neatly aligning him with the assumptions of Sartrian commitment.

Echoing Castellet, Juan Goytisolo also regarded Faulkner as the prime example of the absent author, encouraging the creative intervention of the reader in the text (although Goytisolo said nothing concerning the actual experience of reading one of Faulkner's novels). Faulkner's technique of interior monologue 'participa del relativismo característico de la técnica objetiva de comportamiento externo; al presentar la realidad de un modo informe y como filtrada, obliga al lector a prestar su colaboración para establecerla.'[80] This technical relativism demanded an active reader 'atento a extraer una solución personal del material literario propuesto'. Not only did Goytisolo echo Castellet's Sartrian appropriation of Faulkner, he also adapted directly from Magny the comparison made between the French and the American novel, simply repeating Magny's remarks on the writers' backgrounds and characters. Dismissing the French writer as bourgeois and university trained and identifying himself with the politically more acceptable American writers, autodidacts and far closer to the 'people', he stated: 'Las obras de Faulkner, Hemingway, y Caldwell están llenas de gentes analfabetas (a menudo, de pobres de espíritu) cuya lengua, preocupaciones y visión del mundo son los de un peón, un segador o un mozo de cuadra.' Able to express the concerns and fears of the common man, the American realist novel was far more in tune with the preoccupations of the young Spanish writers; and compared to a novel by Malraux, Faulkner's *The Sound and the Fury* was 'una novela inteligente, no una novela intelectual'. What puzzled Goytisolo was the fact – or so he claimed – that the realism of the American novel, so often regarded as new and challenging in Spain, had formed part of a centuries-old Spanish tradition, only that no one had bothered to say so: 'cabe preguntarse por qué se bautiza novela "a la americana" una forma de narrar que ha sido y es, desde hace siglos, la nuestra.'[81] Here, as before, Goytisolo was reasserting the existence of an indigenous critical realist tradition, best exemplified by the picaresque; that this tradition reflects a highly reductive, selective view of Peninsular literature is left to the reader to deal with. In general then, the two main critics and polemicists of the movement find confirmation in the American realist novel of the sort of features they demanded for a native equivalent. Or to be more exact, they find confirmation in the main theoretical source they liberally exploit, i.e. Magny, whose ideas and comments are frequently reproduced verbatim in Spanish, when not directly glossed. Interestingly, however, where Magny's reading of the Americans is filtered through a philosophical lens, related to existentialism, the Spanish critics stress their social and critical dimensions, even exaggerating the degree of commitment and political purpose in a writer like Faulkner. Obviously, in radically different reading contexts, different demands obtain and novels fulfil different functions in the process of their reception.

On a broader front, in interviews and articles, a number of writers of the movement have confirmed the influence of the American realists, though it is difficult to judge how widely they were read and how far ideas or specific textual features were adapted, incorporated, recycled, etc. In general, as Carmen Martín Gaite has argued, the American stimulus was important in terms of solidarity; that is, Spanish writers were aware that they were not working in isolation, but had available a broadly social literature with which they could identify, particularly in terms of their writing craft.[82] And as Ferres has observed, the American novel was far closer to what Spanish writers wished to develop, in terms of subject matter, i.e. the depictions of the rural south of America, of the poor and downtrodden had Spanish equivalents which were immediately recognizable. Also, as Ferres and Goytisolo point out, Faulkner seems to have been the writer who had most impact on the Spaniards: 'En lo formal', remarks Ferres, 'el descubrimiento de Faulkner fue muy importante para mí y creo para muchos escritores'; talking of the period 1954–5, Goytisolo states: 'la novela de Faulkner *El ruido y el fulgor* fue para mí el hallazgo más interesante de la literatura norteamericana.'[83] By contrast, in technical terms, Sánchez Ferlosio declared, 'me siento afín con John Dos Passos. No por su manera de construir las novelas sino en su modo de narrar los hechos a través de las formas expresivas.' Also, reviewing *El Jarama*, Castellet compared its objectivism with that of the American realists, seeing the novel as inspired by 'el riguroso procedimiento de "narración objetiva", al estilo de los autores norteamericanos'.[84]

The above references indicate that the American realist novel was certainly known about and discussed to some degree in the 1950s. Spanish writers seem to have been aware of the main representatives and of their considerable thematic and technical achievements. Yet, because of the mode of its reception, being mainly filtered through Castellet's and Goytisolo's gloss of Magny, the American novel was viewed in an often narrow, myopic fashion, resulting in some notable absences. Sinclair Lewis, for example – an obvious candidate for the title of 'socially concerned' writer – nowhere figures among the American writers seen as influential, despite his books being easily available in translation. I suspect that Lewis is absent because he is not mentioned by Castellet, and this is so because he is not mentioned by Magny, whom Castellet had faithfully, not to say slavishly, followed. The same might also be true of other writers, far more challenging and 'committed' in their themes and outlook than Faulkner, Hemingway, or Steinbeck, e.g. Upton Sinclair, Theodor Dreiser. One begins to wonder, in fact, just how widely the American texts were really known and thus, beyond the fashionable literary *tertulias*, how influential.

While only a rigorous textual comparison would reveal influence at a specific level, there are certain areas and features of individual Spanish writers in which influence may be discernible. For example, Fiddian notes that 'The predominant social themes of the "lost generation" are echoed in Aldecoa's writing: the decadence of a social jet set exposed by Scott Fitzgerald and Dos Passos; the rebellion of the outsider, exemplified by Kerouac; the exploitation of the unprotected, as indicated by Steinbeck.'[85] Also, let us recall that Aldecoa, in fact, wrote on American literature in the early 1950s; though not producing any theoretical work, he reviewed novels by Faulkner, Hemingway, and Capote, among others. Straightforward and informative, and containing just a hint of existentialist thinking and vocabulary, Aldecoa's pieces are clearly indebted to to the work of Malcolm Cowley, at that time a major specialist on Faulkner and Hemingway.[86] Sobejano suggests the possible influence of Faulkner on Goytisolo's trilogy *El mañana efímero*.[87] Also, Faulkner and Dos Passos may have offered guidance to other social novelists, particularly in terms of structure and modes of narration, e.g. in *El Jarama*, *Las afueras*, and *Fiestas*. Again, however, it is difficult to establish clear-cut textual similarities; indeed, perhaps apart from Benet (at the margins of the social novel movement in the 1950s, but miraculously resurrected as 'avant-garde' in the 1960s), evidence of the American stimulus seems to exist more at an extra-textual than at a textual level.[88] That is, it functions more as a rallying point and polemical device than as a narrative tool kit waiting to be used.

In the late 1950s, among some members of the movement, we find signs of a reaction against the American novel. For example, in 1959, Fernández Santos stated: 'Cuando yo empecé a escribir admiraba mucho a los escritores americanos. Ahora me aburren con igual intensidad.'[89] In the same year, Luis Goytisolo remarked: 'De entre los americanos quizá destacaría a Melville, Dos Passos, Faulkner. La influencia de este último, en cambio, me parece funesta; el faulknerismo sólo se le puede perdonar a Faulkner', adding: 'otros novelistas que me interesan más son Mann y sobre todo Pavese.'[90] Alongside Pavese could go other names, such as Vittorini, Pratolini, Levi, Silone, authors who experienced Italian fascism at first hand, whose work reflected a desire to reveal and criticize that situation and which is increasingly mentioned in discussions and interviews. This displacement of the American novel responded to several factors: it no doubt reflected the greater circulation of fiction and non-fiction texts from other cultures and sources, though perhaps not their greater availability; it corresponded to the entry into the movement's theoretical and critical arsenal of Gramsci's notion of 'literatura nacional popular' and of the entry of Lukács, via the Italian connection. More widely, we find a growing politicization of the movement and a corresponding shift of attention towards those sources identified with the resistance to fascism. Hence, the growing interest in the Italian novel, regarded as a committed literature, but more so than the American, with its roots and practices originating in a country closely comparable to Spain. Also, in the late 1950s, the general standing of the Americans began to slide. In May 1959, for example, at the *Coloquio de Formentor*, famous writers such as Hemingway failed to respond to the invitation to attend.[91] Though their expectations were rather unrealistic, the Spanish organizers and young social novelists were not surprisingly disappointed at the apparent lack of solidarity from their American colleagues with a young struggling realist movement in Spain. American fortunes suffered even further in the Formentor debates, in which foreign critics such as Butor and Robbe-Grillet criticized American realism as an anachronism – and by implication criticized their Spanish hosts for defending it. Indeed, not only was Spain's *novela social* implicitly regarded as dated by foreign spokesmen, its very pretension to intervene in material history and society rather than confine itself to the history of aesthetics and the novel was seen as a fundamental error. Of course, the Spanish writers and critics replied that the situation in Spain, unlike that of France, demanded responsibilities of the novel which in other countries did not apply. Hence, its substitutive, social function, now re-inflected and re-theeorized through more fashionable Marxist notions such as 'realismo histórico' which Castellet, borrowing from Lukács, was now proposing.

Also, in the late 1950s, we see another development in the reception of the American novel, this time in relation to the 'younger generation' of writers of the 1940 and 1950s. In *La Estafeta Literaria*, for example, a number of articles began to appear on such writers as Capote, Styron, Goyen, Saroyan, and McCullers, who were enlisted into an official critical offensive against the growing internal success and international recognition of the *novela social*. Quite simply and in a manner not too dissimilar from that adopted by the French guests at Formentor, critics and writers such as Rodríguez Alcalde and Cunqueiro panned the *novela social* for its anti-aestheticism. They opposed its predictable, uninspiring objective realism and its artistic mediocrity to the well-written, technically sophisticated and highly 'literary' products of the young Americans. Moreover, if the Spanish novel wished to remain up-to-date and responsive to changing literary trends, it had to jettison the lessons of the inter-war realists and return novel writing to its proper task, that of good writing.[92]

To sum up this section, as we have seen, the American realist novel was available in Spain in the 1950s, despite notable absences. It was initially received without any substantive links being made with an indigenous realism, but it quickly attracted the attention of members of the movement of social novelists. It was appropriated, in the main, for its thematics (the lower classes, the poor, the oppressed), its technical sophistication (modes of non-authorial narration, linked with notions of 'reader power') and also perhaps, because it had been influential as a resource in countries which had suffered under Fascism. In Spain, Faulkner (not Hemingway), was presented as the paragon of the absent author, though few people commented on the difficulties of his writing and his evident interest in character interiority and psychological motivation. In fact, he was enlisted into the ranks of committed writers. This appropriation, I would argue, derives from the fact that major critical mediations, such as those of Castellet and Goytisolo, were so dependent on foreign sources, such as Magny. And although Castellet, for example, was quite aware of other sources which might have given a different view (e.g. Frederick Hoffman), it seems that what Magny said was unquestioningly accepted.

Writers not mentioned by her were thus ignored. The American realists were consequently taken up in a highly selective fashion, and made to fit precisely the sort of image of a committed novel being put forward by Castellet and company. Hence their easy incorporation into the discourse and slogans of *engagement*, and their identification with a cinematic objectivism, already seen in Italian neo-realism, which would act as a misleading confirmation of their own supposed 'tough realism'. Yet, the situation is puzzling. In the early days, the American writers were substantially available but not significantly read or exploited as resources. I suspect their influence was more verbal than textual, more a sign of solidarity and identification with the (supposed) gritty autodidact writers, tuned into the voice of the 'people' and able to express, in direct, striking, powerful prose, their problems and pain. However, by the late 1950s, the American novel is partially eclipsed as a stimulus by the arrival of new inputs, particularly Italian, and by a widespread feeling that an objectivist, proletarian realism is no longer sufficient to fulfil the role of a committed literature or to respond adequately to the demands of a changing cultural and political climate. Yet, in the period of the movement's formation, it has to be said that the American novel functions as an important reference-point. It is linked up with Italian neo-realism and Sartrian *engagement* and this combination produces the essential peculiarity of the theory concerning the *novela social*. That is, the idea that commitment in literature is inseparable from a neo-realist aesthetic; in other words, a committed literature demands, by definition, a narrative technique which is neutral, objectivistic, 'non-narrated'. Initially, the American novel would provide guidance precisely on those modes of non-authorial narration required by the theory. But because of this stress on objectivism, the social novelists and their allies would have to take into account the technical developments of a trend I have omitted to mention so far: the French *nouveau roman*. The latter could not be ignored, partly because, from the mid-1950s onwards and in the new, fashionable, and important Biblioteca Breve collection, examples of the trend become available in Spanish translation (e.g. Robbe-Grillet's *El mirón*, 1956). Also, French writers associated with the *nouveau roman*, the so-called 'école du regard', were experimenting with narrative strategies of authorial self-effacement, which seemed to coincide with what their Spanish colleagues were trying to work out. This, not unexpectedly, led to misalignments and mistaken identifications between French and Spanish authors, as if both movements were somehow engaged in the same project. Despite much confusion and the fact that, often through deference and feelings of inferiority, Spanish writers had to applaud their Gallic counterparts, they eventually managed to explain that an apparent similarity of technical outlook did not imply an identity of moral or ideological purpose. While admiring the technical rigour, experimentalism, and innovatory style of Robbe-Grillet, Juan Goytisolo, for example, saw the *nouveau roman* as 'rejuveneciendo, al cabo de setenta años, la teoría wildeana del arte por el arte'.[93] Other writers would echo Goytisolo's view and, in the final analysis, reject the French trend on ideological and political grounds for its unavowed aestheticism and commitment to a rarefied notion of literature rather than to an examination of an historically verifiable reality, the aim and responsibility shouldered by Spain's own *novela social*.[94]

Chapter Five

PATHS TAKEN
AND NOT TAKEN

My aim in this chapter is to consider certain novels that illustrate the sort of narrative paths taken and not taken in the early development of the movement, paths that at times intersect and at others diverge radically, especially in relation to the theories of literary commitment prevailing in Spain in the 1950s. My selection of novels holds no surprises and largely coincides with the choices of other critics, most of whom see the following works as signalling the beginnings of the *novela social: Juegos de manos* (1954) and *Duelo en el Paraíso* (1955) by Juan Goytisolo; *El fulgor y la sangre* (1954) and *Con el viento solano* (1956) by Ignacio Aldecoa, though critical opinion is divided over the validity of Aldecoa's inclusion in the movement; *Los bravos* by Jesús Fernández Santos and, of course, *El Jarama* by Rafael Sánchez Ferlosio.[1]

In certain respects, this is a curious and unusual selection, the paradoxes of which critics have tended to ignore. For example, Goytisolo's first two novels bear little or no relation to the neo-realist narrative style or lower-class subject matter usually associated with the emerging *novela social*. Indeed, we have to wait at least until *Fiestas* (1958) and *La resaca* (1958) for the first significant signs of the above concerns, e.g. greater attention to natural dialogue, focus on the world of Barcelona's sub-proletariat, their particular language and sub-culture. I can only surmise that critics take their bearings on Goytisolo's novelistic realism from these and later texts, such as the travelogues and, projecting this view retrospectively, abusively co-opt his first two novels into the *novela social* as realist works. In the case of Aldecoa, this process appears to work in reverse: In the light of declarations expressing certain reservations towards a politicized realism and in view of the existentialist outlook of his early novels, Aldecoa tends to be relegated to the margins of the movement, if not excluded from the *novela social* altogether.[2] This seems both unfair and historically misleading, in that his first two novels, in their subject matter and thematic concerns, though less so in narrative procedures, place him within the framework of concerns and explorations character-istic of the formation of the *novela social*. For this and other reasons, I propose to comment briefly on his early novel writing. For rather different reasons, I feel Goytisolo should also be retained. This is not because his novels contribute to the development of a novelistic realism, but because they represent a possible option for the *novela social* at a certain moment and express concerns relevant to the offspring of the winning side, who become the protagonists of a newly-emerging intellectual opposition. However, with the possible exception of Ana María Matute, Goytisolo's early work finds little echo among other writers and remains a marginal, if intriguing, contribution to the early writing options found within the movement.

JUAN GOYTISOLO

Goytisolo's first two novels may have found their way into the *novela social* by critical sleight of hand, but they are worth examining briefly as early responses, or more accurately perhaps as gestures, to the problem of how to develop a committed literature. Whereas many social novelists tended to signal their intentions implicitly and indirectly through their technique and thereby mark their literary commitment through the adoption of an objective narrative perspective, Goytisolo's first two novels do almost the reverse. Clearly out of line with the theory of literary commitment, they refuse the conventions of reportage and narrative detachment and choose to explicitly foreground their fictionality and 'perform' the concerns and themes which, in other social novels, would have to be inferred 'between the lines'. In *Juegos de manos*, the explicit dramatization of the problem of political commitment and in *Duelo en el Paraíso*, the critical confrontation with generational revolt and the effects of the civil war obviously echo concerns directly relevant to the emergence of an intellectual opposition and the movement of social novelists. Indeed, well before the much-commented shift of emphasis in the *novela social* towards the so-called 'denuncia de la burguesía', the young Goytisolo was already anatomizing the self-image of the offspring of that very class. Thus, if his first two novels bear little relation to the *style* normally associated with the *novela social*, they none the less take up some of the preoccupations and problems immediately recognizable to a newly-emerging, dissenting intelligentsia.

Juegos de manos (1954)[3]

Goytisolo's first novel is almost unique in the 1950s in Spain in that it directly addresses the question of political commitment in its story-line. This involves the decision of a group of university students to assassinate a very minor political figure, the failure of the chosen assassin to carry out the killing through moral scruples, and the latter's subsequent murder by his best friend, who afterwards hands himself over to the police. Of course, as virtually all the critics point out, the plot of *Juegos* and the picture of Spanish student life it presents lack verisimilitude and are wholly implausible.[4] For example, Betancourt's arrest, which triggers the group's decision to act, arises not from handing out leaflets or painting slogans on university walls (activities one would normally associate with student militancy in the 1950s) but from illegal possession of arms. Also, in terms of left opposition politics of the 1950s, the plan to assassinate someone, let alone a plan masterminded by a group of students, was in reality totally unthinkable. Moreover, the novel lacks any discernible political frame of reference; group members never discuss politics or engage in political theorizing; their political utterances are of the crudest and most elementary kind; the few references that are made to politics in the novel are not to revolutionary political theory by Marx or Lenin, but, as Páez's reading tastes illustrate, to literary sources, 'obras de teatro socialista, novelas francesas y soviéticas'(49). The relations between the novel's student radicals and working-class organizations are built around the totally unbelievable character of 'El proletario', a name significant for its extremely archaic overtones, but a character who quite properly rejects the *señoritos'* proclaimed solidarity with the working classes. In short, in place of any recognizable political framework, related to Spain in the 1950s, *Juegos* draws its inspiration from mainly literary sources, including Gide's *Les Faux monnayeurs*, Cocteau's *Les Enfants terribles*, and perhaps most importantly from Sartre's literature of *engagement*, particularly *Les Mains sales*.[5]

Juegos displays a number of obvious if superficial parallels with Sartre's play: the title of Goytisolo's novel is hardly coincidental and many of its plot elements seem to echo the play, especially the confrontation scene between David and Guarner, which recalls that between Hugo and Hoederer. There are also similarities of characterization, e.g. David's indecision, lack of self-confidence, class guilt, and sexual immaturity correspond to Hugo's; Agustín and Guarner, like Hoederer, represent attractive father figures that only serve to heighten the assassin's oedipal anxiety; Gloria and Ana in the novel also correspond, to some extent, to Jessica and Olga in Sartre's play, where the coquettishness and more self-assured sexuality of the first contrasts with the introversion, seriousness, and devotion to party responsibilities of the second. The obvious and important difference, however, is that the political dimension (i.e. the relation between the middle-class intellectual and party dictates), so central to *Les Mains sales*, is totally absent in *Juegos*. In fact, all we find in Goytisolo's novel is the act of assassination posed in highly abstract, ethical terms and removed from any recognizable historical or political context. Besides, while the characters in Sartre's play are all communists, in *Juegos*, we only have to scratch the surface of the plot to reveal, not communists or indeed any recognizable political grouping, but the *panda* of bourgeois adolescents. Moreover, if we strip *Juegos* of its simplistic philosophizing about commitment, we are left with a basically psychological study of the emotional, sexual, and sado-masochistic ties linking the *panda*: their varying degrees (or lack) of maturity, self-confidence, and independence from parental domination, their jealousies, rivalries, relations of dependence, non-heterosexual preferences, their disaffection with received class values and class guilt, and their need to find a justification, a meaning for lives that are otherwise empty and aimless.

In fairness to Goytisolo, and in the context of the early 1950s in Spain, it would have been extremely difficult, if not impossible, to novelize and publish an account of political commitment based on the relations between the real student opposition and the forces of the political opposition. Having said this, the difficulty still remains of Goytisolo's unusual picture of student life which, while no doubt inspired in some way by his own experience, seems to owe far more to literature than life. This is undoubtedly the case with the handling of the question of political commitment, which in the end has nothing to do with politics. Rather, it functions as a vehicle for the expression of a visceral class hatred and a reaffirmation of a sense of manhood and virility, which has been vitiated by a bourgeois family upbringing and a repressive education. It is here, in its picture of the uselessness of the bourgeois adolescent, that the novel might well connect with the deeper, inner preoccupations of a well-heeled, student elite under Francoism. It gives voice to some of their discontents and repressions, their rejection of family and class values through childish displays of ingratitude and cruelty and their desire to expiate their class guilt through a voluntaristic identification with the lower classes.

In this connection, Goytisolo's attack on the bourgeois family structure and its values is obsessive and relentless. Presented as victims of a secure, but cloying family atmosphere, designed to cocoon them from the real world, the children respond to weak fathers and ambitious, doting mothers by engaging in anti-social behaviour, a mixture of ingratitude, cruelty, and gratuitous violence (e.g. Páez's 'tortura del hijo del peluquero' (66)). Their schooling is also presented in the background stories as repressive, useless, counterproductive and leads them to rebel against unfounded parental aspirations, which they have no part in determining themselves. Above all, these 'rebels without a cause' are tarnished by the sin of privilege, a class guilt which simply nourishes feelings of resentment as well as horror at their physical inadequacies and weaknesses. Hence their unqualified, fetishized admiration for the naturalness, spontaneity, and vitalism of the working class and, as in David's case, their 'deseos de descender, de mezclarse, de olvidar la clase a la que pertenecía'(181). This desire for affiliation can never be fulfilled, however, given the stark social determinism that separates the classes in the novel. Prevented from descending and merging with their desired world, group members channel their visceral populism into the assassination plan, an act that will allow them to 'significarse', transcend their indolence and confirm their solidarity with the class 'other'. It is the latter that informs Ana's revolutionary outlook and links it with the achievement of maturity through the spilling of blood: 'Sólo por medio de la sangre me decía, se puede alcanzar el derecho de ser revolucionario' (97).

Goytisolo's bourgeois adolescents are disaffected, rootless, and unprepared to compromise with a world in which 'hasta el concepto de vida se recibe de prestado' (109). They thus rebel, suffering as a consequence a profound sense of boredom and alienation, which they alleviate through membership of the *panda*, its games and rituals, and the assassination attempt. Of course, as we have seen, the latter has its roots and motivation not in politics, but in a rejection of the 'civilized' world of their parents; the 'golpe' is merely a device, a way of filling a vacuum and demonstrating to the older generation that their offspring can operate independently and affirm a separate, if illusory, identity. Yet, in its lack of foundation in the world of real politics and in its purely visceral, reactive nature, the 'golpe' is but an escape, yet another fantasy designed to stave off confrontation with self-doubt and failure. It also symbolizes the way in which these bourgeois adolescents are invariably trapped in their class position, however much they attempt to transcend it or escape from it. This underlying social determinism is evident in the fact that the killing that does take place, i.e. the substitute killing of David by Agustín, for alleged reasons of cowardice, is kept 'within the family' of the *panda*. The planned 'golpe' is thus reflected back onto the group as if an image in a mirror; it is but a reflection of their own inner desires and conflicts and bears no relation to the outside world. Indeed, it represents a bizarre sublimation of oedipal struggles, where a substitute father punishes a disobedient, 'stand-in' son, in a homo-erotic parody of parental authority. David's murder, an act in which the roles of both executioner and victim merge, is but another means of avoiding confrontation with the self, it is a continuation of those 'juegos de manos', those childish games in which the playground is transformed into the slayground and where commitment is no more than a part of the same game. So even in the face of death, these adolescents are unable to break through their enforced innocence and infantilism to maturity, unable to 'grow up'; they are thus condemned to being 'eternos menores de edad', a state emphatically endorsed and reproduced by the winning side in the Civil War and Francoist repression.

What is significant about *Juegos de manos*, then, is not the failure of these young 'burgueses de izquierda' to be authentic, responsible revolutionaries, as portrayed by Goytisolo. Rather, it is the author's inability, at this stage in his writing career, to envisage and create credible, would-be revolutionary adolescents facing the difficulties of political commitment. Moreover, Goytisolo's characters are already formed and show little inner evolution; attempts to build development into their portrayal through the use of interior monologue in the retrospective sections betray a certain clumsiness in technical control and an overexposure of this literary device. In fact, the tendency to make visible the text's technical devices and thus reveal its fictionality is reflected in the way material is presented to the reader. This is done mainly through the controlling perspective of a dominant, highly visible, and frequently intrusive authorial narrator. Often close to or merging with the characters, often commenting on events from the outside, the narrator exercises a powerful degree of control over character discourse. Even in the clearly differentiated passages of interior monologue (e.g. Mendoza's reflections on his past (142–9), or David's long diary entry which recalls his childhood, adolescence, and student days, (225–31), the narrator's presence is constant and marked, either in the lead-ups to these instances or indirectly during their narration. In other words, reader access to character interiority is heavily mediated, thus making it difficult for the reader to naturalize the text as a plausible representation of mental processes or a real student world. If intrusive formal devices tend to foreground the text's status as a fiction, its 'literary' character is enhanced in no less obvious ways, such as through the widespread use of metaphor, motifs of dissimulation, disguise and masking, interior duplication, foreshadowing, and the text's widely acknowledged vein of lyricism. Even when Goytisolo should be closest to straight mimesis, i.e. in character dialogues, the almost virtuoso use of unusual, stilted words and expressions (e.g. solventar, el decurso, explayarse, inmiscuirse, se levantó con celeridad, etc.), undermine their credibility, making the rendering of speech one of the novel's weakest aspects. However, with its complex, fragmented structure, varied modes of narration and frequent time-shifts between past and present, *Juegos de manos* emerges as a fairly sophisticated, technically up-to-date piece of writing for its time. Shortly after its publication, Castellet was quick to acknowledge the novel's untypical modernity: '*Juegos de manos* aporta a la novelística nacional una preocupación por la técnica, por el sentido estructural de la novela, absolutamente inhabitual en estos últimos años.' At the same time, however, Castellet also noted the novel's lack of realism, not only at the level of character portrayal, but also of language: 'el lenguaje de Goytisolo adolece de envaramiento, de falta de realismo.'[6] At this stage in his career, Goytisolo is still working within a framework of ethical and technical concerns which do not as yet allow him to close the gap between fiction and reality, literature and life. As the author himself states, talking of his early work: 'en la primera etapa exponía una serie de preocupaciones que me atormentaban o que me habían atormentado en la niñez o en la adolescencia, pero lo hacía con un desconocimiento bastante flagrante de la realidad exterior, de lo que me rodeaba.'[7]

Duelo en el Paraíso (1955)[8]

Goytisolo's second novel comes across as very much a re-elaboration of the first, a re-examination of the same issues and preoccupations as before: generational conflict, youth revolt, class determinism, critique of bourgeois values and moral puritanism, escape from oppression through regression to animality and childhood cruelty, etc. On the surface, what seems to distinguish *Duelo* from *Juegos* is that these same concerns are explored against an identifiable historical framework, that of the civil war. The action of *Duelo* takes place in and around the twin locations of the country house *El Paraíso* and the school for refugee children, near Gerona, during the final days of the war in Catalonia. There are a number of textual references that relate to the war in one way or another, such as the radio broadcasts from Barcelona and Seville, the mentions of the fighting at Teruel and Belchite, the fearsome reputation of the *moros* with Republican women, the bombings of Barcelona, and other places, etc. Also, we know from the calendar in the interrogation room that the novel's action takes place on 6 February 1939, being set in the intervening period between the early morning withdrawal of Republican troops and the arrival of the advancing Nationalists later that same day. The various scenarios, i.e. the country house, the school, the forest, and indeed the valley itself, temporarily take on the character of a 'no man's

136

land', divorced from the surrounding conflict. Thus, the main novelistic action is played out in a temporal and spatial vacuum, where time seems to stand still and which, in a sense, directly negates the realism of the historical, war-time backcloth. *Duelo*'s atemporal main settings are thus no less marginal and implausible than the student 'ambiente' of *Juegos*. Indeed, the suspension of time and the parenthesis in the flow of history in *Duelo* are marked by the many references to a luxurious, decadent natural world, presented as an eerie, unreal, magical dreamland: 'Todo era sorprendente y al mismo tiempo mágico' (11); 'Una atmósfera quieta, mágica, parecía suspender milagrosamente todo el valle por encima de la desolación de la guerra' (33). It is in this 'never never land' that Abel Sorzano has been murdered by a group of children for the supposed crime of treason, an act inspired by the war-time example of the older generation. A gun-shot, which awakens the deserter Elósegui, begins the novel's action and also inaugurates the reader's search for a solution to the enigma of Abel's murder, a search conducted through the memories and statements of the different characters.

The novel's magical, poeticized setting, the implausibility of its plot, the parody of the adult war by children, indicate that *Duelo* is not a novel about the historical civil war as such. In *Juegos*, the central problem of generational conflict was presented in entirely fanciful, abstract, ethical terms through the device of the assassination attempt. Similarly, in *Duelo*, the underlying motivation for the conflict is replaced by an equally fanciful but morally more 'respectable' cause: the civil war, which again functions as the vehicle for generational dissent. In short, *Duelo* is not a novel that tries to show what the war did to children, by novelizing the author's own personal experiences and childhood memories. Rather, it proposes a certain theory: that the emergence of a young, rebellious generation in Spain in the 1950s is the direct result of the childhood trauma to which they were subjected in 1936–9; but, perhaps more importantly, dissent arises from a rejection of the corrupt moral values of a bourgeoisie for whom Franco won the war.

In the novel, the war is shown as having divided society into two opposing worlds: children and adults: 'La guerra había abierto entre padres e hijos un abismo difícil de colmar' (130). The latter are so busy killing each other that they have no time for their children. In the case of Abel, who has lost both parents in the war and is fostered by his aunt and uncle, problems of abandonment and alienation are particularly acute. Left to his own devices, this lonely child sublimates family loss, isolation, and boredom into forms of play inspired by the radio reports of the war. At *El Paraíso*, in the face of adult indifference, Abel's fantasies regarding enlistment, fighting, and becoming a war hero help to fill an otherwise desolate existence. However, *El Paraíso*, much to Abel's frustration, is an almost timeless, idyllic, though decaying place, cut off from the realities of the war and where his grandmother, doña Estanislaa, seeks to perpetuate a myth of childhood innocence in her fantasies and nostalgic evocations of her two sons. By contrast, and in imitation of the destruction and violence of the adults, the refugee schoolchildren rebel against authority and take over the school. Enacting Abel's deepest fantasies and longings, they imaginatively re-interpret the codes and cruelties of the adult war in their own forms of play, e.g. Quintana is tried by a mock military court, gang members all wear symbols and insignia of rank, they also adopt the vocabulary of anti-fascism, which they neither understand nor question, and use the term *faccioso* to define the enemy. However, the novel explores not so much the motivations for the primitive and violent behaviour of the schoolchildren as Abel's alienation inside *El Paraíso* and his desire to escape entrapment and by implication the oppressive mystifications and ludicrous attachment to childhood innocence shown by Estanislaa. Not surprisingly, Abel is fascinated by that 'other' world of the schoolchildren, enticed by their liberating animality, hedonism, savagery, and lack of scruples. They represent the real alternative to *El Paraíso*, one which has been repressed by Estanislaa's refined and 'civilized' life-style and on a wider plane, by the moral and sexual puritanism of the class to which she belongs. As in *Juegos*, the shy, introverted, middle-class child finds in his lower-class counterparts the freedom, sensualism and contempt for authority which his own upbringing has denied him. Pablo, who both tempts and betrays Abel, is perhaps the epitome of the cunning, pragmatic, 'street-wise' youngster. Of course, his corruption of Abel is made relatively easy precisely because Abel is itching to be corrupted, to engage in anti-social behaviour, eager to rebel against the norms and values of his class. But, it is the very same class determinism that ensures Abel's fate. Never allowed to become a group member and finally converted into a symbol of what the group is attempting to overthrow, Abel is labelled a *faccioso* and murdered by El Arquero. Yet Abel does not resist, but is the willing sacrificial victim of the schoolchildren's action in their illusory bid for freedom. The boy's death is unanimously represented as meaningless and absurd: to Elósegui, 'la vida se le antojó de pronto, insípida, carente de sentido'(20); Quintana remarks: 'Es absurdo . . . todo es absürdo' (131); the narrator also interjects: 'Imposible de comprender. Todo era absurdo'(81).

The presentation of the war, not directly, but through its parodic and tragic re-enactment by the schoolchildren, serves to underline its irrationality and absurdity, symbolized by the gratuitous killing of Abel. The war is portrayed as a game, waged between arbitrary, opposing sides, with no apparent differentiation between competing forces nor what they stand for; rather the condemnation of war, at least on the surface, is made at an abstract, global level. Both sides are seen as sharing the responsibilities for their children's mimetic behaviour, which has led to destruction of childhood innocence. As Quintana states: 'A esos niños que no tienen ni madre ni padre, es como si les hubiera estafado la infancia. Nunca han sido verdaderamente niños' (131). However, as Jo Labanyi has shown in a provocative re-reading of the novel, *Duelo* cannot simply be regarded as a protest novel at the horrors of war.[9] Indeed, she argues that the novel does take sides and represents an exaltation of the Republic and the values associated with the Fall, values totally at odds with the moral puritanism and bogus freedom represented by the Nationalists in their restoration of order. For Labanyi, the 'fallen' Republic is to be admired, the degeneracy of the schoolchildren being far preferable to the living death represented by the false paradise of 'los vencedores'.[10]

The above view is partially confirmed in the way Goytisolo obsessively returns to the problems that so preoccupied him in *Juegos*, principally his dissatisfaction with the bourgeois family system, represented in *Duelo* by the intercalated story of Estanislaa and her family. As before, the children are presented as innocent victims of parental egotism, self-deception, and a repressive family environment. Estanislaa's own rejection of the real world is motivated initially by her refusal to recognize the fact of her husband Enrique's womanizing. With the accidental death of her first son David, on whom she had doted, she retreats even further into a make-believe world of beauty, refinement, and sensitivity. Compensating for her husband's indifference, she transfers her obsessive love to her second son, Romano. At bottom, Estanislaa's refusal to recognize reality and her jealousy and possessiveness towards Romano are based on a deep-seated fear and horror of heterosexual relations. Indeed, her attitudes prevent Romano from 'growing up', they arrest his psychosexual development and ability to form normal relationships; hence, his predisposition towards sexual ambiguity, represented by his strange relationship with the mysterious, androgynous Claude. Abel can also be seen as a victim of his grandmother's repressions and fantasies, of her constant self-deception which he has imitated and which has rebounded on him. The youngster's death, for which Estanislaa must bear some of the responsibility, does not lead to any new awareness; rather, it is incorporated into her ongoing game of mystifying the past which, in a sense, symbolizes the way her class deals with the awkward and unpalatable aspects of the real world: '[Abel] era un ser extraordinariamente formado para sus pocos años y me quería con un verdadero delirio' (282).

Estanislaa's story serves to reinforce Goytisolo's view of the bourgeois family as a mechanism by which children are exploited by manipulative, self-deceiving parents and thus denied the opportunity to develop their own identity, to 'grow up'. In this sense, Estanislaa's evasions seek to prolong the myth of eternal childhood innocence which Goytisolo is at pains to explode. Denied the freedom to acknowledge their often very mediocre talents and personalities and more importantly, faced with a taboo denying them access to the truths of sex and carnal knowledge (note: it is from the *panda* of refugee children that Abel learns the facts of life), they rebel. They seek to break the rules and to luxuriate in the decadent, animalistic side of human nature, which their family and class have tried to suppress. (Here, Abel's fascination for the *panda* is quite understandable; also at a different level, Goytisolo seems to approve of Enrique's infidelity to his wife as a challenge to bourgeois decency.) Yet, at the same time, youngsters like Abel are victims of the very innocence, naivety, and moral propriety which impels them to covet the class 'other'. Abel's attempt to lose his moral virginity, so to speak, by joining the gang, is already doomed to failure, already negated by the social and class determinism arising out of the sin of privilege by which he is irrevocably tainted.

He admires his executioners for their vitality and wilful cruelty, though he is aware of the gulf that separates them because of his class origins. He willingly accepts the role of victim; it is a masochism which gives him an identity in front of the group members; he thus becomes one of them, but only in his role as scapegoat; unable to fulfil his desire for affiliation any other way, he happily takes on the mantle of sacrificial victim. In a sense, his death provides a means of purging the worst excesses of bourgeois morality, of exorcising the demons of impotence and class innocence. Abel's death is perhaps paradoxically a necessary sacrifice, a way of demonstrating, in an extreme case, the end result of the myriad taboos, repressions, and deceptions by which the bourgeois family conducts the business of upbringing. It is this, rather than the civil war as childhood trauma, which seems to lurk in the deeper recesses of *Duelo* and which Goytisolo wishes to confront. Indeed, Goytisolo seems to be suggesting that the real losers of the civil war were not the Republicans, but the children of the winning side, sentenced to a lingering living death, as Labanyi puts it, by the sexual and moral obsessions of their class.[11] The civil war is no more than a scenario, a theatre of cruelty, in which to indulge all those drives and desires which have been repressed by family and schooling; however, with the Nationalist victory, the brief parenthesis of Republican libertarianism is brought to a halt; order is restored and those 'valores eternos' which once made Spain great are reimposed; in other words, Estanislaa's values, which legitimize the position of children as eternal 'menores de edad' and for which Franco won the war, are set to dominate the false 'paradise' of postwar peace. All in all, *Duelo* emerges as an almost faithful recasting of *Juegos*, simply using a different backcloth against which to explore and legitimate the same concerns. As Marfany has pointed out: 'La necesitat de trobar una justificació per a aquesta revolta i per a la condemnació moral dels adults té, és clar, per a un jove en els anys 50, una sortida obvia: la guerra civil com a exemple de la irresponsabilitat ética dels grans.'[12]

In this attempt to return to the roots of the problem, Goytisolo replaces his adolescents of the 1950s with the children of 1939. But the problem is not so much the ethical condemnation of the civil war as the repudiation of the values of the generation which fought and won the war; it is they who are responsible for an order and a morality which denies their offspring a more libertarian sexuality and places a taboo on the instinctual side of human nature. And it is on these grounds that Goytisolo seems to mount his critique of the adults. Of course, such a visceral revolt lacks any clear sense of direction or focus in social or political terms. Indeed, in *Duelo*, Goytisolo fails even to hint at the fact that the restoration of order in the valley by the (extremely kind, civilized, and understanding) Nationalist troops implies a return to a certain form of economic organization, i.e. capitalism. Subsequent works, however, beginning with the trilogy *El mañana efímero*, reveal a shift in attitudes and a greater awareness of political and class issues (e.g. *chabolismo* and the sub-proletariat). However, the author seems unable to overcome his obsession with the split or multiple self, masks, and metamorphosis, as well as a romanticized vision of 'pueblo', often portrayed as 'noble savage'.

Goytisolo's first two novels may be light years away from proletarian realism, or indeed realism of any description. But they constitute a writing option in the early 1950s that probes the issues of the generation gap, studied earlier, and that offers a certain explanation or rationale for generational revolt. Their importance lies, therefore, less at the referential than at the symbolic or symptomatic levels; they relate to and reveal, not the hidden social realities of a defeated working class, but the emotional and psychosexual obsessions of a privileged elite. But it is a radically disaffected elite, which has cut itself adrift from its own class and is yet to find an adequate anchoring point in relation to a lower class, with which it feels an emotional solidarity.

IGNACIO ALDECOA[13]

Aldecoa clearly accepted the validity of a testimonial function for the novel. This is evident in his attempt, in the first trilogy, to deal with 'tópicos', e.g. the Civil Guard and the gypsies, and to transcend the folkloric and costumbrista dimensions which had, over time, helped to falsify them. His concern was to strip away the layers of myth and prejudice that had encrusted these figures and transformed them into stereotypes and seek to reveal a more authentic, responsible, accurate, and honest view. Whether he achieved this objective is again a matter of opinion, especially in relation to his female characters. Rather than focus directly on the broad social forces and conditions which determined their daily lives, Aldecoa preferred to concentrate on the inner workings of his individual characters, their emotional and psychological make-up, and their behaviour under stress. It would be from this individual experience that the reader could infer more general points regarding environment or historical conditioning. Aldecoa's novelistic plots, then, are little more than a pretext for a study of characters placed in extreme situations. The author is obviously aware of the dramatic potential of such situations, as well as their symbolic and metaphysical implications, which he is careful to cultivate. Indeed, as most critics acknowledge, Aldecoa is acutely concerned with the intricacies of novel construction and style, often to the point of unchecked virtuosity. And it is the visibility of his literary artifice that distances him somewhat from the aesthetics of discretion associated with the *novela social*. Yet, on balance, and particularly in relation to his writings, including the many short stories, Aldecoa would seem to belong to the movement. His explorations of individuals under pressure, limit situations, social determinism, and the lack of horizons of his 'little people' clearly place him in the same novelistic line as *Los bravos* and *El Jarama*. Yet in terms of their treatments, Aldecoa's novels are by no means straightforwardly or predominantly objectivist in their narrative presentation or very explicit in their views on social injustice, but rather more varied and complex. In the 1950s, for the leading figures of the movement and in increasingly politicized conditions, this 'mixed' character of Aldecoa's work may have rendered him less than 'sound' politically, although ultimately more satisfying in literary terms.

El fulgor y la sangre[14]

Most critics recognize the testimonial dimension of Aldecoa's first novel, its realistic portrayal of the Civil Guards and their families, the crushingly tedious routine of daily garrison life in an isolated, rural backwater. But critics such as Borau, Lasagabaster Medinabeitia, Lytra, and to some extent Fiddian, place equal or greater emphasis on the novel's treatment of individual and collective alienation and categorize it as a work of 'existential realism'. Carlisle, however, prefers an archetypal interpretation, stressing the novel's religious and doctrinal implications, while

143

Pérez Firmat, intrigued by the novel's formal composition, regards it as a dramatization of the techniques of novel writing.[15] On the whole, critical readings give prominence to the existentialist/ metaphysical dimension and drawing on the notion of *situation limite*, regard *El fulgor* as fundamentally a study of man's alienated condition, inevitably subject to the whims of a cruel destiny. However, an aspect of the novel which has been somewhat overlooked is that it mainly deals, not with the experiences of the male characters, but of the women, whose stories and memories constitute almost two thirds of the text. These stories give the reader access to the family and cultural backgrounds and the sort of historical forces and conditions of the past that have shaped their lives. Taking this aspect into account, it could be argued that the alienated condition of Aldecoa's characters has less to do with abstract notions of fatality than with the way personal choices are shaped and reproduced by social conditioning, women's roles in traditional communities and the effects of the civil war.

On the surface, Aldecoa seems to paint a sensitive picture of his women characters in their background stories. In the pre-war period, we learn that three of the five held jobs, though in typically female occupations: Carmen was a hairdresser, Ernesta a servant, and María a teacher. Despite these apparent signs of independence, all the women are subjected to the stern advice of parents or grandparents, anxious to inculcate respect for and submission to traditional values. So, while Asún, the liberated hairdresser, decides to fight for the Republic by joining the militias, the five women are made to conform to stereotyped roles, culminating in marriage. Apart from Felisa, the other women enter marriage almost as a reflex-action, as something preordained and taken for granted; Felisa, however, shows her independence and strength of character by deciding to marry Ruipérez, against the wishes of her father and brother, who regard it as a betrayal of family and class allegiances. In all cases, the war situation is the context in which they find their eventual husbands, but in relation to the war, and unlike Asún, they are portrayed as spectators rather than actors; their involvement in politics and the fighting is actively discouraged and as in the cases of Felisa and Sonsoles, they suffer family loss as a direct result of the war. Victims of the war, but also victims of their own choices, their ambitions, jobs, and little scraps of independence are all sacrificed; except in one case, their refuge in marriage is no more than a resigned accommodation to the status quo; this is particularly so in the case of María, the only one of the women to have given up a career and married late for fear ending up 'on the shelf'. Except for Ernesta who, though over twenty, is treated by the others like a baby, Aldecoa's women have made choices whose consequences have deprived them of their earlier margin of freedom and independence, assertiveness and self-sufficiency. And though they complain (Carmen, for example, threatens to leave her husband if no transfer is forthcoming), they seem resigned to their lot, to domestic labour, and fundamentally submissive roles. Even though the war and life in the castle inevitably take their toll on their self-confidence and independence, it is difficult to imagine such active women in the pre-war period being transformed into submissive drudges.

One of the intriguing features of the women's stories is that they deal at some length with the lives, roles, and war-time activities of their fathers. What emerges is a sympathetic and basically positive picture, not of Republican militants or left-wing political activists, but of the non-aligned lower classes, whose attitudes and beliefs are compromised by the pressures of circumstance. In other words, where the choice lies between political integrity and survival, the men opt for survival, even if it means selling out to the other side. Felisa's father, Juan Martín, is jailed at the beginning of the war for supporting the Republic; Felisa believes this basically decent man is a victim of his own generosity and political naivety; his experience of prison, his job in a Nationalist arms factory, his subsequent dismissal from work because of political antecedents – all conspire to inhibit any further political involvement. The case of Juan Martín illustrates the difficulties and contradictions experienced by the working classes, caught in a war situation and tainted by the stigma of their Republican past. Ernesta's peasant father, Paulino, is once again presented as a simple, honest, hard-working soul, but who is sceptical about any sort of politics and happy to accept the status quo. In the end, he inadvertently betrays the names of peasant activists to the local moneylender, which results in severe reprisals on the village. The case of Carmen's father, Santiago, is similar to that of Juan Martín in that his early left-revolutionary outlook is rapidly shelved in return for a job, money, and minimum economic security, which precipitates a remarkable conversion to reactionary politics.

Simple, decent, principled men, salt of the earth, Aldecoa's fathers are portrayed as victims, not only of external forces but of their own good nature and stupidity and thus are easy prey to left political agitators. Their ideals are eventually jettisoned through fear and the need to survive the war and postwar repression. They become compromisers, trimmers, forced by events to sacrifice their integrity. Here, it has to be said, we find in the novel a certain ambiguity of outlook. On the one hand, Aldecoa seems to suggest that the renunciation of principles and class betrayal are the terrible though sadly inevitable consequences of war. On the other, that political involvement simply lands the ignorant working classes in a mess and that what is required is not commitment to a cause but a healthy dose of scepticism towards politics in general. In other words, it is far more sensible not to meddle in politics – a view which could be read as endorsing one of the dominant features of post-civil war life in Spain, i.e. depoliticization. Also, Aldecoa perhaps could have but prefers not to explore the example of the man who resists postwar repression, while holding on to his political ideals in silence; in other words, the classic case of passive though no less real resistance, whose absence from the novel may or may not be significant.

Returning to the main thematic problem posed by the novel, is it history and human agency or cosmic injustice which blight the lives of the inhabitants of the castle? Is the notion of cruel fate, so often invoked by the characters, simply a way of rationalizing the effects of events and conditions which are beyond their control, though perhaps not their comprehension? Despite much critical exegesis on the role of fate in the novel,[16] the historical past, in the shape of the civil war, is a constant source of conversation among the inhabitants: 'El tema inagotable había sido siempre la guerra' (225). Thus, as well as symbolizing abstract notions of entrapment, confinement, and the *huis clos*, the bleak, isolated 'cuartel-convento' is the living emblem of the victors of the civil war, as well as an icon drawn from the regime's propaganda and mythology, representing an ideal Spain and an ideal Spaniard, 'medio-monje, medio soldado'. The castle stands for postwar Spanish society, a society frozen in time, demanding order, discipline, and obedience, even until death. The irony is that the characters do in fact recognize their situation as a product of the civil war. They are victims, not of some abstract destiny, but of their own, admittedly socially-determined, individual choices. Those who advocate an existentialist reading of *El fulgor* should perhaps recall that for the existentialist hero, there are no insurance policies, no way of laying the blame for our conduct on supernatural forces or external agents, such as heredity, environment, nature, or fate. The characters in *El fulgor* are certainly victims, but of the consequences of their choices in a backward, repressive, indifferent, postwar society. Once again, Aldecoa shows his concern with the 'popular' strata of the winning side, taking up the extreme case of the Civil Guards, who represent the very essence of loyalty and sacrifice and whether they like it not, are duty-bound to fulfil: 'Todo por la patria.' The point seems to be that their affiliation to the winning side has left them worse, not better off; their loyalty and devotion to duty have left them no less abandoned, forgotten, or betrayed. This pessimistic conclusion is only relieved by the fact that at the end of the novel, the women seem to overcome some of their petty rivalries and hatreds and begin to take responsibility for each other. The implication is that the only outlet from fear and uncertainty in this 'espera' is to be found, not in individual isolation or in the reassuring straitjacket of duty, but in solidarity with others.

Con el viento solano (1956)[17]

As in the case of *El fulgor*, the spectrum of critical reactions to Aldecoa's second novel seems to divide into three broad camps: the realist, the existentialist and the symbolic. Sobejano, for example, regards *Con el viento solano* as 'la novela realista de los gitanos', a view supported by Senabre but but only partially accepted by Nora, Corrales Egea, and Sanz Villanueva. The latter maintain that the novel is not exactly about gypsies since it fails to analyse them fully as a marginal social grouping and is more concerned with the psychological development of the protagonist.[18] By contrast, Fiddian sees the novel as a 'powerful protest on behalf of a minority group in Spain', its main theme being that of 'cultural conflict and alienation'. However, there is not much textual evidence to show that the novel sets out to campaign on behalf of gypsy rights. The problem is that Fiddian hardly develops his view; he thus stands mid way between the realist reading and its existentialist counterpart.[19] In this connection, Gemma Roberts sees the novel in terms of a *situation limite*, in which the protagonist undergoes an existential conversion to authenticity, signalled by his voluntary surrender to the Civil Guard.[20] The difficulty here revolves round the motivations for Sebastián Vázquez's capitulation/conversion. Is it a question of impulse or rational reflection, a victory for his resolve or an admission of exhaustion and defeat? Fiddian has usefully noted that Sebastián's inability to think for himself conflicts with the customary decisiveness of the existentialist hero and thus puts Roberts' reading somewhat into question.[21] At the symbolic level, and in relation to the matter of alienation, Carlisle argues that the main protagonist suffers as a result of being alienated from God and being subjected to a form of divine retribution for his lack of faith. Recognizing Aldecoa's own agnosticism, Fiddian again casts serious doubt on this view.[22]

As the companion volume to *El fulgor*, *Con el viento solano* takes its point of departure from the same incident that set in motion the action of the first novel: the shooting of the corporal. In the second, we are shown the consequences of this 'fait divers' for the corporal's murderer, Sebastián Vázquez, the gypsy whose story now becomes the novel's main focus of interest. As a result of his act – not a gratuitous crime, but an act committed out of fear – Sebastián enters a new situation, a *situation limite*, as some critics would say. Or rather, he begins to experience in a much more extreme form those pressures and hazards he has always had to cope with: a dangerous existence lived out at the margins of society and harassment from the forces of order. Used to surviving on the edge of the law, his senseless act pushes him over the boundary, to become a fugitive, a true outsider. His week-long flight from the law, during which he searches in vain for support and shelter from his own people is the means by which Aldecoa probes the myth of gypsy clan loyalty. The 'tópico' of the gypsy character is also re-examined in that what Sebastián formerly took for granted is now seen in a very different light; deprived of freedom and support, the gypsy begins to re-evaluate their significance in terms of his own lack and gains a new awareness of their meanings for himself and others. This results in something of a 'toma de conciencia' of a reality to which he had been previously oblivious, a journey of self-discovery which reveals to him and the reader the underside not only of his own character and the gypsy world but also of the strange, exotic, sub-proletarian types who inhabit provincial

Castile, to quote Senabre, 'tipos vulgares, grises, intranscendentes, sin más problemas que los de subsistir día a día y perderse a veces en el mundo añorado de los sueños.'[23] Despite Sobejano's claim, *Con el viento solano* is not quite the novel of the gypsies. We are certainly given sufficient material with which to form a picture, for example, of the gypsy community of Sebastián's village Cogolludo (hunger, poverty, illegal trading, a culture based on a passion for bullfighting, heavy drinking and brawling, clan rivalries, hatred of the Civil Guard, etc.). But the novel's main focus remains the individual figure of Sebastián Vázquez, incarnation of the gypsy *chulo*, and explores what happens to him when his taken-for-granted world is denied him and he is forced to come to terms with his own fear, guilt, and lack of freedom. As Sanz Villanueva correctly argues: 'Parece, por lo tanto, que al autor le interesa el problema en su dimensión humana y se concentra antes en los aspectos psicológicos que en los sociales.'[24]

After the shooting, the first step in Sebastián's psychological development, and indeed in a personal 'toma de conciencia', is an encounter with his old friend Francisco Vázquez. The latter's bravado, self-confidence, and typically arrogant manner remind Sebastián of his former self and give rise to sensations of alienation as the gypsy no longer recognizes himself in that role. However, for fear of being compromised in a manhunt, Vázquez refuses to help; at the same time, Sebastián inwardly regrets having to involve his friend in his misfortune and thus place him in potential danger. Thrust back on his own resources, he begins to see his past life in a different light: 'Nunca recordaba haber vivido alegremente ni tristemente. Había simplemente vivido. Exactamente como un animal cualquiera. Unicamente con una razón animal'(79). Yet, the gypsy's return to origins and to the imagined safety of family and clan respond to that same animal instinct, whose survival value he continues to trust, despite experiences to the contrary. Indeed, the encounters Sebastián has on his journey follow a pattern of alternation between those involving relations and family, who refuse to help him, and those other fleeting acquaintances, who offer their support, but which he ends up rejecting. Among these chance encounters, he meets Pepita, the prostitute, whose life-style and existence on the road resemble his own and Cabeda, the good Samaritan, another outsider with whose fatalistic attitude to life Sebastián identifies and in whom he finds temporary sanctuary: 'Sebastián se encontraba cómodo en compañía del viejo. . . . No sabía por qué pero no tenía miedo junto a él. Parecía que el viejo fuese la clave de la existencia y su voz era el rumor de la vida sosegada, de la vida en calma' (96). Despite his twenty years in prison and a string of personal calamities, Cabeda survives loneliness and isolation and like his colleague Hernández, 'el revolucionario', recognizes the value of friendship and soldarity on the road. Sebastián learns, therefore, that personal tragedy need not lead to despair, a lesson he sees movingly and pathetically repeated in other encounters with Casimiro *el bobo* and Roque the fakir. However, having been made aware of his own 'aburrida, estúpida, monótona limitación' (123) by their example, he also intuits that the freedom of others also has its limitations and that its inevitable concomitants are poverty and loneliness.

Sebastián's reunion with his mother is preceded by his encounter with a muleteer; the latter's invocation of the east wind as a malign force affecting the bad harvests and the backcloth of the gathering storm create an atmosphere of ominous foreboding. The culmination of the gypsy's journey is thus accompanied by a symbol of adverse fate and reinforced by the figurative motif of the threatening skies. The theme of the civil war is reintroduced in the description of the village, which directly echoes that found in *Los bravos*: 'Fachadas de casas en ruinas. Fachadas solas, teatrales. . . . Orografía de ruinas. Gritos de la miseria. . . . Recuerdo, muro de recuerdo, del hogaño triunfal'(175). Nothing has changed; born in poverty, Sebastián returns to exactly the same conditions; and despite savouring some nostalgic moments with his brother, his father sums up his desperation in a remark which accurately foreshadows his son's eventual fate: 'En la cárcel iba a estar más tranquilo que aquí' (180). As the reader might have guessed, especially in the light of Sebastián's own hesitation at finally seeing his mother, she rejects his plea for sanctuary and tells him to leave. The umbilical cord of family and community has now been severed; Sebastián is now totally alone; from a position of supreme self-confidence, he has been transformed into a frightened animal. With nothing left to hope for, he reverts to type and, coming full circle, gets drunk; however, this time he does not become violent, but demands to be taken to the Civil Guard barracks to give himself up.

150

The question of the gypsy's voluntary surrender has given rise to a number of critical readings, most of which can be reduced to two basic lines of interpretation: the surrender corresponds to the working out of fate, of which Sebastián is merely a pawn; and the surrender represents the culmination of an existential conversion to authenticity. Taking the latter interpretation first, and as Roberts has argued, Sebastián could be seen as gaining his freedom by *choosing* to surrender rather than letting his life be ruled by uncertainty.[25] This assumes, however, that his capitulation is an act of self-assertion. But, his reversion to type and his drunkenness, while being signs of an identity he wishes to recapture, do not suggest the actions or rational choices of someone responding to a new self-awareness; rather, they indicate the last pathetic act of a broken man, whose will to carry on has been exhausted. As for the first type of interpretation, if Sebastián is simply acting out what is preordained, then by what or whom is his fate determined? Fate, it seems to me, is just a word used to describe what the gypsy and his kind can expect from their traditional enemies; he knows that, in the end, capture is inevitable, yet the fact is that he has not been caught. Indeed, Sebastián is bothered not so much by the thought of capture as by the persecution complex he suffers. His worst fears remain unfulfilled and it is with the constant torment of uncertainty that he cannot cope. The need to put an end to inner anguish may partly explain his capitulation. At the same time, his week-long persecution has had a positive side, in that his eyes have been opened both to his own suffering and that of others, which has forced him to make a comparison between their freedom and his lack. From this, it could be argued that he surrenders after realizing that if freedom is co-substantial with poverty and misery and this is all the future holds, then, echoing his father, he may as well be behind bars. Sebastián is simply not strong-willed enough to stay on the road, especially when his own community have deserted him. Better the security of the cell, it seems, than the uncertainty of the road. Of course, the irony is that Sebastián stupidly rejects the support of people like Lupe, Pepita, and Cabeda and, in broader terms, the solidarity of the poor, which Aldecoa represents as the only positive feature in this otherwise highly pessimistic novel.

To sum up, in his first two novels, Aldecoa does appear to be concerned, as Fiddian puts it, 'to give a verisimilar representation of contemporary provincial Castile by broadening the range of realistic literature'.[26] His novels do offer a wide panorama of the recent historical past and the social and geographical present, as well as a realistic picture of the lack of horizons and sense of entrapment of his lower class characters. Such are the obvious main points of contact with the *novela social*. Points of difference arise in the way the author tends to set his revelations of social reality in a highly constructed and perhaps even contrived symbolic and archetypal framework, deliberately cueing reading responses at both the referential and metaphysical levels, rather than leaving the deeper implications to the reader to tease out. Also, Aldecoa's picture of oppression is perhaps a little diffuse, complicated by his interest in personal alienation and fatality and thus in the victims of social or political accident. Finally, for the advocates of a critical and hard-hitting realism in the 1950s, Aldecoa was perhaps too much of a stylist, too concerned with producing a work of literature than creating a social document. As Soldevila-Durante observes 'Si se entiende "novela social" en los años cincuenta como un arma de combate, tal vez se puede rechazar la obra de Aldecoa de su pertenencia al movimiento.'[27] None the less, Aldecoa's work can still be considered as yet another strand in the writing options found in the initial stages of the movement, an option certainly motivated by the intention to reveal a hidden social reality, but from a basically humanitarian rather than a concretely political stance. Indeed, both his novels express the author's own personal 'toma de conciencia' of a world and a class to which he does not belong, but whose story demands to be told.

JESUS FERNANDEZ SANTOS: *LOS BRAVOS*[28]

Whether as a precursor or the initiator of the *novela social*, *Los bravos* is generally regarded as a vivid and accurate testimony of Spain's forgotten rural poor, a striking document of the monotonous, immutable pattern of their daily lives in a typical 'pueblo perdido' in the 1940s. For example, Nora states that in the novel, 'no ocurre nada especial: el propósito del novelista parece ser destacar precisamente que en esos pueblos no ocurre nunca nada. Se vive, al mínimo de lo posible.' Sobejano agrees: 'Lo que ha interesado primordialmente al autor ha sido captar la incolora monotonía de la existencia cotidiana de esos hombres y mujeres del agro español.' Reviewing the novel in 1955, Alberto Gil Novales saw it as a testimony, but also as a kind of homage to 'los bravos, los que resisten el paisaje'. Twenty-five years on, Sanz Villanueva makes the same point: 'La verdadera historia de la novela es la del pueblo en su conjunto, la de "los bravos", los que allí viven y resisten.'[29] Not surprisingly, what has tended to galvanize critical attention and polarize interpretations is not the novel's testimonial dimension, whose relevance and importance no one questions; rather, it is the narrative intrigue woven around the character and role of the doctor. At bottom, the question usually posed is: does he replace don Prudencio as the new *cacique* and continue the domination of the village? Gil Casado for example, argues that the doctor's actions are motivated by an unmistakable will to power and that the novel dramatizes: 'el problema central del cacicazgo y subjugación del pueblo bajo el nuevo poder.' Affirming that Gil Casado's substitution argument 'contiene una buena dosis de acertada interpretación', Sanz Villanueva similarly argues that, at the very moment when the villagers have a chance to free themselves from Prudencio's tyrannical power, the village 'por apatía, cae bajo el dominio del médico'. On the other side of this hermeneutic hot spot, Sobejano, for example, finds no justification for the idea that the doctor simply steps into Prudencio's shoes: 'si uno es viejo, terratentiente, lujurioso y egoista y el otro jóven, médico, enamorado y justo, incluso caritativo, no veo posible que éste herede a aquél.'[30]

Such clearly opposed critical reactions not only tend to deflect attention away from other relevant features of the novel; they also oversimplify and obscure more complex attitudes and motivations in the characters, especially in the doctor, whose outlook is by no means wholly consistent with the 'substitution/new tyrant' argument. On the surface, it is true that the doctor's actions (his 'theft' of Socorro, protection of the swindler, decision to stay on, purchase of Prudencio's house, etc.) and the villagers' reactions, suggest that he assumes the position of the new *cacique*. However, his decision to remain and tough it out in adverse circumstances seems motivated not by a will to power (power over what?; the village is poor; Prudencio's wealth is left to his brother), but out of love for Socorro and solidarity with the very people he has antagonized; that is, he wants to regain the confidence and friendship of 'los

153

bravos', become like them, and thus he too chooses to resist. The ongoing development of the doctor's solidarity is a process which is amply recorded in the text and seems to take the form of a series of situations and choices that puts his resolve to the test. Indeed, his decision to commit himself to protecting and curing the swindler exemplfies the contradictions and dilemmas of his position: he is strung between the demands of professional ethics and a basic sense of justice and the equally understandable, though morally indefensible, demands for revenge made by the villagers. By following his conscience and helping 'el prójimo', who is most in need, the doctor/good Samaritan is ostracized by the village. But, though he considers it, he refuses to leave, first because of Socorro, and secondly because of his wish to re-build bridges with the villagers. This whole problem, i.e. the difficulties involved in overcoming the gap between intellectual and 'pueblo', the doctor and the villagers, suggests that underlying *Los bravos*, there is a debate being conducted over the nature of Spanish society, the rigidity of its social structure and the inability of human agents to counteract the effects of social and geographical determinations. At the same time, arising out of the intrigue in the novel, this debate is informed by the role of sexual desire and its impact (disruptive? integrative?) on an entrenched social order.

The opening scene of the novel, involving the amputation of the young peasant's finger, establishes one of the basic traits of the doctor's character:

Comprendió el médico que no les inspiraba mucha confianza. Su juventud y la exigua y vieja cartera donde ahora estaban fijas sus miradas, no debían hablarles ni de una larga práctica ni de su sabiduría en el oficio. Era lo de siempre desde su llegada allí, pero no por conocido le molestó menos. (10–11).

The doctor suffers from a lack of self-confidence, a feature poignantly illustrated by the fact that, even in the oppressive summer heat, he feels compelled to wear a jacket in order to hide his youth and inexperience. He thus takes refuge in his difference from the villagers, hiding behind the mask of his professional identity, wearing it as a form of protective clothing. Inexperienced, naive, lacking in roots, and suffering what Gil Casado sees as an inferiority complex, the doctor is initially presented as having no strong reasons for practising in the village or indeed earning his living as a doctor: 'Lo mismo da un modo que otro' (19), he remarks to a bemused Pepe, who cannot understand why a young, city professional has come to such a God-forsaken place to work. The doctor's apparently casual, indifferent attitude towards his professional calling, underpinned by a deeper sense of aimlessness, are early hints that he is running away from something, that his presence in the village is a form of escape from a city career, lifestyle, and associated values that he is unable or unwilling to pursue. Cut adrift, looking for anchor points and a meaning to his life, the doctor is initially prepared to help others in the village (he helps Pepe to strip the van engine; he does not denounce the wounded Alfredo to the gamekeeper); but he is inevitably regarded as an outsider. And it is the contradictions between his alternating 'insider' and 'outsider' status, i.e. between his detached, professional role and his desire to belong and be regarded on equal terms with the rest of the village, which underpins his character development and gives rise to his first substantive link with the village, in the shape of Socorro.

The character of Socorro is given little elaboration; as in the case of the doctor, her past is something of an enigma; in fact, all we know is that she is not from the village (51). She certainly appears to be an assiduous worker, a faithful housekeeper and servant to don Prudencio, but also extremely shy, modest, passive, and above all a woman of few words: 'Hablaba poco y siempre impersonalmente, como tomando ante la vida una actitud pasiva' (134); 'no concebía otro modo de ser que su mutismo de siempre' (223). Epitome of the uncomplaining, self-denying, submissive companion, Socorro is also willing to cohabit with the *cacique* and be his mistress, there being no hint of coercion. The doctor assumes this is the reason for the village's condemnation of don Prudencio. Pepe explains that this is not the case: 'Cualquiera haría igual si pudiese' (18). Amparo also informs him that, though the situation is immoral, no one is prepared to say so: '¿Y sabe por qué? Porque los hombres tienen tan poca verguenza como él, y si no hacen otro tanto es porque no pueden'(24). For the men of the village, Socorro is obviously a symbol of the power of the *cacique* to establish his own personal moral codes; she is thus a sign of what his commanding position in the village actually allows him to do; she also represents his *droits de seigneur*, something denied to the rest, just like his money and his leisure. At the same time, she constitutes a focus for the men's repressions and sexual fantasies, an imaginary outlet from the tedium of married life, in short an object of desire. Indeed, she is consistently presented as an object of the male gaze, attracting the covetous looks of the asturianos (89), Pepe (67), Manolo (68), Antón (17), as well as the self-satisfied contemplation of don Prudencio himself, proud that his possession is the envy of other men (88). Overall, Socorro or, to be more precise, the physical attraction of her body, both condenses and displaces the envy and contempt the men of the village feel towards don Prudencio. She functions as an object of male desire, which is all the more tempting precisely because she is so apparently unattainable – she belongs to the *cacique*, whose property rights over her have up to now never been challenged. It is left to the doctor to undertake what the other men in the village have always wanted but have been unable to do, i.e. capture Socorro and enjoy the same privileges as don Prudencio. Though he experiences the same desires as the rest of the men, it is precisely his difference from them, his professional status, which gives him access to Prudencio's treasured possession. And by stealing the latter, the doctor precipitates the old man's loss of control over the village and his eventual downfall.

In his initial encounter with don Prudencio, the doctor resents being treated just like another member of the village and ordered to do the old man's bidding; he thus begins by quietly asserting his status. Yet, as soon as he lays eyes on Socorro, this wish to invoke the difference of a separate identity is immediately put under pressure and almost transformed into a barrier. Try as he might to keep his feelings under control and maintain a dignified, professional detachment as he examines her, his inexperience shows through and he is instantly attracted, indeed mesmerized, by her body: 'un cuerpo suave, moreno y duro, de finas venas azules . . . sólo la idea del cuerpo que ante sí tenía reinaba en la mente, atormentándole' (51). The doctor is also overcome by powerful anxieties concerning his own virility and his attractiveness as a man, trapped behind a professional mask: 'Se llamó niño por aquella absurda aprensión, pero persistía en ella en el deseo de hacerla saber que él no era su traje negro, ni la cartera, ni su sabiduría, que era un hombre, sobre todas esas cosas y ahora sufría por causa de su cuerpo' (52). The doctor's development, the process by which he finally decides to stay in the village, thus begins with his physical attraction towards Socorro. And what gives rise to his clash with don Prudencio is not what differentiates him from the village – his education, his professional status, his economic independence, his origins in the same class as don Prudencio – but what identifies him with the men of the village and which is common to all of them: their desire for Socorro. So, in a sense, the ancestral hierarchy and social structure of the village experience their first successful challenge, not from the Asturian invasion during the war, but through the workings of sexual desire, banal though this may appear. And, even when the doctor is living with Socorro and is clearly in love with her, that same desire is still based on a powerful, even fetishized, physical attraction: '[el médico] Se entretuvo contemplándola mientras cortaba el pan, dejando resbalar sobre ella sus ojos como una prolongada caricia' (143).

If Socorro constitutes the doctor's primary link with the village, she is also don Prudencio's only companion, his only contact in an otherwise isolated, enclosed existence. His absence from the village, caused by a visit to his own doctor in the city ironically provides the other, young doctor with the opportunity to move Socorro to a house rented from Baltasar. In another tragically ironic moment, on his return, don Prudencio has bought Socorro the new silk dress she always wanted, convinced that she loves him: 'Tenía que quererle porque siempre se había portado bien con ella' (134). But, on discovering her absence, the old man is totally disconcerted and devastated: 'Nunca le había parecido el pueblo tan vacío y en calma' (138). The wily landlord, clever enough to hide his money from the invading Asturians during the war, has been unable to prevent the theft of his prize possession. A member of the winning side in the war, don Prudencio now experiences for the first time the anguish of losing, the anguish long felt by his subjects in the village. And rather than try to regain Socorro by asserting his authority, he capitulates: 'Entonces se declaró vencido; fue a su cuarto y a tientas, sin encender la luz, se metió en la cama' (138). His new situation of total isolation is one which hastens his death, the responsibility for which obviously falls at the feet of the doctor. Having won a stake in the village by stealing Socorro (a moment which is significantly paralleled by the swindler's theft of the villagers' savings), the doctor now begins to gain an awareness of its wretchedness and poverty.

The first step in the doctor's 'toma de conciencia' occurs when he and Alfredo contemplate the village from a mountain top and reflect on the apparent absurdity of trying to eke a living out of such a barren land. This vain struggle engenders in the doctor a feeling of admiration for the peasants: 'no sabía aún si se quedaría allí un año o dos o toda la vida . . . aunque, desde su joven corazón, admirase a aquellos hombres que, hundidos en su valle, día tras día, trataban de arrancar a su tierra un fruto que se les negaba' (159). This initial identification with 'los bravos' is reinforced by his contact with the shepherds Vidal and Pascual, which helps to strengthen his ethical attachment to those most in need: 'Miró a Vidal. . . . Su prójimo estaba allí, a sus pies, abotonando su camisa cacqui sobre el pecho' (185). The doctor's new-found solidarity with the rural poor is immediately put to the test when he encounters the swindler, bleeding heavily after a severe beating, and decides to take charge of him. Aware of the latter's crime and wishing he could simply remain on the sidelines, cure the man's wounds, and avoid involving himself in the wider problem, the doctor is none the less forced, in spite of himself, to fulfil his ethical responsibilities: 'Sin desearlo, estaba del lado del prójimo que más sufría, del que sufría ante él sobre el caballo'(198). He thus commits himself to protecting the swindler from the anger and clamour for revenge of the villagers, who cannot comprehend his attitude or his actions. Yet, as the narrator points out: 'Sí, la vida podía presentarse fácil en la letra de los libros, en el sí y el no de las gentes, pero para él no era tan sencilla, no era tan fácilmente justa o injusta y no sabía si alegrarse o maldecir de ello'(199).

In protecting the swindler, the doctor pursues the only ethically proper course of action and one that also reflects his basically good intentions: 'estaba seguro de tener un buen corazón y por ahí la vida le tenía cogido' (199). Of course, his action only antagonizes the villagers, whose anger he understands, and leads them to ostracize him and Socorro. At this point, he indeed considers leaving the village; he does not belong there, his situation appears untenable and departure would be the easier option. Yet in an act of free choice, he decides to remain, principally because he loves Socorro but also out of solidarity with the inhabitants and a desire to have them accept him now on equal terms: 'Aquella gente creía odiarle; pensaba que les había perjudicado y sin embargo nunca

había estado su corazón más cerca de ellos que la noche del
suceso . . . ahora venía la ocasión de irrumpir en su mundo,
obligándoles a aceptarle de igual a igual entre sus hombres, entre
las causas de sus penas o alegrías' (212).
Of course, the doctor's decision to stay is interpreted very
differently by others. The men at the station bar are convinced that
only self-interest could possibly explain his choice: 'Vete a
saber. . . . Ese médico debe ser zorro viejo. . . . A mí no hay quien
me saque de la cabeza que si no se mueve es porque espera algo'
(218). That something, according to Pedro, is to take over the
village: 'ese en un par de años se hace dueño del pubelo' (217).
However, such reactions fail to appreciate the more complex
motivations behind the doctor's behaviour, his reservations and
doubts about his actions. The doctor: 'Comprendió que para ellos,
se había convertido ahora en el ladrón de su dinero' (221); yet, he
is prepared to wait in the hope that one day he can regain their
confidence: 'Sólo quedaba esperar, abandonarse al curso de los
días, acechando la primera ocasión de acercarse a la orilla opuesta'
(221). A sign that the process of *rapprochement* might already be
under way emerges from a visit he makes to Amador's bed-ridden
son, who admires him for standing up to the collective rage of the
village (225).
    Of course, as some of the specialist readers of *Los bravos* will be
anxious to point out, the ending of the novel sees the doctor
imitating one of the dead *cacique*'s favourite habits. Previously, don
Prudencio: 'sacó una silla – la misma de siempre – al balcón.
Desde la penumbra de la persiana veía el pueblo a sus pies'(83).
Likewise: 'El médico salió al balcón. Colocó en él una silla y
sentándose, contempló el pueblo a sus pies: la iglesia hueca, la
fragua y el río' (236). The parallel is hardly fortuitous, but
deliberate, striking, and disturbing; for Sanz Villanueva, it
represents 'una imagen clara de sustitución habida en la
dominación'.[31] In other words, it confirms that the doctor becomes
the new *cacique*. On the surface and especially from the point of
view of the aggrieved villagers, this seems to be the case, given the
doctor's theft of Socorro, the swindler, and by implication the
wealth of the village (221); his purchase of don Prudencio's house
and as in the case of the former patriarch, his ostracism from the
village, despite his good intentions. The doctor's position thus
seems uncannily close to don Prudencio's.

However, as I hope the previous discussion will have shown, the doctor's motives for staying on have little to do with a desire for power and control. He does not become the new landowner – so far, at least – and thus has no influence over rents or land distribution or indeed the village economy. Also, unlike don Prudencio, he has no antecedents in the civil war, no allegiances that might give rise to hostility or hatred. And despite protecting the swindler, the doctor has acted justly and professionally within the community. Of course, given that 'para ellos (el médico) se había convertido ahora en el ladrón de su dinero' (221), the inhabitants are unlikely to take such mitigating factors into account and will simply regard the doctor as a substitute for don Prudencio, happy to trust in appearances. However, on closer examination, appearances can be deceptive. In the case of don Prudencio, for example, the author's treatment is not condemnatory but broadly sympathetic; don Prudencio is not portrayed as a heartless tyrant. And though he curses the town, he also tries to be civil; he is not particularly harsh on his tenants; and his treatment of Socorro, though in many ways authoritarian, is also benign; indeed, he loves her and believes she loves him. The fact that she lives with him is not regarded as an act of oppression by the villagers or by her. In the end, don Prudencio's problem, his isolation, is not so much a result of personal failings or character defects, but of the weight of economic, social, and historical conditioning. He is the relatively wealthy landowner (though not the richest in the area); the villagers are the poor tenants and labourers and, in this sense, he is as much a victim of the calcified social structure of the village as they are. He suffers from a gulf between him and them, a gulf that is not of his own making. And because of their particular conditioning, their historically sedimented submission to authority, their time-honoured deference, and their identity as 'bravos' resisting hardship, they cannot escape that structurally cemented role of antagonists of the *cacique*, even when the latter is trying to be friendly. This, I believe, reflects a deep-seated pessimism on the part of Fernández Santos concerning the effects of social and geographical determinism, the idea that the structural backwardness of rural Spain at the time of writing was simply too powerful a determination to be modified by goodwill alone. Equally, as in the case of the young doctor, the gap between him and the villagers is not wholly of his own making. Simply, despite his good intentions, he is not one of them; and his actions, though ethically correct and unimpeachable, have transformed him into their enemy. This is not how he sees himself, but collective resentment and ostracism is the price he has to pay for committing himself to the principle of defending 'el prójimo' and upholding elementary standards of justice – but, even then, he has serious doubts concerning the efficacy and rationale for such choices, given their disastrous consequences. In a sense, he is forced by circumstance and by the cyclical repetition of ancestral antagonisms into occupying the subject position previously held by don Prudencio. However, the novel presents no simple, clear-cut case of substitutionism. The doctor, as much as don Prudencio, is a victim of forces and conditions which are beyond his power to influence or control. The problem of economic and social backwardness in an agrarian community, with its related cultural codes and conventions, is simply too deep-rooted for the doctor to confront successfully. This raises the wider question of the difficulties involved in social and political commitment. These arise not only because of the problem of making people understand the motivations behind commitment; the doctor is aware, for example, that it would serve no purpose to try and explain his actions to the villagers: 'De nada hubiera servido hablarles. ¿Qué palabras hubieran podido explicar su pensamiento, sus razones?' (221). Also, the social structure which creates the gulf between the doctor and the village, intellectual, and *pueblo*, may prove, in the end, to be too big and too entrenched to overcome. If the novel offers a lesson, it may well underlie the epigraph taken from Wasserman, that the destiny of a people is a function of their character – only in this case it is a character forged in the inexorable, unchanging cycle of rural underdevelopment, epitomized by Amparo's desolate existence: 'un pausado encaminarse hacia la nada, entre lejanos ecos de dolor, aburrimiento y deseo . . . la vida valía poco; era preciso seguir el curso de la rueda: girar, girar' (227–8)

RAFAEL SANCHEZ FERLOSIO: *EL JARAMA*[32]

As we saw in previous chapters, Sánchez Ferlosio was clearly influenced in the early 1950s by the writings and programmatic statements of Cesare Zavattini, perhaps above all by the idea that 'lo trivial no existe', i.e. that the banal existence of ordinary working people was an urgent and legitimate subject for artistic treatment and, when truthfully represented, acquired its own particular grandeur, intensity, and aesthetic value. *El Jarama* constitutes something of a homage to the Italian scriptwriter and a practical demonstration in prose of Zavattini's supreme ambition to document the lives of the Italian working class by making a 90-minute film in which absolutely nothing happens. In a similar vein, as Sanz Villanueva has pointed out in relation to the novel's implicit political meaning, what better way to record a society's inertia and stagnation than to write a story in which nothing happens?[33] Sánchez Ferlosio had already found this 'búsqueda del tiempo vulgar' admirably achieved in *Los bravos*, a novel which in no small measure influenced the organization, structure, and language of his own. What impressed the author was not so much the subject matter of *Los bravos*, i.e the oppressive facts of daily life for the villagers, but the ease and simplicity with which they were conveyed. This so minimized the distance between the reader and the writing on the page that such banal facts 'traen su presencia viva a la emoción del lector'. In other words, *Los bravos* had achieved an unusual degree of correspondence to the real through its aesthetics of discretion and its documentary effect, particularly in its use of language: 'Su lenguaje', said Sánchez Ferlosio, in his important review of the novel, 'es por eso, pura y cuidada fidelidad. . . . El autor ha querido hacerse mudo, frente al sagrado mutismo del pueblo que nos revela; se ha colocado detrás de él y lo ha dejado expresarse.'[34] It was precisely this desire to let the people speak for themselves in their own words, thus putting the reader in direct contact with their personal view of the world, which would underlie the distinctive character of *El Jarama* and, having been so spectacularly achieved, establish its importance as the initial, paradigmatic *novela social*.

The reality with which *El Jarama* is concerned and technically geared to document is that of Spain's lower classes, specifically an older generation of mainly rural inhabitants and a younger generation of primarily urban, working-class youth. The comparisons, contrasts, and general interplay between these two groups or sectors and indeed the generational and communicational gaps which exist between them, are the means by which the novel probes certain themes: the nature of class society in post-civil war Spain as well as the role of popular memory and the value of historical consciousness. The terms in which these questions are explored are already subtly indicated by the various elements which frame the narrative text. First, there is the title of the novel itself which, as Marfany points out, has very clear historical associations for the Spanish reader: the river Jarama was the site of one of the major battles of the civil war, waged in February 1937 during Franco's push to encircle Madrid, but resulting in a military stalemate, with over 20,000 casualties approximately on each side.[35] Such associations are echoed in the conversations of the youngsters, who recall the dead bodies floating down the river and later refer to *Paracuellos del Jarama* as the scene of the worst of the fighting. Second, the waters of the river, already identified by their links with the dead of the civil war, are also alluded to in the aphorism taken from Leonardo da Vinci, which expresses the conventional heraclitan notion of the unstoppable course of time. This rhetorical commonplace establishes a direct link between the course of the river and the passage of time and suggests that like 'el agua que tocamos', the novel aims to capture a specific moment within the flow of historical time. That is, a moment in which both past and future are telescoped and which represents the invariable, unchanging nature of the present. This is further emphasized in the way the narrative is bounded by (the author's own edited version of extracts from) Casiano de Prado's factual description of the physical geography of the river Jarama. This gives an account of the river's sources in the Somosierra mountains to its outflow in the Tagus and beyond to the Atlantic ocean, passing through *Puente Viveros*, the verifiable geographical location which acts as the novel's setting. Such a framing device is obviously meant to underline the geographical specificity and reality of the setting; and by its factual nature, it also functions as a means of authorizing the veracity and authenticity of the intercalated fiction, its status as a 'trozo de vida'. At the same time, it gives the impression that the fictional text is but an insertion, a parenthesis, a concrete but fleeting moment in the interminable life-cycle and historical flow of the river. And this reinforces the implications of the da Vinci aphorism: the fiction, which is set in the present in a specific moment in human time, stands in a relation of fixity and stasis to the historical past, as if frozen by its effects and compulsively retreading the blood-stained waters of civil war. Like the river, the fictional slice of life is everywhere informed by the war and destined to repeat itself in an endless, senseless renewal of the same; its main purpose is thus to reveal the stagnant, calcified nature of Spanish society and the determinations responsible for this unchanging present.

El Jarama deals on the one hand with a group of working-class adolescents from Madrid who, on a scorching Sunday in August, flee the 'quema' of the capital to spend the day on the river; the latter has long been regarded by the urban day-tripper as a welcome retreat, an oasis of peace, leisure, and freedom. Consisting of five couples and Daniel, without a partner, the group is a mixture of different personalities and temperaments; yet, they are fairly homogeneous in background, being all members of the urban proletariat. No one character stands out above the rest and they are all convincingly portrayed as typical of their class and social grouping. They work in poorly paid, boring jobs (Sebas is a mechanic, Tito a shop assistant, Santos a factory hand, Lucita sells ice-cream, Daniel works for a cobbler, etc.); and they are all undermined by a sense of weariness, alienation, and emotional suffocation, which they attempt to escape on their Sunday outing. They are not wilfully lazy or apathetic; rather their 'abulia' is primarily a product of the working week: for example, Santos remarks, 'No hijo, no nací cansado; me cansé después. Me canso durante la semana, trajinando' (32); Sebas points out, 'Claro, vosotros vais a la piscina. Yo nunca tengo tiempo'(34), the reason: 'Cada día más trabajo, !qué asco! El dueño tan contento pero nosotros a partirnos en dos' (201); Lucita notes the insuperable tedium of her job: 'Allí estoy yo como un clavo a partir de las diez' (96). However hard they try, the youngsters are unable to leave behind the monotony and oppression of the working week, unable to escape its corrosive effects. Right from the start, their efforts to enjoy themselves are subverted by petty squabbles, rivalries, displays of selfishness, lack of solidarity, and an obsession with the time. Lacking a companion, Daniel is the first to surrender to despair and spends the day getting drunk. Mely, troublesome, trendy, and superficially liberated and independent, is bored almost before she reaches the river. It is Tito who encapsulates the absurdity and tragedy of the situation: 'Total, que hoy no levantamos cabeza. Vamos de una en otra peor . . . ¿Hemos venido a pasarlo bien o a regañar los unos con los otros? A mí me aburre. Es un latazo andar así a cada momento. Menudo plan' (77).

The youngsters show a certain degree of awareness regarding their humdrum lives; some contrast the tedium of village life with life in the city, yet fail to see that the city itself may be just as limiting, if not more so (89). They have also heard of the civil war; Tito seems to be quite knowledgeable, but only beacause an uncle of his was killed during the Jarama offensive: 'Lo supimos cenando. No se me olvida' (40). In Tito's case, indirect experience through family loss functions as an access route to the historical past. However, the youngsters who spend their Sunday bathing in such an historically dramatic setting do not feel part of that experience: 'Y nosotros que nos bañamos tan tranquilos. Como si nada; y a lo mejor donde te metes ha habido un cadáver' (40). The youngsters are thus basically ignorant of the war and its implications; their sense of detachment and isolation from the historical past is complemented by their lack of awareness of contemporary events, such as the Hispano-American military pacts of 1953, indicated by the new American air base at Torrejón (153). With few exceptions, the group regard politics, current affairs and the civil war as something external, peripheral, and basically unimportant; in particular, they see the civil war as having no bearing on their lives, no consequences for them; they make no connections between its results and their alienation. In short, they are unaware of the reasons for the limitations of their lives. Their Sunday outing is simply an ironic, even sarcastic repetition of the working week, their attempts to escape and forget their mediocrity but a continuation of their everyday sense of entrapment. Asked what he would most like, Fernando replies: 'No tener tanto trabajo. No renegarme los domingos, acordándome de toda la semana' (201).

Like the youngsters at the river, the members of the older generation who spend the day at Mauricio's inn represent a fairly typical cross-section of rural inhabitants. We find the self-employed, small businessman, like Mauricio, but mainly the working class, consisting of lorry drivers, shepherds, butchers, bricklayers, etc. and finally the unemployed, like Lucio, who do the occasional odd job. Their presence is complemented by that of Ocaña, the taxi driver, and his family who, like the youngsters, have fled the metropolis in search of peace in an idealized rural setting. At the inn, the older characters engage in conversations that are no less banal and clichéd than those of the youngsters, often on similar topics such as difficulties at work, the pleasures and dangers of drink, the contrast between city and countryside, male pride, etc. Also, like the youngsters, the older generation seem just as subdued, unable to forget their worries and enjoy themselves: 'Poca animación se ve hoy, para ser un domingo'(159), remarks Coca Coña, the cripple.

Within both groups, young and old, we see reflected the same hopes and aspirations, the same lack of horizons and outlets, the same limitations and alienation. And where the youngsters tend to react to their condition with resignation and indifference, the older generation seem gripped by a powerful fatalism. Among the older characters, there is one whose personal experience and attitude to life hint at the reasons which underlie this collective 'abulia'. This is Lucio, Mauricio's first customer, who opens the novel and spends the whole of the day seated in the same position. The wise old man of the novel, Lucio is characterized by his lethargy and inactivity; he has withdrawn to the sidelines of life, from which he looks on as an embittered, sceptical observer. The reasons for his apathy have historical roots: Lucio is a Republican ex-convict who, just after the civil war, was sentenced to a term of imprisonment in Ocaña concentration camp (359). His partner, with whom he ran a bakery, took advantage of his absence and disappeared with the money from the business (65). Lucio is thus a double victim of the civil war, of imprisonment and arising from that, of personal treachery; his 'abulia' is that of the member of the losing side. He is perfectly aware of the reasons for his present condition since he experienced them at first hand. By contrast, the youngsters are ignorant of the historical forces that have conditioned their lives and, lacking that personal experience, they assume that the civil war has not affected them. But, as Marfany points out, 's'equivoquen: són tan vençuts com Lucio'.

With the accidental drowning of Lucita, the youngsters lose their innocence and are given an abrupt acccess to experience. Their direct, first-hand involvement in this tragic and senseless death and its immediate aftermath is an experience in the present analogous to the historical experience of the older generation, specifically their involvement in the war. It arguably forms the beginning of a 'toma de conciencia' which will overcome their ignorance of the past and, with that knowledge, help them make connections with their own situation in the present. Lucita's death generates a range of reactions from different characters, reactions one would expect to emerge from such an event. Here, I disagree with Sanz Villanueva who argues that the event itself is a concession to melodrama and the tone of the scene over-emotional.[36] The initial reactions of the bystanders and the youngsters are those of shock, anger, guilt, grief, despair, etc. and in the circumstances hardly untypical, but quite credible and understandable. Tito, for example, is totally distraught: 'En toda mi puta vida no me vuelvo a bañar en este río. Lo tengo aborrecido para siempre'(288); Sebas, whose idea it was to have a final swim, obviously feels guilty: 'Te digo que dan ganas de pegarse uno mismo con una piedra en la cabeza, te lo juro'(315); Paulina breaks down in flood of tears while Mely swears at the unperturbed Civil Guard and has her name taken. Exactly as one would expect, the youngsters' reactions are heated, anguished, emotional; and they contrast significantly with the cold indifference of 'la Autoridad': 'Demasiado a rajatabla quieren llevarlo. También hay que darse cuenta de que la gente no es de piedra como ellos pretenden'(315), remarks Sebas.

Among the older generation, Faustina puts the accident down to the irresponsibility of the youngsters themselves (318); Mauricio's customers wonder whether more sympathy should be given to the parents rather than the victim (317–18); Amalio's metaphorical view of the river devouring innocent sheep (and by implication innocent people) suggests that Lucita may have been a sacrificial victim, her drowning being the penalty for the lack of moderation of city folk. Amalio's fanciful picture is not to the liking of the barber: 'Usted nos hace pasar buenos ratos, Amalio. . .con todas esas cosas que nos pintas del río, pero hoy les está costando muchas lágrimas a algunas personas'(323). In other words, for the shepherd to wax lyrical in the face of real human tragedy is, for the barber, both inappropriate and irresponsible. Indeed, because of his sensitivity, the barber is so deeply affected that, at the mention of Mauricio's lentils, he vomits, to which Lucio remarks: 'Se te ponen enfermos en cuanto que ocurre un suceso. Aunque los pille al margen, eso no quita' (362). Lucio's observation seems to confirm that the accident is viewed, at least by some of Mauricio's customers, as an accident, a 'suceso', a 'fait divers'; yet this does not lessen its impact even on those who have not directly experienced the tragedy.

If the barber's reaction constitutes one end point of a spectrum of responses, that of officialdom, in the shape of the judge and his secretary, occupies the opposite extreme. The latter not only represent a different social class from that of the rest of the novel's characters but also a remoteness, indifference, and scorn symptomatic of the the winning side in the postwar period. Perhaps it is ironic that of all the characters in the novel, the judge is the only one who seems to be enjoying himself on this *día de fiesta*, attending a function at the *Casino de Alcalá*. Yet, even his pleasure is interrupted by the demands of professional duty, to which a colleague interjects with lofty disdain: 'Encuentro de muy mal gusto el ahogarse a estas horas y además en domingo' (326). At the river, the judge's detached concern with the formalities of the cause of death and the secretary's transcription of proceedings in a stilted, latinate, legalistic jargon (magnificently reproduced by the author), clearly indicate the manner in which the accident is dehumanized and incorporated into the indifferent, neutral discourse of officialdom. The human dimension of Lucita's death is erased and she quickly becomes just one more case of drowning, claimed by the river: 'Con éste – dijo eljuez – ya van a hacer el número de nueve los cadáveres de ahogados que le levanto del Jarama' (330); as the shepherd says, not a year passes without the river being responsible for taking a life, for death by drowning is 'Una desgracia que es ya vieja y notoria; casi una costumbre' (324). And as Lucio puts it, Lucita is a victim, not of malign fate, but of chance, 'Lo mismo que un sorteo' (324). Lucita is simply one more casualty of an alienated existence; but, her demise may be no less tragic than the sense of living death routinely endured by her friends. She thus exemplifies the condition of the postwar generation of working-class Spain, just as her namesake Lucio seems to represent that of the generation which lost the war. Yet, her death may not be altogether meaningless since it does open possibilities among her group for a new awareness; after the accident, and as we would expect, their conversations are more cautious, thoughtful, reflective; the effect of the accident is likely to raise questions concerning why she died and what she was trying to escape from. In this way, it performs a function analogous to that of past experience for the older generation; of course, whether an awareness of one's condition is a prerequisite to changing that condition or, as emerges in Lucio's case, a reinforcement of fatalism is a question which the novel leaves unanswered and in the lap of the reader.

El Jarama certainly presents a gloomy pessimistic picture of the alienation of working-class Spain, but as the novel's ending suggests, the situation is not totally hopeless. Paradoxically, it is the sceptical outsider Lucio who reveals that he has the chance of a part-time job with a baker. His main fear, however, is his age, and that he might be passed over for a younger person. Ironically, this is the first time in the novel that Lucio seems to doubt the value of his experience. Hence, his customary cautious attitude: 'Veremos a ver si no se queda todo en agua de borrajas. Adiós' (364). Yet, he also appears keen to return to the skills he once practised: 'Me agradaría, hombre. No sé los años que no meto estas manos – las enseñaba – entre la harina y la levadura' (364). Lucio opens and closes the novel. His unchanging position as *observer* throughout the day contrasts with what he has just revealed to Mauricio and perhaps invites us to see a symbolic pointer in the ending. That is, in going for the job, Lucio, the dejected loser, is now prepared to raise his head again, to overcome his resignation and return, however indirectly, to his profession. In short, to act. Of course, it is only a tentative beginning, since the job is still uncertain, but in relation to his usual scepticism, it is a significant step. The novel ends with Lucio's interminable urination, which has been variously interpreted as a gesture of disgust and despair and even a symbol of futility.[37] Given that Lucio has apparently spent sixteen hours in the same position, and (as far as we know, incredible though it might seem) has been drinking without relieving himself once, his prodigious discharge seems perfectly in line with the demands of verisimilitude and need not be assigned any ulterior significance. To do so would be to indulge in the very sort of interpretive games that led the critics to assign a symbolic significance to Lucita's death. Yet, the temptation is difficult to resist. In the light of Lucio's chance of a job, and while acknowledging his customary scepticism, his urination could be seen, not as a sign of despair, but as one of vague hope. It suggests a symbolic release from stasis and confinement, from a life rooted in the same position (just like his usual seat in Mauricio's inn); the passing of water is not a repression, but a satisfaction, an overcoming of limitations and controls and this pleasurable projection coincides with Lucio's possible re-entry into the world of work, his possible rehabilitation from the stigmas and determinations of the civil war. So that if Lucita dies because of drinking, Lucio is symbolically restored by it; and in a sense, the youngster's death is the sacrifice that allows the older generation to rediscover life. Such an interpretation is admittedly fanciful, though no less so than some of the other readings available. But, above all, it is unsatisfactory because it attempts to make of a trivial event something far more significant and profound than it actually is: a natural bodily function and a welcome relief after a day spent drinking.

As noted earlier, *El Jarama* has given rise to all sorts of readings. However, the decision to write such a novel as *El Jarama* in Spain, in 1954, and in the literary and intellectual circles in which the author moved, was no accident, but deliberate and ideologically motivated. Indeed, if we see the novel in relation to its own time and making, Castellet's theories, neo-realism and film technique, the publishing/writing context and the role of literary prizes, *Revista Española*, the author's own writing background and his admiration for *Los bravos*, then it is difficult not to conclude that it constitutes an unmistakable *tranche de vie*, a testimony of voiceless, working-class Spain, whose alienation and lack of horizons it implicitly condemns. The point of writing such a work, of course, was to intervene in the ongoing contest of ideas and ideologies in Spain by having a documentary fiction act on the consciousness of the reader and indirectly, eventually, on reality itself, though this could not be preordained. Let us recall that part of the reason Sánchez Ferlosio was so impressed with *Los bravos* was that it constituted 'una nueva manera de narrar', designed to enter 'como una cuña en otras vidas y actuar en ellas', as he put it.[38] *El Jarama* represents a more developed, structurally far tighter and more coherent form of that same mode of presentation. As Goytisolo stated, Sánchez Ferlosio's novel offers us 'una visión de la realidad, abandonándonos al cuidado de tomar – o no tomar – partido frente a ella'.[39] In other words, in the face of such a vision or version of reality, the reader could not remain aloof, he had to take a stand one way or the other. In this sense, *El Jarama* emerges as an exemplary *novela social*, fulfilling the theoretical requirements laid down by Castellet and before him by Sartre. It offered the reader a picture of reality which, because of its mode of presentation, respected his freedom yet at the same time encouraged him to take – or not take – responsibility for that fiction and its equivalent in the real world. Gaining an awareness of the iniquities present in social reality by means of a fiction, the reader might be better disposed to their critique, modification or abolition in the real world.

CONCLUSION

In this study, I have attempted to deal with the *novela social* in terms of the notions of movement and process, analysing the phenomenon as a dynamic development, subject to internal and external determinations, which exist in a mobile, changing interrelationship. In particular, I have tried to identify this process by examining its beginnings and by tracing those specific conditions, publishing platforms, theoretical inputs, groups of writers, etc. that set it in motion and that gave rise to the various writing strands out of which it emerged. In other words, I have been concerned with the historical reconstruction of those elements that restore to the *novela social* a sense of its materiality and that present it as a process rather than a simple linear evolution, informed by a teleological model of coherence. This has meant abandoning the dominant view of the subject based on a progressive recovery of realism and proposing the idea that, in literary and cultural terms, the movement begins in quite varied and disparate ways.

By way of illustration, let us reconsider the previous chapter, which shows the development of the *novela social* as the unfolding of a general process. As already mentioned, given the nature of their work, it is surprising that the early Goytisolo is almost always included in the *novela social*, whilst Aldecoa is left out or placed at the margins. However, both writers have clear points of contact, as well as difference, with the initial development of the movement, not only in terms of personal friendships, but in the nature of their writing. In Goytisolo's case, in his first two novels, there is an attempt, though unsuccessful, to produce a form of committed literature. This is done, not according to the canons of objective realism and film theory, but by exploiting and re-working available literary models, specifically Sartre's *Les Mains sales*. Also, commitment seems to be conceived in basically reactive, visceral terms in the first novel and in abstract, ethical terms in the other; ultimately, Goytisolo's commitment responds to a personal crisis, expressed through the rejection of family and class background. With Aldecoa, a different situation obtains. We find a more mature understanding of social reality, a recognition of the impact of historical and social conditioning on character behaviour, the use of the *situation limite* and an attempt to present a realistic picture of marginal Spain. Yet, at the same time, Aldecoa's highly structured novelistic plots and his abiding concern with stylistic detail and literary symbolism distance him somewhat from the authorless objectivism, seen as a basic requirement of the *novela social*. As the evolution of both writers shows, this situation changes significantly. With Goytisolo, the abstract moralizing of the first two novels gives way to a more socially-aware critique; the problem of revolt, previously conceived in generational terms, is now inflected through the framework of class politics, informed by Marxism, resulting in a shift of writing style. Thus, in the trilogy *El mañana efímero* and in the later travelogues, we see a gradual abandonment of the earlier generational obsessions and 'bookishness' and a shift towards more detached, objective modes of presentation. This is complemented by a change of focus of subject matter towards the *dolce vita* of the bourgeoisie; the latter responds to debates within the movement over the danger for the bourgeois writer of identifying too abusively and voluntaristically with the working classes. Hence, the adoption of a subject matter and a social reality within the area of the writer's own direct experience, as seen in *La isla* (1960) and *Fin de fiesta* (1962). Goytisolo's writing career up to the early 1960s, then, offers a vivid illustration of the various changes and shifts of emphasis in the historical development of the movement. In a sense, Goytisolo catches up with the idea that commitment in the novel is linked to the adoption of a testimonial, objectivist aesthetic. And it is no accident that his own transition towards the latter takes place in the wake of the success of *El*

Jarama, the exemplary, initial point of reference for a new proletarian realism. The notion of process can be appreciated from a slightly different angle in that, while Goytisolo eventually catches up and begins to respond to changes in the movement, Ana María Matute hardly evolves beyond Goytisolo's own early period. Indeed, in 1960, with *Primera Memoria*, she is still writing the same kind of novel as Goytisolo had written with *Duelo en el Paraíso*; this inability to adapt to change perhaps explains why she remained on the margins of the *novela social*.

In the case of Aldecoa, his affiliation to the movement in terms of writing style also indicates the sorts of shift we find in Goytisolo. Having originally embarked on writing a trilogy about the Civil Guards, gypsies and bullfighters, he fails to complete it and goes on to write *Gran Sol*. Like Goytisolo, he seems to respond to the example of *El Jarama* and his third novel, in terms of organization and modes of narration, is far more consistent with the testimonial realism found in Sánchez Ferlosio. Of course, as we have seen, Aldecoa had strong reservations over the use of literature for explicitly political ends:

> Toda la literatura es social, pero hay una literatura social con marcado carácter político-partidista. . . . es la que yo creo debe huir el escritor independiente y generoso, porque esta fácil limitación presupondría mezquindad. El novelista es testigo de excepción. No puede falsificar sus declaraciones a favor del acusado ni en contra'.[1]

Here, while basically faithful to those early Sartrian recommendations on aesthetic distance, Aldecoa finds himself increasingly out of line with the way the movement is developing in the late 1950s and early 1960s. As noted earlier, changes in the strategies of the real political opposition, which filtered into the ranks of their intellectual allies, were translated into the *novela social* in terms of a more combative, politically explicit social realism, which Aldecoa's defence of the *novelista testigo* failed to satisfy. The same could be said, no doubt, of *El Jarama*, the style and purpose of which more or less fulfilled to the letter what theorists such as Castellet were initially advocating for a new committed literature, but whose lack of explicit social critique was out of step with the later evolution of the movement. In the case of both Goytisolo and Aldecoa, I have tried to reiterate the point that the internal development of the *novela social* is irregular, uneven, dynamic, and contradictory; in short, on the move, to the point where, at the end of the 1950s, the narrative technique and proletarian subject matter of *El Jarama* are re-inflected and partly overlaid by a shift of attention to the bourgeoisie. Also, the lack of overt social critique in the early novels is replaced by a more obvious reference to the economic and political reasons for poverty, injustice, and class divisions. So, when we look at such novels as *Nuevas Amistades* (1959) and *Tormenta de Verano* (1961) by Juan García Hortelano, *La piqueta* (1959) by Antonio Ferres, *La mina* (1960) by Armando López Salinas, or *Dos días de septiembre* (1962) by José María Caballero Bonald, which take many of their organizational and technical cues from *El Jarama*, what is striking and perhaps paradoxical is that Sánchez Ferlosio is far closer than the later works to the theory of literary commitment as initially enunciated. This is obviously because the whole notion of commitment is not static, but like the novel, subject to development and change.

In this connection, during the course of this study, as well as internally, I have tried to show the importance of external criteria, as seen principally in chapter 4. Here again, I have emphasized that the influences which informed the beginnings of the *novela social* cannot simply be regarded in terms of given, static, borrowings of ideas or techniques, but as ideological and technical stimuli, adapted to suit specific demands and conditions. I have also tried to indicate that single influences cannot be considered separately but in conjunction and interaction with other such resources. And here, the important factor is the coincidence at a certain moment in time of three such stimuli, complementing and reinforcing each other, but pulled together in the end by the requirements of their receivers. An indication of this interaction can be found in *Los bravos*, which on the one hand marks the entry into postwar Spanish novel writing of Italian neo-realism, i.e. its objectivism, lower-class focus and anti-fascism. In particular, the novel is something of a pioneer in bringing the techniques of film-editing to bear on narrative structure. On the other hand, woven into the intrigue of the novel's plot are elements that seem to relate to Sartrian *engagement*, as seen in the various tests and choices the doctor is obliged to face and overcome. Indeed, *Los bravos* dramatizes the desire as well as the difficulties for the middle-class professional of establishing a solidarity and a *modus vivendi* with a suspicious, hostile, lower-class community. In his review of the novel, Sánchez Ferlosio captured its cinematic foundation and Sartrian roots: 'Es una nueva manera de narrar que implica una posición frente a la vida y que consiste en transmitir los hechos banales de tal manera que sean capaces de introducirse como una cuña en el ánimo del lector.'[2] In other words, like his own novel, *Los bravos* encouraged the reader to take a stand, 'una posición frente a la vida'; and the organization of its narrative was a deliberate strategy to help the reader achieve a 'toma de conciencia'. Moreover, when Sánchez Ferlosio wrote of *Los bravos* that it marked 'una nueva manera de narrar', he was referring to an aim common to the whole of the *novela social*, however differently inflected: the use of literature to transform reader consciousness and to act, however indirectly, on social reality in order to change it.

By the early 1960s, the above notion of literature as an instrument of social and political transformation entered a crisis. This was partly the result of changes taking place in the working-class movements, in relation to which the main opposition party, the Communist Party, was severely out of step, having miscalculated the revolutionary potential and preparedness of Spain's working classes.[3] At the same time, Spain was transforming itself into a modern, industrialized society in the 1960s; changes were taking place, particularly in the economic nature of working-class demands, which went far beyond the ability of the opposition parties and their allies to respond adequately. For the radical writer of the late 1950s and early 1960s, economic and social reality was in a process of change to which his novel writing bore little or no relation; the *novela social* was unable to capture these changes in writing, quite apart from influencing their progress. Thus, the figure of the revolutionary writer and intellectual was rapidly being made redundant by the very reality he had set out to transform. At the same time, in the early 1960s, publishing houses such as Barral Editores, which had been influential in promoting the *novela social* began to discover the commercial potential of the South American novel, beginning with Vargas Llosa's *La ciudad y los perros* (1962). This opened the way for what has become known as the 1960s 'boom' in Latin American fiction. Though stylistically much different, the latter broadly coincided with the testimonial and critical aims of the *novela social*. But, it also gradually captured the sort of market and readership hitherto held by the *novela social* and thus significantly dented its commercial viability.

The demise of the *novela social* is usually seen as coinciding with the publication of *Tiempo de silencio* (1962) by Luis Martín Santos. However, the real defection seems to begin slightly later and in relation to a growing critical disillusionment with the repetitiveness and artistic mediocrity of the *novela social*, voiced even by the guru of the movement himself: 'La novelística española tiene un tono relativamente gris, tiende hacia un naturalismo inconfesable y no alcanza el carácter de "modernidad" que pudiera conseguirle una firme personalidad y una cierta originalidad dentro de la novelística mundial.'[4] This statement appeared in a questionnaire published in *Insula* in December 1963. Curiously, two months earlier, Castellet had delivered a paper at a conference in Madrid organised by the *Club de Amigos de la UNESCO*; his paper was the only one out of a total of five presented which defended a politically committed realism in the novel.[5] Though still prepared to support the movement in public, Castellet's negative response to *Insula* is an indication of private doubts and dissatisfactions with the *novela social*, which would rapidly lead to the abandonment of the whole enterprise. However, explicit declarations to this effect from members of the movement take a little time to emerge. For example, it is only in 1968 and in a journal published abroad that Castellet is prepared to say the following:

Este tipo de literatura testimonial ha desviado la atención de los escritores de su finalidad estricta; se han conformado con hacer un cierto tipo de naturalismo documental que poco tiene que ver con la novela.

No hacen más que un maniqueísmo intelectual . . . que invade la literatura española durante estos años, despojándola de uno de los requisitos elementales de la buena literatura: la presentación del mundo como entresijo de contradicciones.[6]

What is perhaps more significant is that the actual writing of the *novela social* after 1963 came to a virtual standstill and writers such as López Salinas, López Pacheco, Goytisolo, Caballero Bonald, etc. entered a period of silence and reassessment; indeed, García Hortelano abandoned the novel for virtually a decade. This recalls the curious and inexplicable silences of writers such as Sánchez

Ferlosio and to a lesser extent Fernández Santos. Did their silences in the 1950s already indicate a fundamental doubt concerning the ability of literature to modify or transform social reality through the consciousness of the reader?

This is perhaps an appropriate point at which briefly to review the value and impact of *Tiempo de silencio* (1962) by Luis Martín Santos. Supposedly the gravedigger of the *novela social*, *Tiempo de silencio* was a novel that largely went unnoticed at the time of publication and whose impact, for critics such as Alfonso Sastre, has been wildly exaggerated.[7] In fact, it could be argued that the novel became noticed only after the *novela social* had begun to break up and was used to confirm and perhaps even hasten the demise of the trend. Paradoxically, while the critics rush to portray the novel as making the crucial break with the *novela social*, what tends to be forgotten is that *Tiempo de silencio* came not to bury the movement but to enrich and invigorate it, both stylistically and in terms of critical outlook. As the blurb on the dust-jacket of the novel points out: 'Lo más significativo del libro, no obstante, es su decidido y revolucionario empeño por alcanzar una renovación estilística a partir – y no en contra – del monocorde realismo de la novela española actual.'[8]

It attempted to do so by challenging the movement's adherence to a narrative objectivism and an anti-aestheticism which were responsible for an oversimplified, mechanically Marxist view of reality. By contrast, Martín Santos proposed the notion of a *realismo dialéctico*, a more flexible, nuanced narrative strategy, better suited to capturing the complexities and contradictions of social reality and thus, in a sense, more objective and more authentically Marxist. In short, what *Tiempo de silencio* announced and implicitly recommended was the abandonment of the objectivist, document-ary aesthetic of the *novela social*, but the retention of its critical outlook, suitably renovated in theoretical and political terms and at the same time made aesthetically more adequate to the task. However, if *Tiempo de silencio* initially set out to renovate rather than oppose the movement, it began a process which, by the end of the decade, would see the total liquidation and abandonment of the *novela social*. Indeed, if during the 1950s and early 1960s, objective narration was regarded as synonymous with literary *engagement*, it could be argued that the rejection of such a testimonial, documentary realism implied a desertion of that mode of *engagement*, if not a disavowal of the belief in the revolutionary possibilities of the literary text.

Renouncing such features as the collective protagonist, time-space compression, simultaneity of episodes, stress on mimesis through character dialogue and narrative detachment, simple division between the exploiters and the exploited, which had defined the *novela social*, *Tiempo de silencio* constituted a shift to almost the opposite extreme. It was characterized by the return of an omniscient, intrusive, foregrounded narrator and a focus on the inner mental and emotional states of the individual protagonist, Pedro. It also marked an aggressive, self-confident recovery of the basic features of the modernist novel, being clearly indebted to Joyce. Out went the objective mode of narration and in came a literary language, no longer functional and denotative, but highly sophisticated, crammed full of arcane cultural references, ironic asides, and jokes accessible only to the informed, learned reader. Indeed, such was its degree of linguistic and cultural virtuosity that *Tiempo de silencio* implicitly opposed the populist pretensions of the *novela social* by restricting access to a special kind of reader: a man of letters, not unlike Martín Santos himself or one of his colleagues on the Spanish intellectual left. Thus, in its unashamed aesthetic-ism and linguistic excess, *Tiempo de silencio* marked the return of a conception of literature which the practitioners of the *novela social* had rejected as culturally elitist and politically unsound. It was a novel written by an intellectual, about intellectuals and intended to be read by intellectuals; in short, a novel which in some ways was rather more honest than the *novela social* about its bourgeois reading constituency and had no qualms about making concessions to a wider readership. Yet, it would be unfair to see the novel as nothing more than an exercise in self-indulgent word-play. Its language, though only accessible to the *cognoscenti*, was conceived as a means of ridiculing and subverting not only the conventions of official rhetoric, but also the very sociolect and in group ties of Madrid's bourgeois intellectual left, its so-called 'progresía'. Through various modes of irony, parody, and *reductio ad absurdum*, Martín Santos managed savagely to mock the regime's bureau-cracy, taunt the censors and deride those left intellectual circles of which he himself formed a part.

Through the *ingenu* figure of Pedro, the young cancer researcher, Martín Santos presents a picture of the intellectual as effete, useless, and ultimately irrelevant. Generous, kind-hearted, full of good intentions, Pedro is portrayed as a totally ridiculous, superfluous character, as much an embarrassment in the salons of the bourgeoisie as in the *chabolas* of the sub-proletariat, by whom he is mercilessly used and exploited.

The author satirizes his protagonist for trying to find among the poor and destitute a confirmation of his own progressive ideas; his desire to commit himself to helping the disadvantaged turns out, in the end, to be totally counterproductive, as is shown by the abortion incident, as a result of which Florita dies. Pedro is thus as much a victim of his own well-intentioned voluntarism as he is of the cruelty and double-dealing of others; indeed, his altruism is seen as positively dangerous since it supports an image of the working class to which they, in their behaviour, refuse to conform and consistently negate. In short, *Tiempo de silencio* is a novel of lost illusions or, more precisely, of the danger of harbouring illusions about commitment; it unsparingly attacks the intellectual's idealization of the working class; it also seems to negate the idea of a committed literature and suggests that revolution is more than anything a sublimation of the guilt, frustrations and *mala conciencia* of a privileged, intellectual elite.

Tiempo de silencio represented a first major step in the Spanish postwar novel's recovery of aesthetic autonomy. It also became a new and powerful point of reference for subsequent writings, initiating a fashion that would last well into the following decade. In specific terms, the novel made a particular impact on the evolution of such writers as Fernández Santos, whose *Laberintos* (1964) shows many points of contact with *Tiempo de silencio* in thematic, technical, and linguistic terms. *Ultimas tardes con Teresa* (1965) by Juan Marsé is another novel clearly influenced by Martín Santos, especially in its cruel satire of the progressive middle classes. But perhaps the most obvious and symptomatic example of influence, and the one where the notion of the identity between language and social reality is coming under increasing strain, is Juan Goytisolo's *Señas de indentidad* (1966). By the late 1960s, the *novela social* was effectively dead; the movement which had supported it had fragmented and dissolved; its members pursued their individual careers and with few exceptions, lamented their attempts – now regarded as naive and futile – to construct a radical, transformative literature.[9] On a wider plane, the Spanish novel seemed to turn in on itself; it was no longer in the business of revealing the world or writing a story; it was now concerned with the story of a writing, self-absorbed and self-regarding. If the notion of critique survived at all, it was a critique, not of social reality, but of literature itself and at most its language. Commitment now meant something very different; the writer's commitment was no longer to the revelation of the world in order to change it, as Sartre had proposed; rather, it was to the revolution of the word, as Barthes had suggested, which would dominate the novel in the 1960s and 1970s. At best, the only thing that literature could realistically influence was its own evolution and not the world outside it. Reflecting in 1968 on the fortunes of the *novela social*, Carlos Barral noted sceptically: 'Se trataba de una poética de urgencia que se suponía a sí misma determinada por circunstancias pre-revolucionarias. El realismo social fue naturalismo depauperado . . . y uno no puede menos que alegrarse de lo de prisa que cambian las modas.'[10]

NOTES

INTRODUCTION

1 See Roland Barthes, *Le Degré zéro de l'écriture* (Paris: Seuil, 1953), trans. Annette Lavers and Colin Smith (Cape, London, 1967); also Roland Barthes, *Mythologies* (Paris: Seuil, 1957), trans. Annette Lavers (London: Cape, 1972).
2 Nathalie Sarraute, *L'Ère du soupçon* (Paris: Gallimard, 1956).
3 See Edward Said, *Beginnings: Intention and Method* (Baltimore and London: Johns Hopkins University Press, 1973).

CHAPTER 1   PROGRESS OR PROCESS?

1 The secondary bibliography on the postwar Spanish novel is remarkably abundant. The following are but a selective though reasonably representative sample: José María Martínez Cachero, *Novelistas españoles de hoy* (Oviedo, 1945); Federico Carlos Saínz de Robles, *La novela española en el siglo XX* (Madrid: Pegaso, 1957); Domingo Pérez Minik, *Novelistas españoles de los siglos XIX y XX* (Madrid: Guadarrama, 1957); Juan Luis Alborg, *Hora actual de la novela española* (2 vols, Madrid: Taurus, vol. I, 1958). Eugenio de Nora, *La novela española contemporánea (1927–1960)* (3 vols, Madrid: Gredos, 1962), there is a second expanded edition of vol. 3, covering the period 1939–67, published in 1970 to which I shall refer henceforth; Juan Carlos Curutchet, *Introducción a la novela española de postguerra* (Montevideo: Alfa, 1966); Manuel García Viñó, *Novela española actual* (Madrid: Guadarrama, 1967); José Corrales Egea, *La novela española actual (Ensayo de ordenación)* (Madrid: Cuadernos para el Diálogo, 1971); José Domingo, *La novela española del siglo XX. 2. De la postguerra a nuestros días* (Barcelona: Labor,

1973); Fernando Morán, *Novela y semidesarrollo. (Una interpretación de la novela hispanoamericana y española)* (Madrid: Taurus, 1971). Rafael Bosch, *La novela española del siglo XX, vol. II: De la República a la postguerra* (New York: Las Américas, 1971); Juan Luis Alborg, *Hora actual*, vol. 2 (1962); Antonio Iglesias Laguna, *Treinta años de novela española 1938–1968* (Madrid: Prensa Española, 1969); Juan Ignacio Ferreras, *Tendencias de la novela española actual 1931–1969* (Paris: Ediciones Hispanoamericanas, 1970); Santos Sanz Villanueva, *Tendencias de la novela española actual (1950–1970)* (Madrid: Cuadernos para el Diálogo, 1972); Ramón Buckley, *Problemas formales en la novela española contemporánea*, 2nd edn (Barcelona: Península, 1973); Gonzalo Sobejano, *Novela española de nuestro tiempo (En busca del pueblo perdido)* (Madrid: Prensa Española, 2nd edn, 1975); Ignacio Soldevila-Durante, *La novela desde 1936* (Madrid: Alhambra, 1980); Santos Sanz Villanueva, *Historia de la novela social española (1942–1975)* (2 vols, Madrid: Alhambra, 1980). See also, Hipólito Esteban Soler, 'Narradores españoles del medio siglo', in *Miscellánea di studi ispanici* (Universitá di Pisa, 1971–3), pp. 217–370; and Joan-Lluís Marfany, 'Notes sobre la novel. La espanyola de postguerra', *Els Marges*, no. 6 (1976), pp. 29–57. A useful indicator of the sheer volume of available material can be found in the commented bibliographical appendix contained in José María Martínez Cachero, *La novela española entre 1936 y 1980. Historia de una aventura*, 3rd edn (Madrid: Castalia, 1985).

2 Nora, *La novela española*, vol. 3, 2nd edn, pp. 66–7.

3 Pablo Gil Casado, *La novela social española (1942–1968)* (Barcelona: Seix Barral, 1968), p. 2. There is also a 2nd edition, 1973; Corrales Egea, *La novela española*, p. 33; Sobejano, *Novela española*, p. 24.

4 Sanz Villanueva, *Historia*, vol. I, pp. 6 and 61.

5 See Nora, *La novela española*, vol. 2, ii, pp. 7–53.

6 Ibid., p. 12. See also, Corrales Egea, *La novela española*, pp. 26–32; and Sobejano, *Novela española*, pp. 30–9.

7 Sobejano, *Novela española*, pp. 24–5; Corrales Egea, *La novela española*, pp. 33 and 45; Buckley, *Problemas formales*, p. 9; Curutchet, *Introducción*, p. 55; Sanz Villanueva, *Historia*, vol. I, pp. 5 and 6.

8 Sanz Villanueva, *Historia*, vol. I, p. 5.

9 See Gil Casado, *La novela social*, pp. viii and xvi; and Sobejano, *Novela española*, pp. 299–300.

10 Sanz Villanueva, *Historia*, vol. I, p. 10.

11 Edward Thompson, *The Poverty of Theory* (London: The Merlin Press, 1978), pp. 238–9.

12 Nora, *La novela española*, vol 2, i, pp. 281 and 282.

13 Nora, ibid., vol. 2, ii, p 12, vol. 2, i, p. 284.

14 Nora, ibid., vol. 2, ii, p. 48.

15 Ferreras, *Tendencias*, pp. 55 and 130; Domingo, *La novela española*, p. 144; Gil Casado, *La novela social*, pp. xxxvii and xxxviii, n. 32.

16 Gil Casado, *La novela social*, p. 10.

17 Juan Goytisolo, 'Para una literatura nacional popular', *Insula*, no. 146 (1958), pp. 6, 11; Guillermo de Torre, 'Los puntos sobre algunas íes

novelísticas (Réplica a Juan Goytisolo)', *Insula*, no. 159 (1959), pp. 1–2.

18 Torre, ibid., p. 1.

19 Sanz Villanueva, *Historia*, vol. I, p. 15.

20 Corrales Egea, *La novela española*, pp. 28–9;

21 José Ramón Marra-López, *Narrativa española fuera de España* (Madrid: Guadarrama, 1963). See also José Luis Cano, *Insula*, no. 194 (1963), pp. 8–9, who regarded Marra-López's book as having revealed 'un tesoro escondido, una literatura casi totalmente inexplorada por la crítica española'.

22 Sanz Villanueva, *Historia*, vol. I, pp. 44–5; see also Martínez Cachero, *La novela española*, 3rd edn, pp. 114–21; Soldevila-Durante, *La novela desde 1936*, pp. 120–3; also, Jerónimo Mallo, 'Caracterización y valor del tremendismo en la novela española contemporánea', *Hispania*, vol. XXXIX (1956), pp. 49–55; Juan Antonio Gómez Marín, 'Literatura y política. Del tremendismo a la nueva narrativa', *Cuadernos Hispanoamericanos*, vol. LXV, no. 193 (1966), pp. 109–16; Luis López Molina, 'El tremendismo en la literatura española actual', *Revista de Occidente*, no. 54 (1967), pp. 372–8; Julio Rodríguez Puértolas, *Literatura Fascista Española I/Historia*, (Madrid: Akal, 1986), pp. 499–504.

23 Buckley, for example, claims that these three novels represent 'una total renovación del género' and constitute 'el punto de arranque del neorrealismo o realismo social español', *Problemas formales*, pp. 9–10; see also Sobejano, *Novela española*, p. 118; Gil Casado, *La novela social española*, pp. 10 and 261; Martínez Cachero, *La novela española*, pp. 161–2; Sanz Villanueva, *Tendencias*, p. 57; Iglesias Laguna, *Treinta años*, pp. 228–9; Estéban Soler, 'Narradores españoles del medio siglo', p. 293; Corrales Egea excludes *La noria* from the 'giro decisivo' of the 1950s and argues that *Las últimas horas* played no major part in the 'nuevo realismo', *La novela española*, pp. 54–5; Gil Casado, although he includes all three novels in his initial classification (pp. 14–16), later regards *Las últimas horas* as being 'al margen de la novela de tipo social y testimonial', *La novela social española*, p. 260.

24 José María Castellet, *Notas sobre literatura española contemporánea* (Barcelona: Ediciones Laye, 1955), pp. 55–7.

25 See Buckley, *Problemas formales*, pp. 9–10.

26 Castellet, *Notas*, pp. 56–7.

27 Camilo José Cela, *La colmena*, 'Nota a la primera edición', 1st edn (Buenos Aires: Emecé, 1951), cited by Nora, *La novela española*, p. 76.

28 Camilo José Cela, 'Prólogo a Mrs Caldwell' and *Obras Completas*, vol. VII, p. 975, in Camilo José Cela, *La colmena*, Darío Villanueva (ed.), (Barcelona: Noguer, 1983), cited p. 33.

29 Darío Villanueva argues that *La colmena* qualifies as a social novel 'porque refleja – parcialmente por supuesto – el estado material y espiritual de la sociedad urbana en la España de los años 40', ibid., p. 40.

30 See Martínez Cachero, *La novela española*, 3rd edn, pp. 112–13.

31 Martínez Cachero, ibid., p. 113.

32 *Correo Literario*, 28 (1951), p. 9; also reviewed by Gonzalo Torrente Ballester in *Cuadernos Hispanoamericanos*, no. 22 (1951), pp. 96–102.

33 Castellet, *Notas*, p. 63.
34 Juan Goytisolo, *Problemas de la novela* (Barcelona: Seix Barral, 1959), p. 19.
35 José María Castellet, 'Iniciación a la obra narrativa de Camilo José Cela', *Revista Hispánica Moderna*, vol. XXXVIII, nos 2–4 (1962), pp. 107–50.
36 Castellet, ibid., p. 110.
37 For example, 'El figón de la Damiana', *La Hora*, no. 62 (1950); 'Chico de Madrid', *La Hora*, no.66 (1950); 'El libelista Benito', *La Hora*, no. 72 (1950); 'Los bisoñés de don Ramón', *Juventud*, no. 396 (1951).
38 As one of the few writers to be vaguely influenced by Cela, it is interesting that Aldecoa should regard him in just this way, i.e. not as a great novelist, but as 'un gran escritor y sobre todo un tipo literario', *La Estafeta Literaria*, 2a época, no. 51 (7 July 1956).
39 See Gil Casado, *La novela social española*, pp. ix–x.
40 Soldevila-Durante, *La novela española desde 1936*, p. 212.
41 See José-María Martínez Cachero, *Historia de la novela española entre 1936 y 1975*, 2nd edn (Madrid: Castalia, 1980), pp. 230–1, note 15.
42 Joan-Lluís Marfany, 'Notes sobre la novel. la espanyola de postguerra II', *Els Marges*, no. 11 (1977), pp. 3–29, see p. 12.
43 Juan García Hortelano, *Indice de Artes y Letras*, vol. XII, no. 128 (1959), p. 19; Armando López Salinas, cited in Francisco Olmos García, 'La novela y los novelistas españoles de hoy. Una encuesta', *Cuadernos Americanos*, vol. CXXIX (1963), p. 222.
44 See Gil Casado, *La novela social española*, pp. viii and xvi; and in the 2nd edn (1973), p. 19; Sobejano, *Novela española*, p. 299. It is not my intention to comment in detail on these definitions; this has already been done by Marfany, 'Notes sobre la novel. la espanyola de postguerra. II', pp. 13–14.
45 See the declarations by Caballero Bonald, Grosso, and Marsé in Olmos García, 'La novela y los novelistas españoles de hoy. Una encuesta', pp. 214, 217 and 218, cited in Gil Casado, *La novela social española*, p. xxi; see also Ferres and López Salinas, cited in Corrales Egea, *La novela española*, pp. 61 and 62.
46 Gil Casado, *La novela social española*, pp. ix and x; Andrés Amorós, 'Notas para el estudio de la novela española actual (1939–1968)', *Vida Hispánica*, vol. XVI (1968), pp. 7–13; Esteban Soler, 'Narradores españoles del medio siglo', pp. 269–338.
47 Sanz Villanueva, *Historia*, vol. I, pp. 10–11.
48 Juan Goytisolo, 'Literatura y eutanasia', in *El furgón de cola* (Ruedo Ibérico, Paris: 1967), pp. 51–2.
49 Marfany, 'Notes sobre la novel. la espanyola de postguerra. II', p. 19.
50 Juan Goytisolo, 'Literatura y eutanasia', p. 52.
51 Juan Carlos Curutchet, *Cuatro ensayos sobre la nueva novela española* (Montevideo: Editorial Alfa, 1973), p. 98.
52 Castellet, *Notas*, p. 90.
53 See Marfany, 'Notes sobre la novel. la espanyola de postguerra. III,' *Els Marges*, no. 12 (1978), pp 3–22, especially pp. 10–14.

CHAPTER 2   WRITING AND OPPOSITION

1 José María Castellet, 'La joven novela española', *Sur*, (September–October, 1963), pp. 48–54, cited p. 49.

2 Martínez Cachero, *La novela española*, 3rd edn, 1985, p. 174.

3 José María Castellet, 'La novela española quince años después (1942–1957)', *Cuadernos del Congreso por la Libertad de la Cultura*, no. 33 (November–December 1958), pp. 48–52, cited p. 51.

4 Ibid., p. 51.

5 Joan-Lluís Marfany, 'Notes sobre la novel. la espanyola de postguerra. II', *Els Marges*, no.11 (1977), pp. 3–29, cited p. 6.

6 Castellet, 'La novela española quince años después (1942–1957)', p. 51.

7 In reply to A. Carlos Isasi Angulo, 'La novelística de Juan Goytisolo (entrevista con el autor)', *Papeles de Son Armadans*, vol. LXXVI, no. 226 (1975), p. 69.

8 Marfany, 'Notes sobre la novel. la espanyola de postguerra. II', p. 7.

9 Martínez Cachero, *La novela española*, p. 177.

10 Elías Díaz, *Notas para una historia del pensamiento español actual (1939–1973)*, (Madrid: Cuadernos para el Diálogo, 1974), pp. 120–1.

11 See Sheelagh Ellwood, *Prietas las filas. Historia de la Falange Española, 1933–1983* (Barcelona: Crítica, 1984), particularly, chapter 3, pp. 113–54.

12 Díaz, *Notas para una historia*, p. 27.

13 Marfany, 'Notes sobre la novel. la espanyola de postguerra', p. 53.

14 Ibid., p. 54.

15 Martínez Cachero, *La novela española*, p. 178.

16 *Juventud*, no. 573 (4–10 December 1954), p. 8.

17 Cited in Manuel García Viñó, *Ignacio Aldecoa* (Madrid: Epesa, 1973), p. 53.

18 See Robin Fiddian, *Ignacio Aldecoa*, Twayne's World Authors Series, no. 529, (Boston: Twayne Publishers, 1979), pp. 25 and 29.

19 See Paul Preston, 'The anti-Francoist opposition: The long march to unity', in *Spain in Crisis: the Revolution and Decline of the Franco Regime* (Brighton: Harvester Press, 1976), pp. 125–56, particularly p. 143.

20 Gaspar Gómez de la Serna, *Ensayos sobre literatura social* (Madrid: Guadarrama, 1975), p. 89.

21 Fiddian, *Ignacio Aldecoa*, p. 29.

22 Cited in 'Ignacio Aldecoa, programa para largo', *Destino*, no. 956 (3 December, 1955), p. 37.

23 'Literatura social yanquí', *La Hora*, 2a época, no. 3 (19 November 1948), p. 12; and 'El mar y la literatura dramática', *La Hora*, no. 24 (15 May 1949), p. 11.

24 See 'Jesús Fernández Santos', *Destino*, no.492, (27 August 1955), p. 31.

25 David K. Herzberger, *Jesús Fernández Santos*, Twayne's World Authors Series, no. 687 (Boston: Twayne Publishers, 1983), p. 3.

26 See Edouard de Blaye, *Franco and the Politics of Spain* (Middlesex: Pelican Books, 1976), pp. 142–3.

27 Miguel Sánchez Mazas, 'La actual crisis española y las nuevas generaciones', *Cuadernos del Congreso por la Libertad de la Cultura*, no. 26 (September–October 1957), pp. 9–23, cited p. 21.

28 Rafael Sánchez Mazas, in *ABC*, (8 January 1956) p. 52, cited in Darío Villanueva, *El Jarama de Sánchez Ferlosio: Su estructura y significado*, (Santiago: Universidad de Santiago de Compostela, 1973), p. 37, note 72.

29 *Alcalá*, no.4 (10 March 1952), p. 3.

30 *Juventud*, no. 635 (12–18 January 1956), p. 8.

31 Alfonso Sastre, 'Poco más que anécdotas culturales alrededor de quince años (1950–65)', *Triunfo*, número extraordinario II, no. 507 (June 1972), pp. 81–5.

32 Alfonso Sastre, *La revolucíon y la crítica de la cultura* (Barcelona: Grijalbo, 1971), p. 15.

33 *La Hora*, no.8 (24 December 1948), p. 12.

34 *La Hora*, no. 46 (12 February 1950), p. 11.

35 *La Hora*, no. 64 (8 October 1950), p. 11.

36 In Sergio Vilar, *Protagonistas de la España democrática*, (Paris: Ruedo Ibérico, 1969), pp. 266–7.

37 Ibid., p. 296.

38 See *Guía de la literatura catalana contemporània* (Barcelona: Bruguera, 1970), p. 15.

39 Carlos Barral, *Años de penitencia*, (Madrid: Alianza, 1975), p. 206 and note 1.

40 In Vilar, *Protagonistas*, p. 298.

41 Ibid., p. 266.

42 *Juventud*, no. 573 (4–10 November 1950), p. 8.

43 Dionisio Ridruejo, *Escrito en España* (Buenos Aires: Losada, 1962), p. 78.

44 In Vilar, *Protagonistas*, p. 266.

45 Ridruejo, *Escrito en España*, p. 216.

46 See José María Maravall, *Dictatorship and Political Dissent. Workers and Students in Franco's Spain* (London: Tavistock Publications, 1978), chapter 6, pp. 118–43, especially p. 128.

47 Ridruejo, *Escrito en España*, p. 219.

48 Ibid., p. 225.

49 Salvador Giner, 'Power, freedom and social change in the Spanish university 1939–1975', in *Spain in Crisis*, pp. 183–211, cited p. 188.

50 Ridruejo, *Escrito en España*, pp. 217–18.

51 Maravall, *Dictatorship and Political Dissent*, p.126.

52 Barral, *Años de penitencia*, p. 17.

53 Ibid., p. 22.

54 In Vilar, *Protagonistas*, pp. 306–0.

55 Ibid., pp. 307–8.

56 Barral, *Años de penitencia*, p. 235.

57 Maravall, *Dictatorship and Political Dissent*, p. 137.

58 In Isasi Angulo, 'La novelística de Juan Goytisolo (Entrevista con el autor)', pp. 69–70.

59 See Vilar, *Protagonistas*, pp. 310–12, in conversation with José Agustín Goytisolo.

60 Ridruejo, *Escrito en España*, p. 222.

CHAPTER 3 A MOVEMENT IN THE MAKING

1 On *Laye*, see J.M. Castellet, 'Breu història de la revista "Laye"', *L'Avenç*, no. 6 (1977), pp. 46–7; Laureano Bonet, 'La revista "Laye" y la novela española de los años cincuenta', *Insula*, nos 396/397 (November–December 1979), p. 8 and also his *Gabriel Ferrater. Entre el arte y la literatura* (Publicacions i Edicions de l'Universitat de Barcelona, Barcelona: 1983); Carlos Barral, *Años de penitencia*, pp. 216–25 and his second autobiographical volume *Los años sin excusa. Memorias II* (Barcelona: Barral Editores, 1978), pp. 42–4; Barry Jordan, '"Laye": els intel.lectuals i el compromís', *Els Marges*, no. 17 (1979), pp. 3–26. On *Revista Española*, see Martínez Cachero, *La novela española*, 3rd edn, pp. 178–9; Esteban Soler, 'Narradores españoles', pp. 262–3; and Darío Villanueva, *El Jarama de Sánchez Ferlosio*, pp. 25–6. Henceforth, *Laye* will be referred to by the abbreviation *L*.

2 Barral, *Años de penitencia*, p. 225.

3 Ibid., p. 219.

4 Ibid., p. 222.

5 See, for example, José Montagut Roca, 'Sobre polinacionalismo. ¿Conduce el regionalismo al separatismo?', *L*, no. 12 (March–April 1951), centre pages; see also, *L*, nos 8–9 (October–November 1950), p. 1.

6 On Rilke, see *L* no. 21 (November–December 1952), pp. 22–30; Joan Ferrater, '"Stephen Hero" por James Joyce', *L*, no. 23 (April–June 1953), pp. 105–16, 'La terra eixorca', *L*, no. 21 (November–December 1952), pp.44–54, '"El carrer estret": novel.la', *L*, no.7 (September 1950), pp. 41–8, 'Introducción a "Les Elegies de Bierville" de Carles Riba', *L*, no. 23 (April–June 1953), pp. 47–56, '"Cant Espiritual" de Blai Bonet', ibid., pp. 117–19, '"Les hores retrobades" de Joan Vinyoli', *L*, no. 19 (May–July 1952), pp. 51–5.

7 M. Sacristán, 'Una lectura del "Alfanhuí" de Rafael Sánchez Ferlosio', *L*, no.24 (July–September 1953), pp. 11–31.

8 Carlos Barral, 'Poesía no es comunicación', *L*, no. 23 (April–June 1953), pp. 23–6.

9 *L* no. 2 (April 1950), p. 10.

10 Bonet, *Gabriel Ferrater*, p. 29.

11 *L*, no. 19 (May–July 1952), pp.5–10.

12 Juan Goytisolo, 'La piedad y el universo de Guido Piovene', *L*, no. 24 (July–September 1953), pp. 80–4.

13 *L*, no. 1 (March 1950), pp. 6–7; Jesús Ruiz, 'Intelectuales enrolados', ibid., p. 7; J.M. Castellet, 'Intelectual y político', *L*, no. 2 (April 1950), pp. 6–7; Jesús Nuñez, 'Campo de acción del político', ibid., p. 7; M. Sacristán, 'Antístenes y la policía política', *L*, no. 3 (May 1950), pp. 6–7 and 11.

14 Sacristán, 'Antístenes', p. 11.
15 J.M. Castellet, 'Técnicas de la literatura sin autor', *L*, no. 12 (March–April 1951), pp. 39–46, 'Notas sobre la situación actual del escritor en España', *L*, no. 20 (August–October 1952), pp. 10–17, 'El tiempo del lector', *L*, no. 23 (April–June 1953), pp. 39–45.
16 Castellet, 'Notas sobre la situación', p. 15.
17 Castellet, ibid., pp. 13–14.
18 Castellet, ibid., p. 14.
19 Castellet, 'El tiempo del lector', p. 42.
20 Bonet 'La revista "Laye"', p. 8.
21 Castellet, 'Breu història', p. 46.
22 *L*, no. 24 (July–September 1953), p.116.
23 Carlos Barral, *Los años sin excusa*, p. 42.
24 Barral, ibid., p. 43.
25 Alfonso Sastre, 'Poco más que anécdotas', p. 83.
26 Josefina Rodríguez, Prologue to Ignacio Aldecoa, *Cuentos*, (Madrid: Castalia, 1977), p. 19.
27 *Revista Española*, no. 6 (February 1955), end note. Henceforth, the review will be referred to by the abbreviation *RE*.
28 *RE* no. 2 (July-August 1953), pp. 142–7.
29 *RE*, no. 6 (February 1955), pp. 551–7. See also, Alexandro Pinheiro Torres, *O movimento neorealista en Portugal na sua primeira fase*, (Lisbon: Biblioteca Breve, 1977).
30 Carmen Martín Gaite, Prologue to her *Cuentos Completos*, (Madrid: Castalia, 1978), p.7.
31 Rafael Sánchez Ferlosio, 'Niño fuerte', *RE*, no. 1 (May–June 1953), pp. 39–48.
32 Darío Villanueva, '*El Jarama' de Sánchez Ferlosio*, p. 45.
33 *RE*, no. 4 (November–December 1953), pp. 400–5.
34 Ignacio Aldecoa, 'Hablando de "Escuadra hacia la muerte"', *RE* no. 1 (May–June 1953), p. 119; 'A ti no te enterramos', ibid., pp. 27–38; 'Muy de mañana', no. 3(September–October 1953), pp. 270–3.
35 Aldecoa, 'A ti', p. 36.
36 Jesús Fernández Santos, 'Cabeza Rapada', *RE*, no. 1 (May–June 1953), pp. 57–9;
37 Jesús Fernández Santos, 'Hombres', *RE*, no. 3 (September–October 1953), pp. 263–9.
38 Jesús Fernández Santos, 'El sargento', *RE*, no. 5 (January–February 1954), pp. 474–80.
39 Carmen Martín Gaite, 'Un día de libertad', *RE*, no. 2 (July–August 1953), pp. 148–59.
40 Ibid., p. 159.
41 Josefina Rodríguez, 'Voces Amigas', *RE*, no. 2 (July–August 1953), pp. 165–8.
42 Josefina Rodríguez, 'Transbordo en Sol', *RE*, no. 5 (January–February 1954), pp. 485–9.
43 Ibid., p. 489.

44 José María de Quinto, 'Noviembre en los huesos', *RE*, no.1 (May–June 1953), pp. 49–56.
45 José María de Quinto, 'Atardecer sin tabernas', *RE*, no. 3 (September–October 1953), pp. 274–80.
46 Ibid., p. 280.
47 José María de Quinto, 'Noche de agosto', *RE*, no. 6 (February 1955), pp. 558–69.
48 Sastre, 'Poco más que anécdotas', p. 83.
49 See Joan Ferrater, *Dinámica de la poesía*, (Barcelona: Seix Barral, Barcelona, 1982), p. 424.

CHAPTER 4   COMMITMENT, NEO-REALISM, AND PRACTICES

1 Jean-Paul Sartre, *¿Qué es la literatura?*, (Buenos Aires: Losada, 1950). In the summary of Sartre's ideas, I have referred to the original *Situations II. Qu'est-ce que la littérature?* (Paris: Gallimard, 1948, reprinted 1972). All textual references are to the 1972 edition.
2 See, for example, L. Dumont-Wilden, 'Un nuevo "ismo" francés: El existencialismo de Jean-Paul Sartre', *Insula*, no. 3, (15 March 1946), p. 5; Paulino Garagorri, 'Una novela existencialista de Jean-Paul Sartre', *Insula*, no. 14, (15 February 1947), p.2; Marcelo Saporta, 'Entrevistas: Jean-Paul Sartre', *Insula*, no.32 (15 August 1948), p. 3.
3 Constantino Lascaris Conmeno, reviewing Eugenio Frutos, *El humanismo y la moral de Jean-Paul Sartre* (Santander, 1949), in *La Hora*, 2a época, no. 40 (4 October 1949), p. 4.
4 Angel Zuñiga, 'Le Diable et le bon dieu', *Destino*, no. 727 (14 July 1951), p. 18.
5 Alfonso Sastre, 'El teatro existencialista de Jean-Paul Sartre', *La Hora*, 2a época, no. 17 (25 February 1949), p. 11; 'De Sastre a Sartre', *La Hora*, 2a época, no. 18 (4 February 1949), p. 11; 'El teatro existencialista de Jean-Paul Sartre', *La Hora*, 2a época, no. 19 (11 February 1949), p. 11, and subsequently in numbers 20 and 21, pp. 11 and 10 respectively.
6 José María Castellet, *Notas sobre literatura española contemporánea*, (Barcelona: Ediciones Laye, 1955); *La hora del lector* (Barcelona: Seix Barral, 1957).
7 Castellet, *Notas*, p. 31.
8 Ibid., p. 41.
9 Ibid., p. 38.
10 Ibid., pp. 76–7.
11 Ibid., p.68.
12 Ibid., pp. 88 and 90.
13 Castellet, *La hora*, p. 11.
14 Ibid., p. 16.
15 Ibid., p. 33.
16 Ibid., p. 36.
17 Ibid., p. 76.

18 Ibid., p. 83.
19 Ibid., p. 97.
20 Ibid., p. 98.
21 Ibid.,p. 103.
22 Juan Goytisolo, *Problemas de la novela* (Barcelona: Seix Barral, 1959).
23 Ibid., pp. 11–12, 24.
24 Ibid., p. 21.
25 Ibid.
26 Ibid., p. 22.
27 Ibid., p. 26.
28 Ibid.
29 Ibid., p. 39.
30 Ibid., p. 41.
31 The entry of film neo-realism in Spain brought with it the Italian novel, if only indirectly; Spanish writers and intellectuals were at least introduced to some of the major names such as Pavese, Pratolini, Vittorini, Levi, Silone, etc., even though their work was unavailable due to censorship. This would not prevent some of them being read in the original, but more likely in South American editions or in French translations. (In 1953, Enrique Sordo noted the circulation among young intellectuals of a novel by Silone in French translation, i.e. *Une poignée de mûres*, and claimed that the main Italian writers were being read in French.) As regards critical attention towards the Italian novel, it became noticeable only in the mid- and late 1950s, though interest in the Don Camilo series by Guareschi (banned in Spain) was evident earlier. See, for example, Carlo Bo, 'La novela italiana contemporánea', Suplemento, *Insula*, no. 110 (15 February 1955) and Enrique Sordo, 'El neorrealismo en la novela italiana', *Revista*, no. 190 (1–7 December 1958), p. 10. There are signs that the social novelists were vaguely acquainted with the Italian neo-realist novel, but apart from an early piece by Goytisolo on Guido Piovene in *Laye*, no. 24 (August 1953), pp. 80–4, most of the references are fairly late. See the declarations by: Sánchez Ferlosio in *Destino*, no. 962, (10 January 1956), p. 27; Luis Goytisolo in *Destino*, no. 1005 (10 November 1956), p. 40; Josefina Rodríguez in *La Estafeta Literaria*, no. 161 (15 February 1958), p. 5. See also Juan Goytisolo, *Problemas*, pp. 73–8.
32 See, for example, Giulio Cesare Castello, *Il cinema neorealistico italiano*, (Turin: Einaudi, 1962); Roy Armes, *Patterns of Realism: A study of Italian neo-realist cinema* (London: Tantivy Press, 1971); the now indispensable reader edited by David Overby, *Springtime in Italy: A reader on neo-realism* (London: Talisman Books, 1978); also relevant are the papers contained in 'Culture and ideology in postwar Italy', in *Twentieth-Century Studies*, no. 5 (September 1971), in particular the pieces by Tito Perlini, 'Left-wing culture in Italy since the last war', pp.1–15 and Guido Fink, 'Neo-realism revisited', pp. 70–83; see also *Screen*, vol. 14, no. 4 (Winter 1973–4), especially Mario Canella, 'Ideology and aesthetic hypotheses in the criticism of neo-realism', pp. 5–60. I have

also found useful Don Ranvaud (ed.), *Roberto Rossellini B.F.I. Dossier no. 8* (London: BFI, 1981) and the proceedings of a *Coloquio sobre neorrealismo*, (Valencia: Fernando Torres Editor, 1983), sponsored by the Fundació Municipal de Cine de València.

33 Roberto Rosselini, 'A few words about neo-realism', in Overby (ed.), *Springtime*, pp. 89–90.

34 Canella makes some useful points on this question: 'neo-realism took shape under fascism and therefore in a sense rose up against fascism, reflecting all the limitations of cultural opposition to the regime.... Anti-fascist inter-classism compounded the ambiguity of neo-realist anti-fascism or rather, deemed them "progressive" and "revolutionary" and anti-fascism, by mystifying and confusing the examination of its real terms, involved neo-realism in its own crisis'.... The alternatives offered by anti-fascism – unity of the forces for progress and peace, denunciation of poverty and social conditions and the appeal to "values" – were gradually absorbed by the system ... 'Ideology and aesthetic hypotheses in the criticism of neo-realism' (pp. 32–3 and p. 38).

35 Esteban Soler, 'Narradores españoles del medio siglo', p. 276. On the postwar Spanish cinema, see César Santos Fontenla, *Cine español en la encrucijada*, (Madrid: Ciencia Nueva, 1966); José Luis Guarner, *30 años de cine en España* (Barcelona: Kairós, 1971); Román Gubern, *Historia del cine*, 2 vols (Barcelona: Lumen 1971), especially vol. II, pp.213–27, and also his *Un cine para el cadalso: 40 años de censura cinematográfica en España* (Barcelona: Euros, 1976); Doménec Font, *Del azul al verde. El cine español durante el Franquismo* (Barcelona: Avance, 1976); Vicente Molina Foix, *New Cinema in Spain* (London: BFI, 1977).

36 García Seguí, 'El cine español y el neorrealismo', p. 57.

37 Juan Antonio Bardem, 'La crisis del cine americano', *La Hora*, no. 39 (27 November 1949), p. 10.

38 Ricardo Muñoz Suay, during the 'Mesa redonda', reprinted in *Coloquio*, p. 66.

39 Luis G. Berlanga, 'Cuatro pasos por el cine', *La Hora*, no. 33 (5 August 1949), p. 8.

40 Overby, *Springtime in Italy*, pp. 10–11.

41 See Guarner, *30 años de cine*, p. 56.

42 *Revista*, no.4 (8 May 1952), p. 12.

43 Bruno Molinari, 'Vittorio de Sica: otro fiel a sí mismo', *Indice*, no.25 (January 1950), pp. 1–2.

44 Eduardo Ducay, 'Cine italiano hoy', *Insula*, no. 72, (15 December 1951), p. 6.

45 Román Gubern, in *Nuestro Cine*, no. 64 (August 1967), cited by Guarner, *30 años de cine*, p. 56.

46 Angel del Campo, 'Semana del film italiano', *Revista*, no. 48, (12–18 March 1952), p. 14; Luis Gómez Tello, 'Cuidado con el neorrealismo de guardarropia', *Juventud*, no. 14 (6 May 1953), p. 12.

47 Guarner, *30 años de cine*, p. 67.

48 Eduardo Ducay, 'La obra de Zavattini (notas para una

NOTES

interpretación)', *Objetivo*, no. 1 (July 1953) pp. 9–19, cited p. 17.

49 See Ricardo Muñoz Suay, 'En la muerte de Pudovkin', *Objetivo*, no. 2 (January 1954), pp. 24–7, whose obituary for the Russian director is clearly informed by Aristarco's own 'Omaggio a Pudovkin', *Cinema Nuovo* (1 August 1953), cited by Muñoz Suay, p. 27.

50 *Objetivo*, no. 3, (May 1954), p. 3.

51 Ibid.

52 Bardem, in conversation with Antonio Castro, *Cine español en el banquillo* (Valencia: Fernando Torres Editor, 1974), p. 61.

53 Carlo Lizzani, 'El artista frente a la realidad', *Objetivo*, no. 5 (May 1955), pp. 9–14, cited p. 11.

54 Gubern, *Un cine para el cadalso*, pp. 80–4.

55 *Objetivo*, no.5 (May 1955), p. 5.

56 See Gubern, *Historia del cine*, vol. II, p. 216.

57 See José Antonio Bardem, 'Informe sobre la situación actual de nuestra cinematografía', *Objetivo*, no. 6 (June 1955), pp. 7–8, for a slightly expanded version of his address.

58 José María García Escudero, cited by Gubern in an as yet unpublished account of the *Conversaciones* sent to this author, p. 56.

59 See *Objetivo*, no. 4 (August, 1954), p. 2.

60 Guarner, *30 años de cine*, p. 56.

61 Sanz Villanueva, *Historia*, vol. I, p. 99.

62 Rafael Sánchez Ferlosio, 'Una primera novela: "Los bravos"', *Correo Literario*, 2a época, no. 6 (1954), cited by Darío Villanueva, *'El Jarama' de Sánchez Ferlosio*, p. 49.

63 Darío Villanueva, *'El Jarama' de Sánchez Ferlosio*, p. 50.

64 Javier Aguirre, interviewed by Antonio Castro, *Cine español*, p. 38.

65 See G.M. Reeves, 'French windows on modern American fiction', in *Proceedings of the Comparative Literature Symposium*, (Texas University: Texas Technical Press, 1972); Sergio Pacifici, *A Guide to Contemporary Italian Literature. From futurism to neo-realism* (New York: Sphere Books, 1962), especially pp. 162–8.

66 See, for example, Antonio Marichalar, 'William Faulkner', *Revista de Occidente*, vol. XLII (October–December 1933), pp. 78–86.

67 For this brief survey, I have consulted the following: Javier Lasso de la Vega, *Anuario Español e Hispanoamericano del Libro y de las Artes Gráficas*, (Madrid: Editorial Católica) for the period 1944–57; also *Madrid: Catálogo general de la literatura española 1931–1950* (Madrid, 1961); *Libros españoles* (Madrid) for the period 1953–7; *Libros en venta. Servicio informativo de Bowker* (New York, 1964); also of interest is Valeriano Bozal, 'La edición en España', *Cuadernos para el diálogo*, Extra (1969), XIV, pp. 85–93.

68 Antonio Vilanova, 'William Faulkner, Premio Nobel', *Destino*, no. 693, (18 November 1950), p. 11; Ricardo Gullón, 'La irrupción de la literatura americana', *Insula*, no.69 (15 September 1951), pp. 1 and 6; Francisco Ynduráin, 'La literatura norteamericana: notas de un lector', *Insula*, no. 83 (15 November 1952), p. 3.

69 Antonio Vilanova, 'La novela de William Faulkner', *Destino*, no. 694

(25 November 1950), p. 16.

70 Gullón, 'La irrupción de la literatura norteamericana', p. 1.

71 Ynduráin, 'La literatura norteamericana: notas de un lector', p. 3.

72 Ricardo Gullón, 'William Faulkner, Premio Nobel', no. 60 (15 December 1950), p. 3.

73 Antonio Vilanova, 'William Faulkner y la epopeya del sur', *Destino*, no. 698 (23 December 1950), p. 31.

74 Claude-Edmonde Magny, *L'Âge du roman américain* (Paris: Editions du Seuil, 1948).

75 Ibid., p. 57.

76 Ibid., p. 59.

77 Ibid., p. 60.

78 José María Castellet, 'Faulkner y el lector', *Revista*, no. 85 (26 November–2 December 1953), p. 10.

79 In his prologue to Frederick J. Hoffman, *La novela moderna en norteamérica 1900–1950*, (Barcelona: Seix Barral, 1955), p. 11.

80 Juan Goytisolo, 'Los límites de la novela', *Destino*, no. 1021 (2 March 1957), p. 27.

81 Juan Goytisolo, 'Novela francesa, novela americana', *Destino*, no. 1061 (7 December 1957), p. 35.

82 Carmen Martín Gaite, in her prologue to *Los bravos*, (Biblioteca Breve, Salvat, Madrid, 1971), p. 9.

83 'Encuentro con Antonio Ferres', p. 6; Juan Goytisolo, cited by Maurice Edgar Coindreau, in 'La joven literatura española', *Cuadernos del congreso por la Libertad de la Cultura*, no. 24 (May–June 1957), p. 40.

84 See Sánchez Ferlosio in *Destino*, no. 962 (10 January 1956), p. 28; and J.M. Castellet, 'La novela española, quince años después', *CCLC*, no. 33, (November–December 1958), p. 51.

85 Fiddian, *Ignacio Aldecoa*, p. 42.

86 See Ignacio Aldecoa, 'Arpa de hierba', *Cuadernos Hispanoamericanos*, no. 45 (September 1953), pp. 375–6; 'Requiem para una monja', *CH*, no. 47 (November 1953), pp. 237–8; 'Hemingway y sus mitos', *CH*, no. 50 (February 1954), pp. 268–9; 'Los novelistas jóvenes americanos', *CH*, no. 53 (May 1954), pp. 235–36.

87 Sobejano, *Novela española*, p. 349.

88 However, see Phyllis Zatlin Boring, 'Faulkner in Spain: the case of Elena Quiroga', *Comparative Literature Studies*, vol. XIV, no. 2 (June 1977), pp. 166–76.

89 *Insula*, no. 148 (15 March 1959), p. 4.

90 *Insula*, no. 146 (15 January 1959), p. 4.

91 See, for example, José María Espinas, 'El Primer Coloquio Internacional de novela de Formentor', *Destino*, no. 1139, (6 June 1959), pp. 13–15; J.M. Castellet, 'Coloquio internacional sobre novela en Formentor', *CCLC*, no. 38, (September–October, 1959), pp. 82–6.

92 See, for example, 'El momento actual de las letras americanas', *La Estafeta Literaria*, no. 114 (1 February 1958), p. 3 and, in the same review, no. 138 (19 July 1958), pp. 1–2 on Saroyan, and no. 141 (9 August 1958), p. 6 on Capote.

93 Goytisolo, *Problemas*, p. 66.

94 Ramón Nieto states: 'el *nouveau roman* veo que nos ha servido para conseguir una enorme depuración de estilo y de enfoque, pero no sucede lo mismo cuando se trata de asuntos, intenciones y actitudes, pues un Robbe-Grillet, vgr., soslaya "los males del mundo, los de Europa, los de Francia" y convierte sus novelas "en piruetas arquitectónicas, en malabarismos de circo, en equilibrios de mago mental: se cogen tres bolas de colores — el tiempo, el espacio, el objeto — se tiran al aire, varias veces, sin que ninguna caiga al suelo y se espera el aplauso', in 'Encuentro con Ramón Nieto', interviewed by Antonio Núñez, *Insula*, no. 221 (April 1965), p. 4.

CHAPTER 5   PATHS TAKEN AND NOT TAKEN

1 See, for example, Corrales Egea, *La novela española actual*, pp. 65–81; Nora, *La novela española contemporánea*, vol. III, 2nd edn, p. 246; Sobejano, *Novela española de nuestro tiempo*, p. 311; and Sanz Villaneuva, *Historia*, vol. I, pp. 10–11.

2 See Martínez Cachero, *La novela española entre 1936 y 1980*, p. 176; Gil Casado, *La novela social española*, p. xiii; Manuel García Viñó, *Ignacio Aldecoa* (Madrid: Epesa, 1972), pp. 18–22; Sanz Villanueva, *Historia*, vol. I, pp. 319–26; Corrales Egea, *La novela española actual*, p. 127; all these critics regard Aldecoa as marginal while Sobejano, op. cit., and Nora, op. cit., p. 302, locate his early work firmly within the 'nueva oleada'.

3 Juan Goytisolo, *Juegos de manos* (Barcelona: Destino, 1954). All subsequent references are to the 5th edition, 1975.

4 See Castellet's review in *Revista*, no. 157 (14–20 April 1955), p. 10; Antonio Vilanova, '"Juegos de manos" de Juan Goytisolo', *Destino*, no. 916 (26 February 1955), p. 10; and a review by M.A. in *Alcalá*, no. 70 (25 April 1955), p. 11; see also the opinions of Nora, *La novela española contemporánea*, vol. III, 2nd edn, p. 292; Sobejano, *Novela española de nuestro tiempo*, pp. 348–9; Martínez Cachero, *La novela española*, pp. 200–2; and Kessel Schwartz, *Juan Goytisolo*, Twayne's World Authors Series, no. 104 (Boston: Twayne Publishers, 1970), pp. 35–7. On Goytisolo, see the relevant sections in Gonzalo Navajas, *La novela de Juan Goytisolo* (Madrid: SGEL, 1979); and Héctor R. Romero, *La evolución literaria de Juan Goytisolo* (Florida: Ediciones Universal, 1979).

5 Jean-Paul Sartre, *Les Mains sales* (Paris: Gallimard, 1948). See W.D. Redfern's useful introduction to his edition of the play in the series Methuen's Twentieth-Century Texts (London: Methuen Educational, 1985), pp. 1–46; see also the reference to the Sartrian influence in José-Carlos Pérez, *La trayectoria novelística de Juan Goytisolo: El autor y sus obsesiones*, (Zaragoza: Ediciones Oroel, 1984), p. 27.

6 José María Castellet, *Revista*, no. 157, p. 10.

7 Interviewed by Emir Rodríguez Monegal, in *Mundo Nuevo*, no. 12 (June 1967), p. 45; see also the interview with A. Carlos Isasi Angulo, 'La

novelística de Juan Goytisolo (Entrevista con el autor)', in *Papeles de Son Armadans*, vol. LXXVI, no. 226 (1975), pp. 65–87.

8 Juan Goytisolo, *Duelo en el Paraíso* (Barcelona: Planeta, 1955). All references are to the Destinolibro edition of 1979.

9 Jo Labanyi, 'The ambiguous implications of the mythical references in Juan Goytisolo's "Duelo en el Paraíso"', *Modern Language Review*, vol. 80, part 4 (October 1985), pp. 845–57.

10 Labanyi, 'The ambiguous implications', p. 847.

11 Ibid, p. 851.

12 Marfany, 'Notes . . .II', p. 9.

13 Apart from the relevant sections in the panoramic works on the postwar novel, see the following essays and monographic studies on Aldecoa: Gaspar Gómez de la Serna, *Ensayos de literatura social* (Madrid: Guadarrama, 1971), pp. 65–240; Manuel García Viñó, *Ignacio Aldecoa*, op cit.; Pablo Borau, *El existencialismo en la novela de Ignacio Aldecoa* (Zaragoza: Talleres Gráficos, "La Editorial", 1974); Charles R. Carlisle, *Ecos del viento, silencios del mar. La novelística de Ignacio Aldecoa* (Madrid: Playor, 1976); Robin Fiddian, *Ignacio Aldecoa*, Twayne's World Authors Series, no. 529 (Boston: Twayne Publishers, 1979); José María Lasagabaster Medinabeitia, *La novela de Ignacio Aldecoa. De la mimesis al símbolo* (Madrid, SGEL, 1978); Drosoula Lytra, *Soledad y convivencia en la obra de Aldecoa* (Madrid: Fundación Universitaria Española, 1979); Ricardo Landeira and Carlos Mellizo (eds), *Ignacio Aldecoa. A collection of critical essays*, (Laramie: University of Wyoming Press, 1977); Drosoula Lytra, *Aproximación crítica a Ignacio Aldecoa*, (Madrid: Espasa Calpe, 1984); also relevant is José-Luis Martín Nogales, *Los cuentos de Ignacio Aldecoa* (Madrid: Ediciones Cátedra, 1984).

14 Ignacio Aldecoa, *El fulgor y la sangre* (Barcelona: Planeta, 1954). All references are to the Planeta edition of 1973.

15 Borau, *El existencialismo*, pp. 91–5; Lasagabaster Medinabeitia, *La novela de Ignacio Aldecoa*, pp. 162–8; Lytra, *Soledad y convivencia*, pp. 31–54; Fiddian, *Ignacio Aldecoa*, pp. 45–7; Carlisle, *Ecos del viento*, pp. 17–38; Gustavo Pérez Firmat, 'The structure of "El fulgor y la sangre"', *Hispanic Review*, vol. 45, no.1 (Winter 1977), pp. 1–12.

16 See, for example, the monographs by Borau, Carlisle, and Lytra.

17 Ignacio Aldecoa, *Con el viento solano* (Planeta, Barcelona, 1956).

18 Sobejano, *Novela española de nuestro tiempo*, p. 392; Ricardo Senabre, 'La obra narrativa de Ignacio Aldecoa', *Papeles de Son Armadans*, vol. XV, no. 66 (1970), pp. 5–24; Nora, *La novela española contemporánea*, vol. III, 2nd edn, p. 305; Corrales Egea, *La novela española actual*, p. 131; Sanz Villanueva, *Historia*, vol. I, p. 330.

19 Fiddian, *Ignacio Aldecoa*, pp. 61 and 63.

20 Gemma Roberts, *Temas existenciales en la novela española de postguerra* (Madrid: Gredos, 1973), pp. 99–128.

21 Fiddian, *Ignacio Aldecoa*, pp. 58–9.

22 Carlisle, *Ecos del viento*, pp. 35–49; Fiddian, *Ignacio Aldecoa*, p. 39.

23 Senabre, 'La obra narrativa de Ignacio Aldecoa', p. 8.

NOTES

24 Sanz Villanueva, *Historia*, vol. I, p. 330.
25 Roberts, *Temas existenciales*, p. 102.
26 Fiddian, *Ignacio Aldecoa*, p. 64.
27 Soldevila-Durante, *La novela desde 1936*, p. 226.
28 Jesús Fernández Santos, *Los bravos*, (Valencia: Castalia, 1954). All references are to the Destinolibro edition of 1973. On the author, see David K. Herzberger, *Jesús Fernández Santos*, Twayne's World Authors Series, no. 687 (Boston: Twayne Publishers, 1983), p. 6.
29 Nora, *La novela española contemporánea*, vol. III, 2nd edn, p. 289; Sobejano, *Novela española de nuestro tiempo*, p. 321; Alberto Gil Novales, *Insula*, no. 120 (December 1955), p. 6; Sanz Villanueva, *Historia*, vol I, p. 336.
30 Gil Casado, *La novela social española*, p. 76; Sanz Villanueva, *Historia*, vol. I, p. 336; Sobejano, *Novela española*, p. 325.
31 Sanz Villanueva, *Historia*, vol. I, p. 336.
32 Rafael Sánchez Ferlosio, *El Jarama*, (Barcelona: Destino, 1956). All references are to the 6th edition of 1979. On *El Jarama*, see Edward C. Riley, 'Sobre el arte de Sánchez Ferlosio: aspectos de "El Jarama"', *Filología*, no. IX (1963), pp. 201–21; Salvador Bacarisse, 'Rafael Sánchez Ferlosio: Literatura sub specie ludi', *FMLS*, no. 1 (January 1971), pp. 52–9; Medardo Fraile, 'El Henares, El Jarama y un bautizo', *Revista de Occidente*, no. 122 (May 1973), pp. 125–47; José Schraibman and Walter T. Little, 'La estructura simbólica de "El Jarama"', *Philological Quarterly*, vol. LI, no. 1 (1972), pp. 329–42; Patrick Gallagher, 'Una nota sobre temporalidad y acción en "El Jarama"', *Cuadernos Hispanoamericanos*, vol. XCV, no. 285 (1974), pp. 631–4; Antonio Risco, 'Una re-lectura de "El Jarama" de Sánchez Ferlosio', *Cuadernos Hispanoamericanos*, vol. XCV, no. 288 (1974), pp. 700–11; Ricardo Gullón, 'Recapitulación de "El Jarama"', *Hispanic Review*, vol. XLIII, no. 1 (1975), pp. 1–25; Gregorio Martín, 'Juventud y vejez en "El Jarama"', *Papeles de Son Armadans*, vol. LXXXVII, no. 229 (1975), pp. 9–33; Francisco García Sarriá, '"El Jarama", Muerte y Merienda de Lucita', *Bulletin of Hispanic Studies*, vol. LIII, no. 4 (1976), pp. 323–37; see also F.Z.S. Medendorp, '"El Jarama", sus símbolos e imágenes', *Neophilologus*, vol. LXV, no. 1 (January 1981), pp. 62–8; and in a rather different vein, David Frier, 'The feminist theme in Rafael Sánchez Ferlosio's "El Jarama"', *Spanish Studies*, no. 6 (1984), pp. 57–65.
33 Sanz Villanueva, *Historia*, vol. I, p. 354.
34 Rafael Sánchez Ferlosio, '*Los bravos*: una primera novela', *Correo Literario*, no. 6 (1954), cited in Darío Villanueva, '*El Jarama*" de Sánchez Ferlosio, p. 50.
35 See Hugh Thomas, *The Spanish Civil War* (London: Pelican Books, 1974), pp. 485–92.
36 Sanz Villanueva, *Historia*, vol. I, p. 363.
37 See, for example, García Sarriá, '"El Jarama", Muerte y Merienda de Lucita', p. 334; and John Butt, *Writers and Politics in Modern Spain* (London: Hodder and Stoughton, 1978), p. 58.

197

38 Rafael Sánchez Ferlosio, '*Los bravos*: una primera novela', see note 50.
39 Juan Goytisolo, *Problemas*, p. 26.

CONCLUSION

1 See Marino Gómez Santos, 'Entrevista con Ignacio Aldecoa', *Madrid* (18 January 1955), cited in Drosoula, *Soledad y convivencia*, p. 23.
2 Rafael Sánchez Ferlosio, '*Los bravos*: una primera novela', cited in Darío Villanueva, '*El Jarama*' *de Sánchez Ferlosio*, p. 49.
3 See Paul Preston, 'The anti-Francoist opposition: The long march to unity', in Preston (ed.), *Spain in Crisis*, pp. 125–56; and Jordi Solé Tura, 'Unidad y diversidad en la oposición comunista al franquismo', in Josep Fontana (ed.), *España bajo el Franquismo*, (Editorial Crítica, Barcelona, 1986), pp. 123–41.
4 J.M. Castellet, *Insula*, vol. XVI, no. 205 (1963), p. 3. See also the declarations by Marra López and Batlló, cited by Martínez Cachero, *La novela española entre 1936 y 1980*, p. 261.
5 See Martínez Cachero, *La novela española*, pp. 266–7.
6 J.M. Castellet, 'Tiempo de destrucción para la literatura española', *Imagen* (Caracas, 15 August 1968), cited in Martínez Cachero, *La novela española*, p. 264.
7 Alfonso Sastre, 'Poco más que anécdotas culturales', p. 84.
8 Luis Martín Santos, *Tiempo de silencio* (Seix Barral, Barcelona, 1961), quote taken from jacket of 13th edition, 1973.
9 See the many revealing declarations of López Salinas, Grosso, Caballero Bonald, and García Hortelano, collected by Eduardo G. Rico, *Literatura y Política (en torno al realismo español)* (Edicusa: Madrid, 1971), especially pp. 20, 21, 26, 34 and 38.
10 Carlos Barral, 'Reflexiones acerca de las aventuras del estilo en la penúltima literatura española', pp. 39–42 of *30 años de Literatura. Narrativa y Poesía Española 1936–69*, número extraordinario, XIV, *Cuadernos para el diálogo*, (Madrid, May 1969), cited p. 42.

SELECT BIBLIOGRAPHY

PRIMARY SOURCES

Catalogues consulted

Lasso de la Vega, Javier, *Anuario Español e Hispanoamericano del Libro y de las Artes Gráficas* (Madrid: Editorial Católica) for the period 1944–57.
Catálogo General de Librería Española 1931–1950 (Madrid, 1961).
Libros españoles (Madrid) for the period 1953–7.
Libros en venta, Servicio informativo de Bowker (New York, 1964).

Main fictional works cited

Aldecoa, Ignacio, *El fulgor y la sangre*, (Barcelona: Planeta, 1954).
——, *Con el viento solano* (Barcelona: Planeta, 1956).
——, *Gran Sol* (Barcelona: Noguer, 1957).
Cela, Camilo José, *La colmena* (Buenos Aires: Emecé, 1951).
Fernández Santos, Jesús, *Los bravos* (Valencia: Castalia, 1954).
Goytisolo, Juan, *Juegos de manos* (Barcelona: Destino, 1954).
—— *Duelo en el Paraíso* (Barcelona: Planeta, 1955).
—— *El circo* (Barcelona: Destino, 1957).
—— *Fiestas* (Buenos Aires: Emecé, 1958).
—— *La resaca* (Paris: Club del Libro Español 1958).
—— *La isla* (Barcelona: Seix Barral, 1961).
Martín Santos, Luis, *Tiempo de silencio* (Barcelona: Seix Barral, 1961).
Romero, Luis, *La noria* (Barcelona: Destino, 1952).
Sánchez Ferlosio, Rafael, *El Jarama* (Barcelona: Destino, 1956)
Sartre, Jean-Paul, *Les Mains sales* (Paris: Gallimard, 1948).
Suárez Carreño, José, *Las últimas horas*, (Barcelona: Destino, 1950).

199

Main non-fictional works cited

Barral, Carlos, *Años de penitencia. Memorias* (Madrid: Alianza, 1975).
—— *Los años sin excusa, Memorias II* (Barcelona: Barral Editores, 1978).
Castellet, José María, *Notas sobre literatura española contemporánea* (Barcelona: Ediciones Laye, 1955).
—— *La hora del lector* (Barcelona: Seix Barral, 1957).
Goytisolo, Juan, *Problemas de la novela* (Barcelona: Seix Barral, 1959).
—— *El furgón de cola* (Paris: Ruedo Ibérico, 1967).
Magny, Claude-Edmonde, *L'Âge du roman américain* (Paris: Editions du Seuil, 1948).
Ridruejo, Dionisio, *Escrito en España* (Buenos Aires: Losada, 1962).
Sartre, Jean-Paul, *Situations II. Qu'est-ce que la littérature?* Paris: Gallimard, 1948).
Sastre, Alfonso, *La revolucíon y la crítica de la cultura* (Barcelona: Grijalbo, 1970).
Vilar, Sergio, *Protagonistas de la España democrática. La oposición a la dictadura 1939–1969* (Paris: Ruedo Ibérico, 1969).

Publications consulted

The following journals and reviews have been my main source of information. Below, I list them in alphabetical order, noting in parenthesis the period of coverage and their respective locations, marked according to the following code: Biblioteca Nacional, Madrid (BNM); Hemeroteca Municipal, Madrid (HMM); Biblioteca de Cataluña (BC); Archivo Histórica Municipal, Barcelona (AHMB); University of Liverpool (UL). I do not list separately any items referred to in these publications.

Acento Cultural (1958–61) (HMM)
Alcalá (1952–5) (HMM)
Ateneo (1952–9) (BNM)
Correo Literario (1951–5) (BNM)
Cuadernos del Congreso por la Libertad de la Cultura (1957–62) (UL)
Cuadernos Hispanoamericanos (1948–61) (UL]
Destino (1950–63) (BC)
El Ciervo (1951–3) (AHMB)
Indice (1950–9) (HMM)
Insula (1946–66) (UL)
Juventud (1942–59) (HMM)
La Estafeta Literaria (1956–63) (HMM)
La Hora (1945–60) (BNM)
Laye (1950–3) (HMM)
Objetivo (1953–5) (HMM)
Revista (1952–8) (AHMB)
Revista Española (1953–4) (UL)

SELECT BIBLIOGRAPHY

Articles

Castellet, José María, Prologue to Frederick J. Hoffman, *La novela moderna en Norteamérica 1900-1950* (Barcelona: Seix Barral, 1955), pp. 5–11.

—— 'Notas para una iniciación a la lectura de "El Jarama"', *Papeles de Son Armadans*, no. 2 (May 1956), pp. 205–17.

—— 'Iniciación a la obra narrativa de Camilo José Cela', *Revista Hispánica Moderna*, vol. XXVIII, nos 2–4 (1962), pp. 107–50.

—— 'Veinte años de novela española (1942–1963)', *Cuadernos Americanos*, no. 126 (February 1963), pp. 290–5.

—— 'La joven novela española', *Sur*, (September–October, 1963), pp. 48–54.

——, 'Breu història de la revista *Laye*', *L'Avenç*, no. 6 (1977), pp. 46–7.

Isasi Angulo, A. Carlos, 'La novelística de Juan Goytisolo (entrevista con el autor)', *Papeles de Son Armadans*, vol. LXXVI, no. 226 (1975), pp. 65–87.

Marichalar, Antonio de, 'William Faulkner', *Revista de Occidente*, vol. XLII (October–December 1933), pp. 78–82.

Martín Gaite, Carmen, Prologue to *Los bravos* (Madrid: Biblioteca Breve Salvat, 1971).

——, Prologue to her *Cuentos Completos* (Madrid: Castalia, 1978).

Olmos García, Francisco, 'La novela y los novelistas españoles de hoy. Una encuesta', *Cuadernos Americanos*, vol. CXXIX, no. 4 (1963), pp. 211–37.

Rodríguez, Josefina, Prologue to Ignacio Aldecoa, *Cuentos*, Madrid: Castalia, 1977).

Rodríguez Monegal, Emir, 'Entrevista con Juan Goytisolo', *Mundo Nuevo*, no. 12 (June 1967), pp. 44–60.

Sastre, Alfonso, 'Poco más que anécdotas culturales alrededor de quince años (1950–1965)', *Triunfo*, número extraordinario II, no. 507 (June 1972), pp. 81–5.

SECONDARY SOURCES

Books

Abellán, Manuel L., *Censura y creación literaria en España (1939–1976)* (Barcelona: Península, 1980).

Alborg, Juan Luis, *Hora actual de la novela española* (2 vols, Madrid: Taurus 1958).

Armes, Roy, *Patterns of Realism. A study of Italian neo-realist cinema* (London: Tantivy Press, 1971).

Barrero Pérez, Oscar, *La novela existencial española de postguerra* (Madrid: Gredos, 1987).

Barthes, Roland, *Le Degré zéro de l'écriture* (Paris: Editions du Seuil, 1953)

201

—— *Mythologies* (Paris: Editions du Seuil, 1957).

Blaye, Edouard de, *Franco and the Politics of Spain* (Middlesex: Pelican Books, 1976).

Bonet, Laureano, *Gabriel Ferrater. Entre el arte y la literatura* (Barcelona: Publicacions i Edicions de l'Universitat de Barcelona, 1983).

Borau, Pablo, *El existencialismo en la novela de Ignacio Aldecoa* (Zaragoza: Talleres Gráficos, 'La Editorial', 1974).

Bosch, Rafael, *La novela española del siglo XX. vol. II. De La República a la Postguerra* (New York: Las Américas, 1971).

Buckley, Ramón, *Problemas formales en la novela española contemporánea*, 2nd edn (Barcelona: Península, 1973).

Butt, John, *Writers and Politics in Modern Spain* (London: Hodder and Stoughton, 1978).

Carlisle, Charles R., *Ecos del viento, silencios del mar. La novelística de Ignacio Aldecoa* (Madrid: Playor, 1976).

Castello, Giulio Cesare, *Il cinema neorealistico italiano* (Turin: Einaudi, 1962).

Castro, Antonio, *Cine español en el banquillo* (Valencia: Fernando Torres Editor, 1974).

Corrales Egea, José, *La novela española actual (Ensayo de ordenación)* (Madrid: Cuadernos para el Diálogo, 1971).

Curutchet, Juan Carlos, *Introducción a la novela española de postguerra* (Montevideo: Alfa, 1966).

Díaz, Elías, *Notas para una histora del pensamiento español actual (1939–1973)* (Madrid: Cuadernos para el Diálogo, 1974).

Domingo, José, *La novela española del siglo XX. 2. De la postguerra a nuestros días* (Barcelona: Labor, 1973).

Ellwood, Sheelagh, *Prietas las filas. Historia de la Falange Española 1933–1983* (Barcelona: Crítica, 1984).

Ferrater, Joan, *Dinámica de la poesía* (Barcelona: Seix Barral, 1982).

Ferreras, Juan Ignacio, *Tendencias de la novela española actual 1939–1969* (Paris: Ediciones Hispanoamericanas, 1970).

Fiddian, Robin, *Ignacio Aldecoa*, Twayne's World Authors Series, no. 529 (Boston: Twayne Publishers, 1979).

Font, Doménec, *Del azul al verde. El cine español durante el Franquismo* (Barcelona: Avance, 1976).

García Viñó, Manuel, *Novela española actual* (Madrid: Guadarrama, 1967).

—— *Ignacio Aldecoa* (Madrid: Epesa, 1973).

Gil Casado, Pablo, *La novela social española (1942–1968)*, 1st edn (Barcelona: Seix Barral, 1968), 2nd edn, 1973.

Gómez de la Serna, Gaspar, *Ensayos sobre literatura social* (Madrid: Guadarrama, 1975).

Guarner, José Luis, *30 años de cine en España* (Barcelona: Kairós, 1971).

Gubern, Román, *Historia del cine* (2 vols, Barcelona: Lumen, 1971).

—— *Un cine para el cadalso: 40 años de censura cinematográfica en España* (Barcelona: Euros, 1976).

Herzberger, David K., *Jesús Fernández Santos*, Twayne's World Authors Series, no. 687 (Boston: Twayne Publishers, 1983).

Iglesias Laguna, Antonio, *Treinta años de novela española 1938–1968* (Madrid: Prensa Española, 1969).

Landeira, Ricardo and Mellizo, Carlos (eds), *Ignacio Aldecoa. A collection of critical essays* (Laramie: University of Wyoming Press, 1977).

Lasagabaster Medinabeitia, José María, *La novela de Ignacio Aldecoa. De la mimesis al símbolo* (Madrid: SGEL, 1978).

Lizcano, Pablo, *Le generación del 56. La Universidad contra Franco* (Barcelona: Grijalbo, 1981).

Lytra, Drosoula, *Soldedad y convivencia en la obra de Ignacio Aldecoa* (Madrid: Fundación Universitaria Española, 1979).

—— *Aproximación crítica a Ignacio Aldecoa* (Madrid: Espasa Calpe, 1984).

Maravall, José María, *Dictatorship and Political Dissent. Workers and Students in Franco's Spain* (London: Tavistock Publications, 1978).

Marra-López, José Ramón, *Narrativa española fuera de España* (Madrid: Guadarrama, 1963).

Martín Nogales, José Luis, *Los cuentos de Ignacio Aldecoa* (Madrid: Cátedra, 1984).

Martínez Cachero, José María, *Novelistas españoles de hoy* (Oviedo, 1945).

—— *La novela española entre 1936 y 1980. Historia de una aventura*, 3rd edn (Madrid: Castalia, 1985).

Molina Foix, Vicente, *New Cinema in Spain* (London: BFI, 1977).

Morán, Fernando, *Novela y semidesarrollo, (Una interpretación de la novela hispanoamericana y española)* (Madrid: Taurus, 1971).

Navajas, Gonzalo, *La novela de Juan Goytisolo* (Madrid: SGEL, 1979).

Nora, Eugenio de, *La novela española contemporánea (1927–1960)* (3 vols, Madrid: Gredos, 1962), 2nd edn, vol. 3 (1970).

Overby, David, *Springtime in Italy: A reader on neo-realism* (London: Talisman Books, 1970).

Pacifici, Sergio, *A Guide to Contemporary Italian Literature. From futurism to neo-realism* (New York: Sphere Books, 1962).

Pérez, José Carlos, *La trayectoria novelística de Juan Goytisolo. El autor y sus obsesiones* (Zaragoza: Ediciones Oroel, 1984).

Pérez Minik, Domingo, *Novelistas españoles de los siglos XIX y XX* (Madrid: Guadarrama, 1957).

Pinheiro Torres, Alexandro, *O movimento neorealista en Portugal na sua primeira fase* (Lisbon: Biblioteca Breve, 1977).

Preston, Paul (ed.), *Spain in Crisis: The evolution and decline of the Franco regime* (Brighton: The Harvester Press, 1976).

Ranvaud, Don, *Roberto Rossellini*, BFI Dossier no. 8 (London: BFI, 1981).

Rico, Eduardo G., *Literatura y Política (en torno al realismo español)* (Cuadernos para el Diálogo, Suplemento 19, Madrid, 1971).

Roberts, Gemma, *Temas existenciales en la novela española de postguerra* (Madrid: Gredos, 1973).

Rodríguez Puértolas, Julio, *Literatura Fascista Española I/Historia* (Madrid: Akal, 1986).

Romero, Héctor R., *La evolución literaria de Juan Goytisolo*, Florida: Ediciones Universal, 1979).

Said, Edward, *Beginnings: Intention and Method* (Baltimore and London: Johns Hopkins University Press, 1973).

Saínz de Robles, Federico C., *La novela española en el siglo XX* (Madrid: Pegaso, 1957).

Santos Fontenla, César, *Cine español en la encrucijada* (Madrid: Ciencia Nueva, 1966).

Sanz Villanueva, Santos, *Tendencias de la novela española actual (1950–1970)* (Madrid: Cuadernos para el Diálogo, 1970).

—— *Historia de la novela social española (1942–1975)* (2 vols, Madrid: Alhambra, 1980).

Sarraute, Nathalie, *L'Ère du soupçon* (Paris: Gallimard, 1956).

Schwartz, Kessel, *Juan Goytisolo*, Twayne's World Authors Series no. 104 (Boston: Twayne Publishers, 1970).

Sobejano, Gonzalo, *Novela española de nuestro tiempo (En busca del pueblo perdido)*, 2nd edn (Madrid: Prensa Española, 1975).

Soldevila-Durante, Ignacio, *La novela desde 1936* (Madrid: Alhambra, 1980).

Thomas, Hugh, *Tha Spanish Civil War* (London: Penguin Books, 1965).

Thompson, Edward, *The Poverty of Theory* (London: The Merlin Press, 1978).

Vázquez Montalbán, Manuel, *La penetración americana en España* (Madrid: Cuadernos para el Diálogo, 1974).

Villanueva, Darío, *'El Jarama' de Sánchez Ferlosio. Su estructura y significado* (Universidad de Santiago de Compostela, 1973).

Articles

Amorós, Andrés, 'Notas para el estudio de la novela española actual', *Vida Hispánica*, vol. XVI (1968), pp. 7–13.

Bacarisse, Salvador, 'Rafael Sánchez Ferlosio: Literatura sub specie ludi', *Forum for Modern Language Studies*, no. 1 (January 1971), pp. 5–29.

Barral, Carlos, 'Reflexiones acerca de las aventuras del estilo en la penúltima literatura española, in *30 años de literatura. Narrativa y poesía española 1936–1969*, número extraordinario XIV, *Cuadernos para el Diálogo* (May 1969), pp. 39–42.

Canella, Mario, 'Ideology and aesthetic hypotheses in the criticism of neo-realism', *Screen*, vol. 14, no. 4 (Winter 1973–4), pp. 5–60.

Esteban Soler, Hipólito, 'Narradores españoles del medio siglo', in *Miscellánea di studi ispanici* (Universitá di Pisa, 1971–3), pp. 217–370.

Fink, Guido, 'Neo-realism revisited', *Twentieth Century Studies*, no. 5 (September 1971), pp. 70–83.

Fraile, Medardo, 'El Henares, "El Jarama" y un bautizo', *Revista de Occidente*, no. 122 (May 1973), pp. 125–47.

Frier, David, 'The feminist theme in Rafael Sánchez Ferlosio's "El Jarama"', *Spanish Studies*, no. 6 (1984), pp. 57–85.

Gallagher, Patrick, 'Una nota sobre temporalidad y acción en "El Jarama"', *Cuadernos Hispanoamericanos*, vol. XCV, no. 285 (1974), pp. 631–4.

SELECT BIBLIOGRAPHY

García Sarriá, Francisco, '"El Jarama", Muerte y merienda de Lucita', *Bulletin of Hispanic Studies*, vol. LIII, no. 4 (1976), pp. 323 37.

Giner, Salvador, 'Power, freedom and social change in the Spanish University, 1939–1975', in Preston (ed.), *Spain in Crisis*, pp. 183–211.

Gómez Marín, José Antonio, 'Literatura y política. Del tremendismo a la nueva narrativa', *Cuadernos Hispanoamericanos*, vol. LXV, no. 193 (1966), pp. 109–16.

Gullón, Ricardo, 'Recapitulación de "El Jarama"', *Hispanic Review*, vol. XLIII, no. 1 (1975), pp. 1–25.

Jordan, Barry, '"Laye": els intel.lectuals i el compromís', *Els Marges*, no. 17 (1979), pp. 3–26.

Labanyi, Jo, 'The ambiguous implications of the mythical references in Juan Goytisolo's "Duelo en el Paraíso"', *Modern Language Review*, vol. 80, part 4 (October 1985), pp. 845–57.

López Molina, Luis, 'El tremendismo en la literatura española actual', *Revista de Occidente*, no. 54 (1967), pp. 372–8.

Mallo, Jerónimo, 'Caracterización y valor del tremendismo en la novela española contemporánea', *Hispania*, vol. XXXIX (1956), pp. 49–55.

Marfany, Joan-Lluís, 'Notes sobre la novel.la espanyola de postguerra', *Els Marges*, no. 6 (1976), pp. 29–57.

—— 'Notes . . . II', no. 11 (1977), pp. 3–29.

—— 'Notes . . . III', no. 12 (1978), pp. 3–23.

Martín, Gregorio, 'Juventud y vejez en "El Jarama"', *Papeles de Son Armadans*, vol. LXXXVII, no. 229 (1975), pp. 9–33.

Medendorp, F.Z.S., '"El Jarama", sus símbolos e imágenes', *Neophilologus*, vol. LXV, no. 1 (January 1981), pp. 62–8.

Pérez-Firmat, Gustavo, 'The structure of "El fulgor y la sangre"', *Hispanic Review*, vol. 45, no. 1 (Winter 1977), pp. 1–12.

Perlini, Tito, 'Left-wing culture in Italy since the last war', *Twentieth-Century Studies*, no. 5 (1971), pp. 1–15.

Preston, Paul, 'The anti-Francoist opposition: the long march to unity', in Preston (ed.), *Spain in Crisis*, pp. 125 56.

Reeves, George Macmillan, 'French windows on modern American fiction', in *Proceedings of the Comparative Literature Symposium*, (Texas University: Texas Technical Press, 1972), pp. 5–18.

Riley, Edward C., 'Sobre el arte de Sánchez Ferlosio: aspectos de "El Jarama"', *Filología*, no. IX (1963), pp. 201–21.

Risco, Antonio, 'Una re-lectura de "El Jarama" de Sánchez Ferlosio', *Cuadernos Hispanoamericanos*, vol. XCV, no. 288 (1974), pp. 700–11.

Schraibman, José and Little, Walter T., 'La estructura simbólica de "El Jarama"', *Philological Quarterly*, vol. LI, no. 1 (1972), pp. 329–42.

Senabre, Ricardo, 'La obra narrativa de Ignacio Aldecoa', *Papeles de Son Armadans*, vol. XV, no. 166 (1970), pp. 5–24.

Sole Tura, Jordi, 'Unidad y diversidad en la oposición comunista al Franquismo', in Josep Fontana (ed.), *España bajo el Franquismo* (Barcelona: Crítica, 1986), pp. 123–41.

Zatlin Boring, Phyllis, 'Faulkner in Spain: the case of Elena Quiroga', *Comparative Literature Studies*, vol. XIV, no. 2 (June 1977), pp. 166–76.

INDEX

207

INDEX